P9-BJM-043

ALSO BY THE AMERICAN HEART ASSOCIATION

The American Heart Association Cookbook, 4th Edition

The American Heart Association Low-Fat, Low-Cholesterol Cookbook

The American Heart Association Low-Salt Cookbook

Portions of this publication were adapted from *Cooking Without Your Salt Shaker* © 1978, American Heart Association, Northeast Ohio Affiliate, Inc., Cleveland, Ohio.

THE AMERICAN HEART ASSOCIATION LOW-SALT COOKBOOK

A COMPLETE GUIDE TO REDUCING SODIUM AND FAT IN THE DIET

RODMAN D. STARKE, M.D.
MARY WINSTON, ED.D., R.D.
EDITORS

ILLUSTRATIONS BY REGINA SCUDELLARI

TIMES BOOKS
RANDOM HOUSE

Copyright © 1990 by American Heart Association
Illustrations copyright © 1990 by
Regina A. E. Scudellari
All rights reserved under International and Pan-American Copyright Conventions. Published in the United States by Times Books, a division of Random House, Inc., New York, and simultaneously in Canada by Random House of Canada Limited, Toronto.

Note to Doctor and Dietitian:
This cookbook is designed for those who wish to restrict their salt or sodium intake mildly, to approximately 2,000 milligrams per day. If further restrictions are necessary, the recipes here can easily be adapted to a lower level of sodium.

Library of Congress Cataloging-in-Publication Data
American Heart Association low-salt cookbook: a complete guide to reducing sodium and fat in the diet/by the American Heart Association.
p. cm.
ISBN 0-8129-1852-5
1. Salt-free diet—Recipes. I. American Heart Association. II. Title: Low-salt cookbook.
RM237.8.A45 1990
641.5′632—dc20 90-10823

DESIGNED BY BARBARA MARKS
CUT-PAPER ILLUSTRATIONS BY REGINA SCUDELLARI
ART DIRECTION BY NAOMI OSNOS

Manufactured in the United States of America

9 8 7 6 5 4 3 2

First Edition

PREFACE

Cutting down on sodium in your diet is a good idea for a lot of reasons. But most people make this change only when they have to, when advised to by their doctor, to help treat high blood pressure, also known as hypertension.

About 60 million Americans have high blood pressure. Many of them follow medical treatment their doctors have recommended. But over the past decade, concern over the potential danger of lifelong drug therapy for all hypertensives has grown. Shouldn't there be ways to reduce high blood pressure in some cases without resorting to drugs?

Fortunately, there are. Two of the best treatments today seem to be reducing the amount of sodium in the diet and controlling weight.

While it may be impossible to know how effective a sodium-restricted diet would be for *all* hypertensive patients, it does appear that a sizable group of them could benefit greatly from this approach. We wrote this cookbook for those patients.

Actually, research is beginning to show that *most* of us—not just hypertensives—would benefit from reducing the sodium in our diets. Studies of people around the world have indicated that habitual high sodium intake may "set the stage" for hypertension in certain people who are genetically prone to it. Many Americans want to reduce their sodium intake—either as a preventive measure or because their doctors have advised them to do so. If you are one of these people, this book can help you do just that.

It is well established that the chance of developing cardiovascular disease increases if you have high blood pressure. Sometimes people with high blood pressure are also fighting high blood cholesterol. In *The American Heart Association Low-Salt Cookbook,* we've acknowledged and addressed that problem; all the recipes are not only low-sodium, but low-modified-fat and low-cholesterol, too. Without extra effort, you can help control both high blood pressure and high blood cholesterol with the recipes here and cut your risks of cardiovascular disease even further.

You'll also find in this book a nutrient analysis of each recipe, its calorie count per serving, tips on buying and preparing foods and two easy-to-follow eating plans, the Step-One and Step-Two diets (see Appendix A, pages 284–326).

Best of all are our newly created and revised recipes. If your idea of low-sodium cooking has been "cardboard on a plate," you're in for a wonderful surprise! Featuring fresh ingredients, herbs, spices and spirits, these recipes pack flavor into each dish. You'll be so dazzled by these taste sensations, salt may seem almost bland by comparison.

Most of us know from experience that change—any change—is hard. Changing longtime eating habits is no exception. So take it slowly, one step at a time. In a few months, you'll wonder why you didn't start eating this way years ago.

To health and happiness.

RODMAN D. STARKE, M.D.
Senior Vice President
Office of Scientific Affairs
American Heart Association
National Center
Dallas, Texas

Acknowledgments

The credit for recognizing the need for a low-sodium, low-modified-fat, low-cholesterol cookbook—and for the hard work and dedication that goes into developing such a book—goes to the American Heart Association Northeast Ohio Affiliate's Low Sodium Cookbook Task Force.

The teamwork and expertise of those volunteers resulted in the publication of *Cooking Without Your Salt Shaker,* the first edition of this book, in 1978. The Task Force members and significant contributors were: Sharon Reichman, R.D., chairperson; Charlene Krejci, R.D.; Karen Wilcoxon Izso, R.D.; Grace Petot, R.D.; Sally Gleason, R.D.; Tab Forgac, R.D.; Rosemary Manni, R.D.; Auretha Pettigrew, R.D.; Robert Post, M.D.; Mary Ann Weber, R.D.; and Cleveland Dietetic Association, Diet Therapy Section.

That cookbook was available only through the American Heart Association. But its popularity convinced us to offer it to a wider audience. At the same time, changes in science and trends in food preparation prompted us to update and expand the book significantly.

Kudos to Mike Semon for creating delicious new recipes and modifying existing ones for more flavor and variety, as well as for analyzing each for protein, carbohydrate, fat, cholesterol, sodium, potassium, calcium and calories per serving.

Sincere thank-yous go to Jane Ruehl for the excellent but tedious task of copyediting and to Pat Covington for copywriting.

Thanks also go to Lynne Scott, M.S., R.D., for her expertise and undying efforts in developing the diet plan.

Finally, without Ann Yanosky's untiring efforts to keep all of us on schedule and attention to every detail, this book would never have been published.

MARY WINSTON, ED.D., R.D.
Senior Science Adviser
Office of Scientific Affairs
American Heart Association
National Center
Dallas, Texas

Contents

Preface vii
Acknowledgments ix
Introduction 3
When You Go Shopping 7
Food Preparation Ideas 17
Ingredient Substitutions 23
How to Use These Recipes 26

Recipes 29
Seasoning Blends 31
Soups 39
Salads 53
Salad Dressings 71
Fish 83
Poultry 97
Meats 121
Vegetarian Entrées 137
Vegetables 151
Sauces 175
Breads 193
Desserts 213
Appetizers and Snacks 249

Appendix *265*

A: The Low-Sodium Diet *266*

The Step-One Diet *285*

The Step-Two Diet *307*

B: Herb, Spice and Seasoning Guide *327*

C: American Heart Association Affiliates *330*

D: For More Information *333*

Index *335*

The American Heart Association Low-Salt Cookbook

INTRODUCTION

Congratulations.

You are about to do something exciting: learn to cook without salt. Maybe you picked up this book because your doctor recommended reducing your sodium intake to control your high blood pressure. Or maybe you decided on your own that you'd like to cut down on salt. Whatever the reason, this cookbook will help you do just that.

THEY SAID IT COULDN'T BE DONE

People often claim that food cooked without salt is boring, flat and tasteless. Well, they're wrong.

With no-salt cooking you'll learn to use your imagination. You'll try spices and herb combinations you've never heard of . . . and be glad you did. You'll create new taste sensations with wines and spirits and with exotic spices and oils. Cooking without salt may be as easy or as elaborate as you wish to make it, but it can always be deliciously flavorful.

SALT, FAT AND HEART DISEASE

At the American Heart Association, we've learned a lot about the many possible causes of heart attack and stroke—and what can be done to try to prevent them.

The top three ways to help prevent these and other cardiovascular diseases are: avoid smoking, try to achieve a desirable blood cholesterol level and control high blood pressure.

By the millions, Americans have stopped smoking. Millions more are cutting down on total fat, saturated fat and cholesterol in their diets. Now, Americans in record numbers are helping control their high blood pressure by reducing—or eliminating—the salt in their diets.

WHAT IS HIGH BLOOD PRESSURE?

Blood pressure describes the pressure exerted by the blood against the artery walls. The heart creates this pressure as it pumps blood. A blood pressure measurement is written in two numbers, such as 120/80. It is read as "one-twenty over eighty."

The first, or upper, number represents systolic pressure—the blood pressure in the arteries when the heart is pumping blood. The second, or lower, number represents diastolic pressure, the pressure in the arteries when the heart is at rest between beats.

As a general rule, any blood pressure greater than 140/90 is considered to be high. And the higher your blood pressure above this point, the greater your risk of stroke, heart attack, kidney failure and other cardiovascular complications. That's why treating high blood pressure is so important.

The cause of 90 percent of all high blood pressure is unknown. All the same, it has been found that too much salty food may contribute to high blood pressure in certain "genetically susceptible" people. Occasionally, high blood pressure is caused by another medical problem and will disappear once the problem is corrected.

IS THERE A CURE?

Unfortunately, there is no cure for hypertension. But there are many things you can do to help bring your blood pressure under control. You can keep your weight at a normal level, get regular exercise and use this cookbook to help you reduce your sodium intake. Hypertension and high blood cholesterol are both risk factors for heart attack. This cookbook will show you how to help reduce both of these risks by limiting your intake of sodium, saturated fat and cholesterol.

Too much sodium in your system holds water in your body and puts an extra burden on your heart and blood vessels. That's why low-sodium diets are often effective for treating high blood pressure. Eating more foods that contain potassium or calcium may help lower blood pressure in some people. (See the list of these foods in "Potassium Sources" on page 272.)

THE SALT-SODIUM CONNECTION

Many people use the words *salt* and *sodium* as if they were the same thing. Not quite. Salt is actually sodium chloride, a chemical compound that is about half sodium.

Sodium is a mineral found in nature and in almost all the food we eat. Everyone needs some sodium to live, but this need can be met easily without adding even a pinch of salt to food. The foods themselves contain all we need.

The average American eats an estimated ten times more sodium than he or she actually needs for good health. One way to reduce that intake is to cut down on ordinary table salt even if you have no health problem. If you have high blood pressure, your doctor will probably advise you to do that. It's one way to help keep your blood pressure under control to reduce your risk of stroke, heart attack and kidney failure.

WATCHING YOUR HEART—AND YOUR WAISTLINE

This low-sodium cookbook was also designed with fat in mind. "Low" fat, to be exact. Each recipe and recommended serving size was created to be low in total fat, saturated fat and cholesterol.

Watching your fat intake does more than just help your heart. It helps your waistline, too. If you're counting calories, look for the calorie content of each serving size listed in the analysis of each recipe.

In this cookbook, we use "acceptable" margarines and vegetable oils wherever fats are called for. Acceptable margarine is unsaturated and unsalted. Acceptable vegetable oils include polyunsaturated cooking oils such as corn and safflower, or monounsaturated oils such as canola and olive. You'll learn more about these oils later in the cookbook. (See the list of recommended oils on page 14.) Just remember that they provide flavor—with the added benefit of contributing to a cholesterol-lowering eating plan.

WHEN YOU ARE FOLLOWING SPECIAL DIET INSTRUCTIONS

If your doctor or dietitian has given you a low-sodium diet instruction sheet, check it against the ingredients in these recipes. If there is a difference, follow the instructions on your instruction sheet. If, for example, your instructions tell you to use only unsalted bread, use that in place of the regular bread listed in the ingredients list of our recipes. Such substitutions will result in slightly different values from those listed in our nutrient analysis for that particular recipe.

If you have not received a diet instruction sheet from your doctor or dietitian, we offer our own low-sodium diets to help you reach your goal. (See pages 284–326 in the Appendix.) Follow the recipes in the book closely, and be sure to use the ingredients specified.

EATING WITH YOUR HEART IN MIND

When you reduce the amount of sodium in your foods and change the kind and amount of fat in your diet, you can help lower your risk of heart and blood vessel disease.

It's never easy to change old cooking habits. You may find it difficult at first. But when you savor the exotic taste of our Lamb Curry or a light but flavor-filled bite of Herbed Fillet of Sole, you'll realize that it is worth the effort. Creative, help-your-heart cooking can be "just what the doctor ordered" for you and your family.

So go ahead. Take the salt shaker off the table. Then pick up this cookbook. Consider it the beginning of a great culinary adventure. If you have questions, ask your doctor or call your American Heart Association. We're here to help.

Bon appétit!

When You Go Shopping

Shopping for a low-sodium menu is easier than you might think, now that many familiar items are available in no-salt or low-salt varieties.

With a little effort, you can learn to cut the sodium, change the kind of fat and reduce the amount of fat and cholesterol in your diet. As part of that effort, you'll have to start reading the product labels on prepared foods to make sure they're really low in sodium, total fat, saturated fat and cholesterol.

CHECK FOR SODIUM

Check ingredient lists for salt and other high-sodium additives. Be alert to any food label that has the word *sodium* on it. Watch especially for these sources of "hidden salt" in foods:

- Monosodium glutamate (MSG) (flavor enhancer)
- Sodium bicarbonate (leavening agent)
- Sodium nitrite (meat curing agent)
- Sodium benzoate (preservative)
- Sodium propionate (mold inhibitor)
- Sodium citrate (acidity controller)

When you see the phrase *sodium-free* on a label, it means the item has less than 5 milligrams of sodium per serving. *Very low sodium* means less than 35 milligrams per serving. *Low sodium* means less than 140 milligrams per serving, and *reduced sodium* means the product was processed to reduce the usual sodium level by 75 percent.

Unsalted, no salt added and *without added salt* mean the product is made without the salt that is normally used in processing, but the product still contains the sodium that is a natural part of the food.

DOWN WITH CHOLESTEROL

When you see the phrase *no cholesterol* on a label, it means the product does not contain any cholesterol. But it may still contain saturated fat, which raises blood cholesterol. Basically, any product that does not contain ingredients from an animal source is naturally cholesterol-free. But coconut, palm and palm kernel oil—the "tropical oils"—are three plant sources that contain saturated fat.

A few product labels will give you the percent of calories derived from fat. Peanut butter and margarine labels often give this information, alerting you to the fact that these products contain primarily fat.

Most of the recipe ingredients called for in this cookbook are readily available in your local grocery store. Some, such as no-salt-added tomato paste and sauce, will be found in the usual section of the grocery store. Other unsalted foods can be found in the special diet section. If the items you want are not in stock, ask your grocer to order them for you.

COUNTING CALORIES

The words *low-calorie* mean the product contains no more than 40 calories per serving. *Reduced calorie* means the product has at least one-third fewer calories than the product for which this food is substituted.

When you shop, be sure to compare labels. Some premixed, frozen or prepared foods have a lower sodium, saturated fatty acid or cholesterol content than others. Now that many products list their sodium, fat and cholesterol content, shopping for low-sodium, low-saturated-fatty-acid, low-cholesterol foods is easier than ever before.

HOW TO READ A LABEL

This is important. First, look at the ingredients listed. All food labels list the product's ingredients in order by weight. The ingredient present in the greatest amount is listed first. The ingredient present in the least amount is listed last.

As a rule, if salt and several sodium compounds are listed as ingredients, the product contains more salt than is advisable on a low-sodium diet. To avoid too much total fat or saturated fatty acids, limit your use of products that list a fat or oil first, or that list many fat and oil ingredients.

The nutrition label also tells you what types of nutrients the product provides, the relative proportions of those nutrients and their contributions to the U.S. Recommended Daily Allowances for protein, vitamins and minerals.

WHAT TO SHOP FOR

Now make your shopping list. The key to a healthful diet is to make sure you eat a variety of foods. Your daily food choices should include:

- No more than 6 ounces of lean meat, fish or poultry
- Dried beans, peas, lentils or soybean curd (tofu) in place of meat a few times a week
- Whole grain or enriched bread or low-sodium cereal products
- 3 or more servings of fruit and 3 or more servings of vegetables (include 1 serving of citrus fruit or vegetable high in vitamin C and 1 serving of dark green, leafy or deep yellow vegetables)
- 2 or more servings of skim milk or low-sodium, low-fat milk products for adults; 3 to 4 servings for children or adolescents
- 5 to 8 teaspoons of polyunsaturated and monounsaturated fats and oils in the form of unsalted margarine, cooking oil and unsalted salad dressing (this amount may vary according to caloric needs)

DAIRY PRODUCTS

For a balanced diet, include two or more servings of skim milk (0 to 1 percent milk fat) or low-sodium, low-fat milk products every day.

With the exception of buttermilk and cheese, most milk and milk products do not contain added salt—but do watch out for the cholesterol and saturated fats found in whole milk and whole milk products. Try to make your dairy selections from the wide variety of low-fat dairy products on the market instead.

It's amazing how much fat and cholesterol you can eliminate from your diet by using low-fat or nonfat milk products. One ounce of plain, low-fat yogurt, for example, has 0.28 grams of saturated fat and 1.70 grams of cholesterol, while the same amount of plain, nonfat yogurt has just 0.03 grams of saturated fat and 0.57 grams of cholesterol.

The comparison can become even more dramatic. Look at regular sour cream: It has 3.41 grams of saturated fat and 18.71 grams of cholesterol per ounce, compared with low-fat sour cream, with just 1.15 grams of saturated fat and 6.39 grams of cholesterol per ounce.

Whole-milk products can be replaced with the following:

- Skim milk, evaporated skim milk, nonfat dry milk
- Dry-curd cottage cheese that has no salt added
- Cheese made from skim or partially skim milk with no salt added (no more than 5 grams of fat and 150 milligrams of sodium per ounce)
- Low-fat yogurt or low-fat frozen yogurt
- Ice milk and sherbets
- Polyunsaturated nondairy creamers or whiteners
  Note: Imitation sour cream, nondairy whipped toppings and nondairy coffee whiteners that contain saturated fat are not recommended.

EGGS

One large egg yolk contains almost the entire daily allowance for cholesterol, approximately 213 to 220 milligrams. It's a good idea to limit your egg yolk consumption to three per week.

On the other hand, egg whites contain no cholesterol and are an excellent source of protein. You often can use egg whites in place of whole eggs. In fact, in most recipes two egg whites and a little acceptable vegetable oil will substitute nicely for a whole egg. (See our recipe for No-Cholesterol Egg Substitute on page 149.)

Be sure to eat only cooked eggs and egg whites—not raw.

MEAT PRODUCTS

A balanced diet requires some protein foods every day. With meats, keep your sodium intake to a minimum by buying only unsalted fresh or frozen lean meat. And because meats contain cholesterol and saturated fat, you'll want to limit yourself to six ounces per day.

The best meats for you are lean cuts with less fat around the outside and less marbled fat throughout. Some of the leanest cuts are round steak, sirloin tip, tenderloin and extra-lean ground beef. All cuts of veal are lean except cutlets. Look for lean pork, such as low-sodium fresh center-cut ham, tenderloin and loin chops.

Pay particular attention to ground beef. It's best to select a lean cut of meat and ask the butcher to trim and grind it for you. This is usually done at no extra charge.

Fresh poultry pieces cooked without skin is an excellent protein choice. When using whole chickens and turkeys, roast them with the skin on. This will help prevent the meat from drying out. Be sure to remove the skin before eating. Stay away from self-basting turkeys, because commercial basting fats are highly saturated. Even when the turkey is basted in broth, the broth is usually high in sodium. It's much better to baste your own turkey with an unsalted broth.

In general, steer clear of the following meats, which contain large amounts of one or more of the things we are trying to limit (sodium, fat and cholesterol): luncheon meats; frankfurters; sausage; spareribs; corned beef; salt pork; liver and other organ meats; smoked, cured or dried meats such as ham and bacon; and canned meat or poultry, unless packed without salt.

FISH

Fish is a versatile low-sodium favorite. While not free of cholesterol, fish generally contains less than red meat. For a cholesterol-lowering diet, this gives fish a slight edge over lean red meat and a definite edge over fatty red meat. For this reason, many authorities recommend that fish be eaten two or three times a week.

Fish itself can be either fatty or lean. Omega-3 fatty acids, found in some varieties of fatty fish, are currently being studied for potential lipid (blood fat)-lowering benefits. Some fish high in Omega-3 fatty acids are: Atlantic and coho salmon, albacore tuna, mackerel, carp, lake whitefish, sweet smelt, and lake and brook trout.

Shrimp, lobster, crab, crayfish and most other shellfish are very low in fat. However, ounce for ounce, some varieties contain more sodium and cholesterol than do poultry, meat or other fish. Even these, however, can be eaten occasionally within the recommended guidelines of 300 milligrams of cholesterol per day.

FRUITS, VEGETABLES, GRAINS AND LEGUMES

With few exceptions, fresh foods in these categories have no cholesterol, tend to be low in sodium and fat and, in many cases, are high in fiber and vitamins.

The exceptions include coconut meat, avocados and olives. Coconut meat is high in saturated fatty acids. Both avocados and olives are high in fat, although the fat is largely unsaturated. Green olives are high in sodium (800 milligrams in 10 small), and ripe olives are moderately high in sodium (250 milligrams in 5 extra-large). Stay away from vegetables that have been packed in brine, such as pickles and sauerkraut, because they're loaded with sodium.

In this category, always read the labels on frozen and processed foods. Many of them contain added salt, butter or sauces.

Also note that fruits that are fresh or canned in water are lower in calories than fruits canned in juice or in syrup.

NUTS AND SEEDS

These are tasty snacks and most kinds are available in their natural state: unsalted. But remember that although the fat in nuts and seeds is mostly unsaturated, there's lots of it, so the calorie count is higher than most people realize. Nuts and seeds are good sources of incomplete proteins and can replace other high-protein foods to some degree—especially when eaten with beans, legumes and grains, which are also incomplete proteins. Together, they provide complete protein.

BREADS, CEREALS AND PASTA

Whole-grain or enriched breads, cereals and pastas are an important part of a balanced diet. They provide plenty of nutrients and relatively few calories. (But avoid the high-fat or salty sauces and condiments that often accompany them.)

Go ahead and experiment with different kinds of breads, such as whole or cracked wheat, rye, French, Italian and pumpernickel. They do contain some sodium and a small amount of fat, but not enough to outweigh their natural goodness for you.

Check the labels on crackers for sodium, fats and oils. Look for soda crackers without salt, or try matzo, melba toast or bread sticks if you want something crunchy. Scandinavian-style rye crackers and other whole-grain crackers are often made without fats or oils and with little or no salt. Also look for unsalted popcorn, pretzels and bread sticks.

Be wary of commercially baked goods and mixes such as muffins, biscuits, sweet rolls, cakes, cookies and pastries. They contain significant amounts of sodium and/or cholesterol and saturated fat. It's 100 percent better to bake your own: Just use the recipes in this book or adjust your own favorites by omitting the salt and using the ingredient substitutions listed on pages 23–25.

Cereals are great for anyone on a low-sodium, low-modified-fat diet. Most cereals don't have saturated fat or cholesterol. (One of the few exceptions is granola.) Most do, however, contain sodium. Be sure to read the label and choose those that are low in sodium and are made with the kinds of fats recommended in the following section on fats and oils. Look for the word *sodium* on the label, because it appears disguised in many different sodium compounds. (These are listed in the Appendix, on page 278.)

Hot cereals, rice and pastas contain almost no sodium—just remember to leave the salt out of the cooking water when you prepare these foods.

FATS AND OILS

Polyunsaturated and monounsaturated fats and oils are the kinds of fats you'll want to include in your daily diet. In fact, 5 to 8 teaspoons of these fats and oils daily is a reasonable amount.

You can use them in the form of unsalted salad dressing, unsalted margarine or oil used in cooking. Oils are cholesterol-free and do not contain sodium. Mayonnaise and most margarines, on the other hand, do contain some salt, but they're still okay to use occasionally. Most commercial salad dressings contain large amounts of salt and should be avoided.

WHAT KIND OF FAT IS IT?

When reading the labels on packaged goods, pay particular attention to the kinds of fats and oils present.

Saturated Fat. Fats and oils high in saturated fatty acids tend to become hard at room temperature. Butter, lard and tallow from animals, and coconut, palm and palm kernel oils from plants are common examples. These saturated fats raise blood cholesterol and should be avoided.

Monounsaturated and Polyunsaturated Fat. Oils that stay liquid at room temperature are high in unsaturated fats. They include corn, safflower, soybean, sunflower, olive and canola (rapeseed) oils. All are low in saturated fatty acids and can be used to help lower blood cholesterol. They do not contain sodium, either.

Hydrogenated Oils. These are ordinarily found in liquid form at room temperature but have been artificially hardened to produce margarines and shortenings. Their effect on blood cholesterol depends on how much they are hydrogenated. It's best to look for margarines that have the hydrogenated oil listed as the second ingredient.

As a rule, keep your total fat intake to no more than 30 percent of your total diet, and use the following lists to help you identify recommended fats and oils.

FATS AND OILS	
Recommended:	***Not recommended/saturated:***
Safflower oil	Butter
Sunflower oil	Vegetable shortening
Corn oil	Vegetable fat
Soybean oil	Bacon, salt pork
Sesame seed oil	Suet, lard
Canola oil	Chicken fat, meat fat
Olive oil	Coconut oil
Polyunsaturated margarine	Palm kernel oil
Unsalted oil-based salad dressing (using recommended oils)	Palm oil
	For occasional use only:
	Peanut oil

BEVERAGES

When you're thirsty, look for beverages that are not high in sodium, fat or cholesterol. These include skim milk and low-sodium fruit juices, fruit drinks and carbonated beverages. Some diet soft drinks and mineral waters are high in sodium. Be sure to read the label before selecting your beverage. The sodium content of tap water varies widely from one location to another. If your water supply is high in sodium, use low-sodium bottled water for drinking and for making drinks such as tea and coffee.

If you're trying to lose weight, steer clear of sugared carbonated beverages, fruit drinks, beer, wine and alcohol.

Alcohol has been erroneously credited with preventing heart disease. In moderation, alcohol does not appear to be harmful. But the ill effects of excessive alcohol consumption are well established. If you drink, it's smart to limit your alcohol intake to one ounce per day.

MISCELLANEOUS FOODS AND FLAVORINGS

On a low-sodium eating plan, be careful of the many commonly used commercial seasonings and sauces containing large amounts of sodium or salt. These include: soy sauce, Worcestershire sauce, steak sauce, ketchup, chili sauce, monosodium glutamate, meat tenderizer, flavored seasoning salts and bouillon cubes. Look for low-sodium versions of these items, or use the recipes we've included in this cookbook to make your own.

Try making your own salad dressings from herbs, oil and vinegar. Cook with spices, flavorings, freshly ground horseradish, hot pepper sauce, garlic, herbs and fruit juices.

Many snack foods, commercial soups, green olives, relishes and pickles contain lots of salt. Some of them are available commercially in no-salt varieties. Try the recipes in this cookbook for soups and sauces and even pickles.

You'll want to substitute unsweetened cocoa powder for baking chocolate and chocolate chips. Chocolate and cocoa butter contain lots of saturated fat, but most of the fat has been removed from cocoa powder.

SNACKS

Many snack products, such as chips and rich crackers, are high in sodium and saturated fatty acids. However, some chips are cooked in unsaturated oil. Choose only those labeled as having lower salt and more polyunsaturated than saturated fatty acids. Better yet, make your own cookies, cakes and snack foods without salt and with acceptable oils or margarines.

Food Preparation Ideas

Now you know what kinds of foods are part of a low-salt, low-modified-fat, low-cholesterol eating plan. That's great, but it's just the beginning. It's not enough just to *buy* healthful foods. You also need to know how to prepare them so that they *stay* that way.

All cooking methods are not created equal. Some are better than others for retaining vitamins and minerals and for cutting cholesterol, fat and calories. Basically, stay away from cooking techniques that add fat or allow food to cook in its own fat, such as deep-fat frying or pan frying.

Instead, look for cooking techniques that enhance flavor, preserve basic nutrients, and keep added fat and sodium to a minimum. To get you started, here are a few examples of cooking methods that will help you help your heart.

Roasting. Always place a rack on the bottom of the roasting pan so the meat or poultry doesn't sit in its own fat drippings. Be sure to roast at a low temperature, about 350° F., to avoid searing the meat or poultry and sealing in the fat. For basting, use low-sodium, fat-free liquids such as table wine, no-salt-added tomato juice or fresh lemon juice.

Baking. Poultry, fish and meat can be baked in covered cookware with a little additional liquid. The moisture that the liquid adds makes this method particularly good for fish or chicken breasts, which tend to be a little dry.

Braising or Stewing. This method uses a little more liquid than baking does. Try it in a covered container on top of the stove (using low heat) or in the oven (using medium temperatures, 300°–325° F.). If you're braising or stewing meat or poultry, begin a day ahead of time and refrigerate the dish overnight. The next day, when the chilled fat has congealed, you can remove it easily before reheating. Braising is also an excellent way to cook vegetables.

Poaching. To poach chicken or fish, immerse it in a pan of simmering liquid on top of the stove. This method works especially well when you serve the food with a sauce made of pureed vegetables and herbs.

Grilling or Broiling. Placing food on a rack and cooking with either of these methods allows the fat to drip away from meat or poultry. It's also a tasty way to cook fish steaks or whole fish. For extra flavor, try marinating food before putting it over the coals or under the broiler. Skewered vegetables also taste great browned over an open flame.

Sautéing. Fish, poultry and vegetable dishes can be sautéed in an open skillet with little or no fat; the high temperature and motion keep food from sticking. Try sautéing with a tiny bit of unsaturated oil rubbed onto the pan with a paper towel. Better still, use vegetable oil spray or sauté in a small amount of low-sodium broth or table wine.

Steaming. Cooking food in a basket over simmering water leaves the natural flavor, color and nutritional value of vegetables intact. Try adding herbs to the steaming water or using low-sodium broth instead of water to add even more flavor to the finished dish.

Stir-frying. Done in a Chinese wok, this method relies on the same principle as sautéing. The high temperature and the constant movement of the food keep it from sticking and burning. Try stir-frying vegetables and diced poultry or seafood with a tiny bit of peanut oil Use the low-sodium version when your recipe calls for soy sauce.

Microwave Cooking. This is a fast, easy cooking method that requires no added fat. You don't have to add fat to keep the food from sticking to the pan because foods don't tend to stick in the moist heat of microwaving. In fact, you can drain food of fat as it cooks by placing it in the microwave between two paper towels.

If you want to adapt a recipe for microwaving, try cutting the cooking time to one-fourth to one-third of the conventional time. If the food needs more cooking, increase it a little at a time. You might also look for a microwave recipe similar to the one you're trying to adapt. Keep the following in mind when microwave cooking:

- Choose foods that cook well in moist heat: chicken, fish, ground meat, vegetables, sauces and soups.
- Pieces that are about equal in size and shape will cook uniformly.
- You can reduce the liquid used in cooking beverages, soups, vegetables, fruits and main dishes by about one-third because less evaporates in microwave cooking.
- Choose a microwave-safe container slightly larger than the dish required for cooking the recipe in a conventional oven.
- Use a high setting (100 percent power) for soups, beverages, fruits, vegetables, fish, ground meat and poultry. Use a medium-high setting (70 percent power) for simmering stews. And use a medium setting (50 percent power) for baking breads, cakes and muffins and for cooking less tender cuts of meat.
- To create a crusty look on baked items, grease pans with an acceptable vegetable oil and add ground nuts or crumbs. (Be sure to calculate the values for the fat and/or sodium in these added nuts when deciding how these foods fit into your dietary plans.)
- Add low-fat, low-sodium cheese and other toppings near the end of cooking to keep them from becoming tough or soggy.
- Don't try coating meat with flour if you will be adding liquid for cooking. The coating only becomes soggy.
- Use quick-cooking instead of long-grain rice.

COOKING TIPS

Keep the taste, but trim the fat and salt. That's the challenge you'll face cooking for a low-sodium, low-modified-fat, low-cholesterol eating plan. Here are a few helpful hints.

- Use a nonstick skillet so that you can cook with a minimum of oil, or cook with vegetable oil spray, another good fat-cutting technique.
- Trim all visible fat from meat before cooking.
- After you roast meat or poultry, chill the drippings in the refrigerator. Once they are cooled, the fat will rise to the top and harden; it can be removed easily and the broth saved to use in stews, sauces and soups.
- Buy only the leanest ground beef, pork and turkey (no more than 15 percent fat). After browning it, put ground meat into a strainer or

colander lined with paper towels. Allow fat to drain out. "Ground" meat is generally higher in fat than nonground meat. Even the leanest ground beef contains more fat than is recommended for those on the Step-Two Diet (see pages 307–326). Instead of buying packaged ground beef, have your butcher grind a sirloin steak for you. Be sure to have him remove all visible fat and clean the grinder to remove any fat from previous grindings.

- When figuring serving sizes, remember that meat loses about 25 percent of its weight during cooking. (For example, 4 ounces of raw meat will be about 3 ounces cooked.)
- To make gravy without fat, blend a teaspoon of cornstarch with a cup of room-temperature, low-sodium broth by shaking the two together in a jar with a tight-fitting lid. Then heat the rest of the defatted broth in a saucepan and add the blended liquid. Simmer until thickened.
- Make a habit of skinning chickens before cooking and removing all visible fat below the skin. The skin will be easier to remove if you use paper towels or a clean cloth to take hold of it. Be certain to scrub the cutting surface and utensils well with hot sudsy water after preparing poultry for cooking.
- Fresh fish should be cooked for 10 minutes per inch of thickness. Add 5 minutes if it's wrapped in foil. Frozen fish requires 20 minutes per inch of thickness, plus 10 minutes if it's wrapped in foil. Cooking time may vary, depending on the cooking method used, but fish is done when the flesh is opaque and it flakes easily.
- Prepare scrambled eggs or omelettes so that only one egg yolk per portion is used. Add a few extra egg whites to the mixing bowl to make more generous servings.
- Seal natural juices into foods by wrapping them in foil before cooking. Or try wrapping foods in edible pouches made of large steamed lettuce or cabbage leaves and placing them seam-side down in the baking dish before cooking.
- Cook vegetables just long enough to make them tender-crisp. Overcooked vegetables lose both flavor and important nutrients.
- Clean mushrooms as you use them by wiping them with a damp cloth. A quick rinse in cold water is fine, but never soak them or they'll get soggy.

- Be sure to wear rubber gloves when handling hot peppers or wash hands thoroughly after handling. Skin, especially around the eyes, is very sensitive to the oil from peppers.
- Cut down on cholesterol by using more vegetables and less poultry or meats in soups, stews and casseroles. Finely chopped vegetables are great for stretching ground poultry or meat, too.
- Cut down on fat in creamy salad dressing by mixing it with plain, low-fat or nonfat yogurt.
- Sweeten plain, low-fat or nonfat yogurt with pureed fruit or applesauce instead of buying prepared fruit yogurt.

ENHANCING FLAVORS WITHOUT USING SALT

Spicing up low-salt cooking is easy when you know a few good tricks. The following ideas will help you enhance the flavor of a variety of foods without using salt. After trying a few of these techniques, you'll agree that the best things in life are salt-free.

- To remove oils and salty liquids, drain canned salmon, tuna or sardines. Then add water to the can and drain again to rinse.
- Toast seeds, nuts and whole spices to bring out their full flavor. Cook them in a dry skillet over moderate heat or on a baking sheet in a 400° F. oven.
- Roasting vegetables in a hot oven will caramelize their natural sugars.
- Pound garlic, chilies and fresh herbs and spices with a mortar and pestle to release their flavors.
- Use citrus zest. The zest is the part of the peel without the white pith; it holds the true flavor of the fruit. Either grate it with a flat, sheet-type grater or remove it with a vegetable peeler and then cut the piece into thin strips.
- Grate fresh ginger with a flat, sheet-type grater. Use a food processor to grate fresh horseradish, which packs more punch than the salted, bottled kind.
- Use fresh herbs instead of dried when possible. Chop and add them at the last moment for fresher, more "alive" taste.
- Add dried herbs such as thyme, rosemary and marjoram for more pungent flavor, but use them sparingly.
- Sprinkle vinegar or citrus juice for a wonderful flavor enhancer, but

add it at the last moment. Vinegar is wonderful on vegetables such as greens, citrus on fruits such as cantaloupe. Either is great on fish.

- Use dry mustard or salt-free mustard. Mix the dry mustard with water to make a very sharp condiment. You can also find bottled, salt-free mustard that's just as powerful as the kind that contains salt.
- For a little more "bite," add fresh hot peppers to your dishes. Remove the membrane and seeds before finely chopping. They are fine raw, and a small amount goes a long way.
- Vegetables and fruits are easy to season without salt. Fill an herb shaker with a combination of fresh herbs and spices. Use that in place of a salt shaker. One of our favorites can be found on page 35.
- Some vegetables and fruits, such as mushrooms, tomatoes, chilies, cherries, cranberries and currants, impart a more intense flavor when dried than when fresh. And if they are soaked in water and reconstituted, you get as a bonus a natural "broth" to work with.
- Buy the best and the freshest whole spices and grind them in a spice grinder. You'll taste a big difference.

Ingredient Substitutions

No need to toss out old family recipes and holiday treats because you're watching your salt intake. You can keep many of your favorite recipes if you're willing to make a few simple ingredient substitutions. Just by making these few changes, you will reduce enough of the sodium and fat to make almost any recipe fit right into your new eating plan.

If your own recipe calls for:	Use:
Broth or bouillon	Unsalted bouillon cubes according to package directions; commercially prepared low-sodium broth; Chicken Broth (page 42); or Beef Broth (page 43).
Tomato juice	No-salt-added tomato juice; or dilute 1 6-ounce can of no-salt-added tomato paste with 3 cans of water.
Tomato puree	Combine 1 6-ounce can of no-salt-added tomato paste with 1 can of water.
Salt	See "Seasoning Blends" (pages 31–37).
Flavor salts such as onion salt, garlic salt and celery salt	Onion powder, garlic powder, celery seed or flakes as indicated in the recipe or according to your preference.
Sour cream	Mock Sour Cream (page 178); plain low-fat or nonfat yogurt; unsalted low-fat cottage cheese plus low-fat yogurt for flavor; unsalted ricotta cheese made from part-skim milk (thinned with yogurt or low-fat buttermilk, if desired); 1 can of chilled evaporated skim milk whipped with 1 teaspoon of fresh lemon juice; or low-fat buttermilk. *Note:* When using yogurt in sauces, mix 1 tablespoon cornstarch with 1 tablespoon of yogurt and then mix into remainder of yogurt. This prevents the yogurt from separating.
Whipped cream	Mock Whipped Cream (page 179). Evaporated skim milk (thoroughly chilled before whipping).

If your own recipe calls for:	Use:
Unsweetened baking chocolate	Unsweetened cocoa powder or carob powder blended with unsaturated oil or unsaturated, unsalted margarine (1 1-ounce square of chocolate = 3 tablespoons of cocoa or carob plus 1 tablespoon polyunsaturated oil or unsaturated, unsalted margarine). Because carob is sweeter than cocoa, reduce the sugar in the recipe by one-fourth.
Butter	Unsaturated, unsalted margarine or oil (1 tablespoon butter = 1 tablespoon unsaturated, unsalted margarine or ¾ tablespoon oil); if you wish to substitute margarine for oil, use 1¼ cups unsaturated, unsalted margarine for 1 cup of oil; use 1¼ tablespoons of unsaturated, unsalted margarine for 1 tablespoon of oil.
Melted butter or shortening	Vegetable oil or melted unsaturated, unsalted margarine.
Eggs	Use commercially produced, cholesterol-free egg substitutes according to package directions; or use 1 egg white plus 2 teaspoons of unsaturated oil for each egg. For every 2 whole eggs requested in baking recipes, substitute 3 egg whites. For 1 whole large egg, substitute 2 egg whites. The table on page 289 shows the approximate whole egg content of various prepared foods.
Whole milk	Use 1 cup of skim or nonfat milk plus 1 tablespoon of unsaturated oil as a substitute for 1 cup of whole milk.
Cream cheese	Blend 4 tablespoons of unsaturated, unsalted margarine with 1 cup dry, unsalted, low-fat cottage cheese. Add a small amount of skim milk if needed in blending mixture. Vegetables such as chopped herbs and seasonings may be added for variety.
Cream	Polyunsaturated coffee creams; undiluted evaporated skim milk; double-strength reconstituted nonfat dry milk powder; or skim milk.
Evaporated milk	Evaporated skim milk
Ice cream	Ice milk; fruit ice; sherbet; or low-fat frozen yogurt.

MORE SUBSTITUTION IDEAS

- Use low-fat buttermilk in place of sour cream in salad dressing recipes.
- Thicken soups, stews or sauces that have been defatted, with cornstarch or flour dissolved in cold liquid, or with pureed vegetables.
- Substitute chopped vegetables for some of the bread when you make poultry stuffing.
- Since most recipes include more sugar than necessary, you can usually reduce the amount of sugar by one-fourth to one-third.
- Reduce salt in nonyeast baking recipes.
- Add a drop of fresh lemon juice to the water you cook pasta in and eliminate the salt.
- Substitute brown rice for white rice to add whole-grain fiber.
- Use a blend of whole-wheat flour and all-purpose flour in recipes that call for regular flour.
- Use wheat germ, bran and whole-wheat bread crumbs in place of buttered crumbs to top casseroles.
- Using vegetable oil for shortening in cakes that require creaming will affect the texture, so use unsaturated, unsalted margarine instead. Do use vegetable oil in recipes calling for melted butter.

How to Use These Recipes

When planning menus, remember to read the analysis following each recipe to help you keep track of your sodium, fat, cholesterol and calorie intake. (Also calculated there are protein, carbohydrate and potassium values.) The recipes were all calculated by the American Heart Association using the Nutrient Data System developed by the University of Minnesota School of Public Health's Nutrition Coordinating Center. All values are rounded to whole numbers. Note that the values for saturated, monounsaturated and polyunsaturated fatty acids will not add up precisely to the total fat value in the recipe. That's because the total fat report includes not only fatty acids but other fatty substances and glycerol as well.

Each analysis is based on a single serving unless otherwise indicated. The analyses include all the ingredients listed, including the optional ones. They do not, however, include ingredients listed as suggested accompaniments unless there's a note to that effect on the analysis.

When figuring portions, remember that the serving sizes are divided equally; they're not listed as a measured amount. All figures for the total amount made are approximate.

The calories in alcohol evaporate when heated, and this reduction is reflected in the calculations. When a marinade is used in a recipe, some of the liquid is discarded. This is also accounted for in our calculations.

All of the recipes were analyzed using mostly unsalted or low-sodium ingredients. We used unsalted margarine, no-salt-added tomato sauce, low-sodium soy sauce, etc. In a few instances where we used "regular" ingredients, you may wish to use the low-salt version.

A few examples of these are baking powder, bread crumbs and mayonnaise.

Caloric values reflect physiological energy values. (This means they represent the energy values remaining after the losses in digestion and metabolism have been deducted from the total.) The caloric values are based on the Atwater system for determining energy values.

In recipes calling for vegetable oil, choose corn, safflower, soybean or sunflower oils because they contain polyunsaturated fat. Canola and olive oils are acceptable monounsaturated oils. You also may use peanut oil occasionally for variety.

Finally, although specific ingredients are listed for each recipe, feel free to experiment or substitute when necessary—as long as your ingredient substitutions do not add sodium or fat. Interchanging herbs, spices, spirits, vinegars and kinds of vegetables can give you variety and can customize the recipe to your taste and will not change the nutritional value of the dish substantially. Above all, remember the cardinal rule of cooking and eating: have fun!

RECIPES

SEASONING BLENDS

Herb Seasoning

Lemon Herb Seasoning

Salad Herb Blend

Chili Powder

So you've thrown away your salt shaker. "But what *else,*" you ask, nervously rifling the kitchen shelves, "can make my food taste good?"

Don't panic. There are hundreds of alternatives to salt. You are limited only by your imagination. Start by borrowing from some exotic cuisines: use spices to create the taste of foods from India, Vietnam, China and Thailand; use wines for a European flavor. Consider the cornucopia of taste sensations you can create from ginger, sesame seeds, orange rind, fresh horseradish, dried mushrooms and dozens of other things.

And that's only the beginning. Not only can you combine these tastes endlessly, your cooking methods can be varied also. For example, baked apples with cinnamon and margarine enhance the sweetness of the apples; orange juice on chicken or apple juice concentrate on pork enhance the flavors of those meats beautifully. Using foods with a natural sweetness rounded out with herbs and spices is especially delicious. Also using foods with contrasting textures and presenting them beautifully can delight the senses—and the appetite!

Here's an easy way to keep your favorite seasonings on hand: place a mixture of herbs in an herb shaker. Use that instead of your salt shaker. You'll find three of our favorite combinations here, or invent an herb-shaker combination custom-made for your tastebuds.

And don't forget the possibilities of using wine, vinegar and oil or unsalted salad dressings to create delicious marinades.

Although table wines contain no salt, "cooking wines" do. Read the labels carefully and use only those without salt.

For meats, soups and vegetables, try fresh lemon juice, hot pepper sauce, vinegar or unsalted liquid smoke for a variety of flavors.

To get you started, try cooking with the herbs and other items suggested for certain foods on the chart in Appendix B. They're guaranteed to add spice to your life!

HERB SEASONING

MAKES APPROXIMATELY ⅓ CUP

½ teaspoon cayenne pepper
1 tablespoon garlic powder
1 teaspoon dried basil
1 teaspoon dried marjoram
1 teaspoon dried thyme
1 teaspoon dried parsley
1 teaspoon dried savory
1 teaspoon mace
1 teaspoon onion powder
1 teaspoon freshly ground black pepper
1 teaspoon powdered sage

Place all ingredients in a medium bowl. Toss gently with spoon until well blended. Store in an airtight container in a cool, dry, dark place for up to 6 months.

This mix is perfect for keeping on hand at the table as an all-purpose replacement for the salt shaker. It's good on casseroles, stews, fresh vegetables and meats.

LEMON HERB SEASONING

MAKES APPROXIMATELY 1 CUP

4½ tablespoons dried basil
3¾ tablespoons dried oregano
1½ tablespoons finely ground black pepper
1½ tablespoons dried onion flakes
1½ tablespoons whole celery seed
1¼ tablespoons powdered basil
½ teaspoon garlic powder
½ teaspoon grated lemon rind

Place all ingredients in a medium bowl. Toss gently with spoon until well blended just before using. (For a more lemony flavor, add fresh lemon juice). Store in an airtight container in a cool, dry, dark place for up to 6 months. This seasoning is good on fish, poultry and salads.

SALAD HERB BLEND

MAKES APPROXIMATELY 1 CUP

1/4 cup dried parsley
1/4 cup dried marjoram
2 1/2 tablespoons dried basil
1 1/2 tablespoons sesame seeds
1 1/2 tablespoons chili pepper flakes
1 1/2 tablespoons powdered rosemary
1 1/4 tablespoons powdered celery seed
2 1/2 teaspoons dried savory
2 1/2 teaspoons powdered sage
2 1/4 teaspoons dried thyme
2 teaspoons granulated onion
2 teaspoons dried dill weed
1 1/4 teaspoons fine ground black pepper
3/4 teaspoon garlic powder

Place all ingredients in a medium bowl. Toss gently with spoon until well blended. Store in an airtight container in a cool, dry, dark place for up to 6 months.

CHILI POWDER

MAKES APPROXIMATELY 4 TABLESPOONS

3 tablespoons paprika
2 teaspoons finely crushed oregano
1 teaspoon ground cumin
1 teaspoon ground turmeric
1 teaspoon garlic powder
1/4 teaspoon cayenne pepper

Place all ingredients in a medium bowl. Toss gently with spoon until well blended. Store in an airtight container in cool, dark, dry place for up to 6 months.

Use in place of packaged chili powder.

Soups

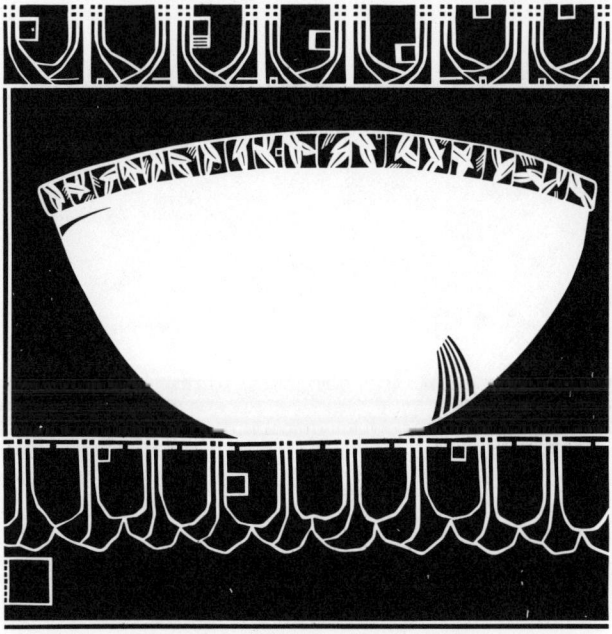

Chicken Broth

Beef Broth

Beef Vegetable Soup

Minestrone

Turkey Vegetable Soup

Onion Soup

Split Pea Soup

Lentil Soup with Lemon

Gazpacho

New England Fish Chowder with Thyme

An old Spanish proverb says, "Of soup and love, the first is best." A strong sentiment to some, perhaps—but one perfectly understood by those of us who love good soup. Whether it's homemade Beef Vegetable Soup simmering on a winter's day or a spicy, crunchy, cold Gazpacho, soup is diversity in a bowl.

Your greatest challenge in cooking soups is to get the zest and flavor you want—without the salt you don't want. Steer clear of canned, dried or frozen soups and soup mixes always. They're among the saltiest foods available. Instead, make your soup just like Grandma did—from scratch.

It's easy, really. Just remember that soup is composed basically of three elements—liquids, solids and seasonings—and the sky's the limit on herb and spice combinations.

The liquid base or broth is critical. It is best prepared by cooking the protein source you plan to use: low-fat beef, poultry or fish. It may be tempting to use bouillon cubes or flavor packets, but they contain lots of salt. Instead, use our recipes for Beef or Chicken Broth, or, if you must, unsalted bouillon cubes or canned low-sodium broth.

Here's an easy trick for removing a lot of the fat in your soup: Just prepare the soup a day in advance and chill it overnight. The fat will rise to the top, and you can easily remove it. If you can't prepare the broth in advance, try to skim off as much fat as possible before adding your vegetables, grains, beans, pastas and seasonings. Some kitchenware stores carry inexpensive gadgets to help you with this, and while they aren't strictly necessary, they can make the job easier.

Finally, inventive toppings can add further interest and flavor to your soups. Garnish them with lemon slices, low-fat yogurt, chopped onions, chives, a sprinkling of herbs or Seasoned Croutons (page 211).

So, go ahead. Try Onion Soup as an appetizer at a small dinner party. Serve Lentil Soup with Lemon for a deliciously different lunch. Or try New England Fish Chowder with Thyme at dinner. You'll love the variety of flavors soup can provide.

CHICKEN BROTH

MAKES 2½ QUARTS

NUTRIENT ANALYSIS*	
CALORIES	319 KCAL
PROTEIN	30 GM
CARBOHYDRATE	38 GM
TOTAL FAT	6 GM
SATURATED	2 GM
POLYUNSATURATED	1 GM
MONOUNSATURATED	2 GM
CHOLESTEROL	68 MG
SODIUM	327 MG
POTASSIUM	1591 MG
CALCIUM	211 MG

*FOR ENTIRE RECIPE.

3 pounds chicken, skinned, all visible fat removed
3 quarts cold water
1 medium onion, chopped
2 large carrots, chopped
2 stalks celery, chopped
5 or 6 peppercorns
1 bay leaf
1 teaspoon dried thyme

Rinse chicken and pat dry.

In a large stockpot, combine all ingredients and bring to a boil. Reduce heat and simmer 1 to 2 hours for a lightly flavored soup. For a richer, more flavorful soup simmer the broth for 3 to 4 hours. Skim the froth off the top of broth. Remove chicken and strain broth. Refrigerate until the fat hardens on the surface. Remove fat and discard.

This dish may be served as a light soup or used in recipes calling for chicken broth.

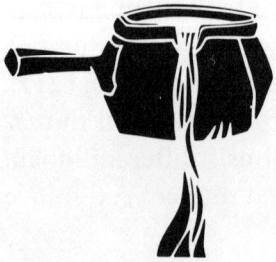

BEEF BROTH

MAKES 2 QUARTS

4 pounds beef or veal bones (preferably shank or knuckle bones)
3 quarts water
1 medium onion, coarsely chopped
1 bay leaf
2 whole cloves
1 teaspoon dried thyme
5 or 6 peppercorns
8 sprigs fresh parsley

Preheat oven to 400° F.

Place bones in a roasting pan and bake 25 to 30 minutes, turning bones once. Pour off collected fat.

Transfer bones and remaining ingredients to a large stockpot. Simmer 4 to 6 hours; do not boil. Skim fat off the top. Strain through a fine strainer lined with cheesecloth. Refrigerate. Fat will harden on the surface when chilled. Skim fat from top.

This dish may be served as a light soup or used in recipes calling for beef broth.

NUTRIENT ANALYSIS*

CALORIES	402 KCAL
PROTEIN	35 GM
CARBOHYDRATE	51 GM
TOTAL FAT	7 GM
SATURATED	3 GM
POLYUNSATURATED	0 GM
MONOUNSATURATED	3 GM
CHOLESTEROL	81 MG
SODIUM	237 MG
POTASSIUM	1839 MG
CALCIUM	247 MG

*FOR ENTIRE RECIPE.

BEEF VEGETABLE SOUP

SERVES 4; APPROXIMATELY 8 OUNCES PER SERVING

NUTRIENT ANALYSIS	
CALORIES	107 KCAL
PROTEIN	5 GM
CARBOHYDRATE	12 GM
TOTAL FAT	5 GM
SATURATED	1 GM
POLYUNSATURATED	1 GM
MONOUNSATURATED	2 GM
CHOLESTEROL	10 MG
SODIUM	53 MG
POTASSIUM	425 MG
CALCIUM	62 MG

1 tablespoon olive oil
1/2 cup chopped onions
1/2 cup diced celery
1/2 cup sliced carrots
1/2 teaspoon oregano
1/2 teaspoon thyme
2 cloves garlic, minced
4 cups low-sodium beef broth
Freshly ground black pepper to taste
1/2 cup cut fresh green beans
1/2 cup chopped fresh tomatoes

Place oil in a medium stockpot over medium heat. Add onions, celery, carrots, oregano and thyme and sauté until soft, about 5 to 7 minutes. Add garlic and cook for another minute. Add beef broth, pepper and the rest of the vegetables. Simmer 30 to 45 minutes, or until vegetables are soft.

MINESTRONE

SERVES 6; 1 CUP PER SERVING

4 tablespoons olive oil
½ cup chopped onions
½ cup sliced carrots
½ cup diced celery
1 to 2 cloves garlic, minced
6 cups low-sodium chicken broth
1 cup canned no-salt-added tomatoes
1 cup cooked macaroni (no salt added)
1 cup cooked white beans (no salt added)
2 tablespoons chopped fresh parsley
½ teaspoon freshly ground black pepper
¼ cup grated Parmesan cheese

Heat olive oil in a large pot over low heat. Add onions, carrots, celery and garlic. Cook 5 to 7 minutes, or until soft. Next add the chicken broth, tomatoes, pasta, white beans, parsley and black pepper. Cook 5 minutes, or until thoroughly heated. Pour into individual bowls and garnish with Parmesan cheese.

NUTRIENT ANALYSIS

CALORIES	162 KCAL
PROTEIN	7 GM
CARBOHYDRATE	15 GM
TOTAL FAT	8 GM
SATURATED	2 GM
POLYUNSATURATED	1 GM
MONOUNSATURATED	6 GM
CHOLESTEROL	2 MG
SODIUM	104 MG
POTASSIUM	371 MG
CALCIUM	82 MG

TURKEY VEGETABLE SOUP

SERVES 6; 1 CUP PER SERVING

NUTRIENT ANALYSIS	
CALORIES	219 KCAL
PROTEIN	26 GM
CARBOHYDRATE	6 GM
TOTAL FAT	10 GM
SATURATED	3 GM
POLYUNSATURATED	3 GM
MONOUNSATURATED	4 GM
CHOLESTEROL	63 MG
SODIUM	139 MG
POTASSIUM	479 MG
CALCIUM	46 MG

2 tablespoons acceptable margarine
½ cup chopped onions
¼ cup diced celery
6 cups low-sodium chicken broth
1 cup canned no-salt-added tomatoes
1 pound cooked and diced turkey meat
½ teaspoon freshly ground black pepper
¼ teaspoon hot pepper sauce
½ cup frozen peas, thawed

Melt margarine in a large pot over low heat. Add onions and celery and cook 5 minutes, or until soft. Add chicken broth and tomatoes. Cook 10 minutes, or until vegetables are soft. Add turkey, black pepper and hot pepper sauce. Cook 5 more minutes. Add the peas and cook another 5 minutes. Serve hot.

ONION SOUP

SERVES 3; APPROXIMATELY 1 CUP PER SERVING

2 tablespoons acceptable margarine, melted
1 tablespoon acceptable vegetable oil
2 medium onions, sliced
1/8 teaspoon sugar
2 teaspoons all-purpose flour
2 1/2 cups low-sodium beef broth
2 tablespoons vermouth or dry white table wine
1/8 teaspoon freshly ground black pepper
1/2 cup Seasoned Croutons (see recipe, page 211) or 1 slice bread, toasted and cut into cubes

NUTRIENT ANALYSIS	
CALORIES	210 KCAL
PROTEIN	6 GM
CARBOHYDRATE	17 GM
TOTAL FAT	13 GM
SATURATED	3 GM
POLYUNSATURATED	4 GM
MONOUNSATURATED	6 GM
CHOLESTEROL	9 MG
SODIUM	72 MG
POTASSIUM	329 MG
CALCIUM	55 MG

Combine margarine, oil and onions in a saucepan. Cover and cook over low heat 15 minutes.

Add sugar and cook uncovered 10 minutes, stirring occasionally, until the onions are a deep, golden brown.

Add flour and mix thoroughly. Stir in broth. Add vermouth and pepper and simmer 15 to 30 minutes.

Place soup in cups and top with Seasoned Croutons or cubes of toast.

SPLIT PEA SOUP

SERVES 6; APPROXIMATELY 1½ CUPS PER SERVING

NUTRIENT ANALYSIS	
CALORIES	52 KCAL
PROTEIN	3 GM
CARBOHYDRATE	10 GM
TOTAL FAT	0 GM
SATURATED	0 GM
POLYUNSATURATED	0 GM
MONOUNSATURATED	0 GM
CHOLESTEROL	0 MG
SODIUM	8 MG
POTASSIUM	195 MG
CALCIUM	14 MG

1 cup (½ pound) dried split peas
2 quarts water
1 carrot, chopped
2 stalks celery, chopped
1 medium onion, chopped
½ teaspoon unsalted liquid smoke
1 tablespoon chopped fresh parsley or 1½ teaspoons dried parsley flakes
¼ teaspoon onion powder
⅛ teaspoon garlic powder
⅛ teaspoon freshly ground black pepper

Place all ingredients in a large pan. Cover and simmer 2½ to 3 hours. If soup becomes too thick, add more water, stirring it in slowly.

If a smooth soup is desired, remove from heat and process in a blender or force through a sieve. Serve immediately.

LENTIL SOUP WITH LEMON

SERVES 8; APPROXIMATELY 1¼ CUPS PER SERVING

2 cups lentils, dry
½ yellow onion, diced
2 cloves garlic, minced
2 tablespoons olive oil
8 cups water or no-salt-added vegetable broth
1 medium potato, diced
½ teaspoon oregano (optional)
2 tablespoons fresh lemon juice
Freshly ground black pepper to taste

Rinse lentils and drain.

Place onion, garlic and oil in a medium stockpot over medium heat. Sauté until soft. Add all ingredients except lemon juice and pepper. Simmer 45 to 60 minutes, or until the lentils are soft. Stir in lemon juice and pepper and serve immediately.

NUTRIENT ANALYSIS

CALORIES	109 KCAL
PROTEIN	5 GM
CARBOHYDRATE	15 GM
TOTAL FAT	4 GM
SATURATED	0 GM
POLYUNSATURATED	0 GM
MONOUNSATURATED	3 GM
CHOLESTEROL	0 MG
SODIUM	5 MG
POTASSIUM	260 MG
CALCIUM	17 MG

GAZPACHO

SERVES 8; APPROXIMATELY 1 CUP PER SERVING

NUTRIENT ANALYSIS	
CALORIES	48 KCAL
PROTEIN	2 GM
CARBOHYDRATE	12 GM
TOTAL FAT	0 GM
SATURATED	0 GM
POLYUNSATURATED	0 GM
MONOUNSATURATED	0 GM
CHOLESTEROL	0 MG
SODIUM	29 MG
POTASSIUM	575 MG
CALCIUM	36 MG

1 medium fresh tomato
1 small green bell pepper
2 medium cucumbers
1 small zucchini
1/4 cup chopped onion
1/4 cup chopped green onions, with tops
1/4 cup chopped fresh parsley
2 cloves garlic, minced
1 teaspoon freshly ground black pepper
1 teaspoon Worcestershire sauce
4 cups no-salt-added tomato juice
1 tablespoon fresh lemon juice (optional)

Finely chop all vegetables. Place in a large bowl. Add remaining ingredients. Stir to mix well. Cover and refrigerate. Serve cold.

NEW ENGLAND FISH CHOWDER WITH THYME

SERVES 6; 1 CUP PER SERVING

4 tablespoons acceptable margarine
½ cup diced onions
4 tablespoons flour
6 cups low-sodium fish stock or chicken broth
2 medium potatoes, peeled and cut into small cubes
1 cup low-fat (2 percent) milk
1 teaspoon thyme leaves
⅛ teaspoon white pepper
1 pound boneless fish fillets (haddock, cod or other firm white fish) cut into ½-inch cubes

Melt margarine in a large pot over low heat. Add onions and cook 5 minutes, or until soft. Add flour and cook 2 minutes. Next, add fish stock, stirring vigorously. Add potatoes and simmer 20 to 25 minutes, or until potatoes are tender. Add milk, thyme leaves, white pepper and fish. Cook 10 more minutes. Serve immediately.

NUTRIENT ANALYSIS

CALORIES	230 KCAL
PROTEIN	20 GM
CARBOHYDRATE	14 GM
TOTAL FAT	10 GM
SATURATED	3 GM
POLYUNSATURATED	3 GM
MONOUNSATURATED	4 GM
CHOLESTEROL	43 MG
SODIUM	143 MG
POTASSIUM	522 MG
CALCIUM	84 MG

SALADS

Three-Bean Salad

Texas Caviar (Black-eyed Pea Salad)

Spicy Marinated Vegetables

Summer Pasta Salad

Potato Salad

Macaroni Salad

Creamy Coleslaw

Pineapple Coleslaw

Cucumber Raita

Waldorf Salad

Ambrosia

Orange-Grapefruit Salad

Chicken Salad

Hawaiian Chicken Salad

Tuna Salad

Seafood Salad

If your picture of a salad is iceberg lettuce with a tomato, you'll be delighted with the variety of these recipes. From Texas Caviar (Black-eyed Pea Salad) to Hawaiian Chicken Salad or creamy Cucumber Raita, salads can mean exciting tastes and textures.

Of course, tossed green salads *are* a staple of healthful cuisine. But insiders know the trick to making them magnificent every time: using more than one variety of lettuce. Today your grocer probably offers a dozen kinds to choose from. Consider using romaine of Caesar Salad fame; or the soft, velvety leaves of Boston, bibb or endive; or green- or red-leaf lettuce with its curly, narrow leaves. And don't stop there! Experiment with beet, dandelion and mustard greens—even nasturtium leaves. Add watercress, chicory and spinach to your "standard" salad. With such a wealth of greens, a tossed salad need never be boring.

Upon this delicious foundation, you can add nearly endless varieties of vegetables, seeds, nuts and sprouts. Also consider chopped hard-cooked egg whites, cooked chicken or turkey, marinated fish and croutons. For even more variety, look for unusual toppings such as alfalfa sprouts or other fresh sprouts, jicama, fresh jalapeños, cilantro or fresh raw peas.

Virtually any food can be made into a salad. Just look at our Summer Pasta Salad, Orange-Grapefruit Salad and Spicy Marinated Vegetables. One of the nicest things about salads is that you can enjoy them as a side dish or, with soup and bread, make them an entire meal.

Best of all, salads with fresh ingredients are naturally low in salt. As long as you stay away from salt-filled accompaniments such as green olives, pickles, sardines, luncheon meats, cheeses and commercial dressings, salads can be one of the tastiest staples of your low-salt eating plan.

THREE-BEAN SALAD

SERVES 14

THREE-BEAN SALAD NUTRIENT ANALYSIS

CALORIES	118 KCAL
PROTEIN	2 GM
CARBOHYDRATE	17 GM
TOTAL FAT	5 GM
SATURATED	1 GM
POLYUNSATURATED	3 GM
MONOUNSATURATED	1 GM
CHOLESTEROL	0 MG
SODIUM	8 MG
POTASSIUM	142 MG
CALCIUM	37 MG

BEAN AND SPROUT SALAD NUTRIENT ANALYSIS

CALORIES	124 KCAL
PROTEIN	2 GM
CARBOHYDRATE	18 GM
TOTAL FAT	6 GM
SATURATED	1 GM
POLYUNSATURATED	3 GM
MONOUNSATURATED	1 GM
CHOLESTEROL	0 MG
SODIUM	9 MG
POTASSIUM	166 MG
CALCIUM	40 MG

3/4 cup dried kidney beans
4 cups water
1 10-ounce package frozen or 1 pound fresh cut green beans
1 10-ounce package frozen or 1 pound fresh cut yellow beans
1/2 cup cider vinegar
3/4 cup sugar
1/3 cup acceptable vegetable oil
1/2 teaspoon freshly ground black pepper
1 clove garlic
1 medium onion, sliced
1/2 green bell pepper, chopped

Place kidney beans and water in a saucepan. Bring to a boil and cook for 2 minutes. Set aside for 1 hour without draining.

Return beans to heat and simmer for 1 hour or until beans are very tender. Drain, rinse and set aside.

Cook green and yellow beans until tender. Drain.

Heat vinegar and sugar together to dissolve sugar. Add oil, pepper and garlic and mix.

Toss vinegar mixture with beans, onion and green pepper. Cover and chill 6 hours or overnight. Remove garlic clove before serving.

BEAN AND SPROUT SALAD

Add 1 cup fresh bean sprouts to the cooked bean, onion and green pepper mixture.

TEXAS CAVIAR (BLACK-EYED PEA SALAD)

SERVES 6

2 cups black-eyed peas, dry
½ cup diced green bell pepper
¼ cup diced white onion
2 tablespoons finely chopped canned jalapeño peppers
2 tablespoons acceptable vegetable oil
2 tablespoons red wine vinegar
1 clove garlic, minced
¼ teaspoon freshly ground black pepper

Sort black-eyed peas and soak overnight in 6 cups of water. Drain. Cook peas in 4 cups of fresh water until done but still firm, about 1½ hours.

Rinse in cold water and drain. In a medium bowl, combine all remaining ingredients and mix well. Add peas and chill.

NUTRIENT ANALYSIS

CALORIES	113 KCAL
PROTEIN	5 GM
CARBOHYDRATE	13 GM
TOTAL FAT	5 GM
SATURATED	1 GM
POLYUNSATURATED	3 GM
MONOUNSATURATED	1 GM
CHOLESTEROL	0 MG
SODIUM	39 MG
POTASSIUM	199 MG
CALCIUM	18 MG

SPICY MARINATED VEGETABLES

SERVES 4

NUTRIENT ANALYSIS	
CALORIES	107 KCAL
PROTEIN	3 GM
CARBOHYDRATE	11 GM
TOTAL FAT	7 GM
SATURATED	1 GM
POLYUNSATURATED	1 GM
MONOUNSATURATED	5 GM
CHOLESTEROL	0 MG
SODIUM	25 MG
POTASSIUM	470 MG
CALCIUM	44 MG

½ cup julienned yellow onion
1½ cups diced raw broccoli
1½ cups diced raw cauliflower
1 cup sliced yellow squash
1 cup sliced carrots
½ cup red wine vinegar
2 tablespoons olive oil
1 teaspoon garlic powder
½ teaspoon cayenne pepper

Combine vegetables in a large glass or ceramic bowl.

In another bowl, mix remaining ingredients. Pour over vegetables and stir to mix thoroughly. Cover and refrigerate 6 to 8 hours. Serve cold.

SUMMER PASTA SALAD

SERVES 4

3 cups pasta spirals
1½ cups broccoli florets
½ cup sliced carrots
1½ cups sliced zucchini
¾ cup plain nonfat yogurt
¼ cup cider vinegar
2 tablespoons Parmesan cheese
2 tablespoons mayonnaise
½ teaspoon garlic powder
½ teaspoon freshly ground black pepper

Cook pasta according to package directions, omitting salt. Drain and rinse under cold water and set aside.

Blanch vegetables in unsalted boiling water for 2 to 3 minutes, or just until tender crisp. Drain, rinse under cold water and set aside.

In a small bowl, mix yogurt, vinegar, Parmesan cheese, mayonnaise and seasonings. Set aside.

In a large bowl, combine pasta, yogurt mixture and vegetables. Mix well. Chill thoroughly and serve cold.

NUTRIENT ANALYSIS

CALORIES	269 KCAL
PROTEIN	11 GM
CARBOHYDRATE	42 GM
TOTAL FAT	7 GM
SATURATED	1 GM
POLYUNSATURATED	3 GM
MONOUNSATURATED	2 GM
CHOLESTEROL	7 MG
SODIUM	138 MG
POTASSIUM	507 MG
CALCIUM	168 MG

POTATO SALAD

SERVES 6

NUTRIENT ANALYSIS	
CALORIES	121 KCAL
PROTEIN	2 GM
CARBOHYDRATE	20 GM
TOTAL FAT	4 GM
SATURATED	1 GM
POLYUNSATURATED	2 GM
MONOUNSATURATED	1 GM
CHOLESTEROL	3 MG
SODIUM	54 MG
POTASSIUM	371 MG
CALCIUM	39 MG

5 medium red potatoes, cooked, peeled and diced
3/4 cup chopped celery with leaves
1/2 cup sliced radishes
2 green onions, diced
2 tablespoons mayonnaise
2 tablespoons plain nonfat yogurt
1 teaspoon dry mustard powder
1 tablespoon sugar
1/4 teaspoon freshly ground black pepper
1/4 teaspoon turmeric
1/2 teaspoon celery seed (optional)
2 1/2 tablespoons white vinegar
3 tablespoons skim milk

Combine potatoes, celery, radishes and onions.

In a separate bowl, mix together mayonnaise, yogurt, mustard powder, sugar, pepper, turmeric and celery seed. Add vinegar and milk and stir until mixed.

Combine with potato mixture and stir to mix well. Chill before serving.

MACARONI SALAD

SERVES 4

1 cup uncooked macaroni
2 tablespoons mayonnaise
2 tablespoons plain nonfat yogurt
1 tablespoon sugar
2 teaspoons cider vinegar
1/8 teaspoon freshly ground black pepper
1/4 cup chopped cucumber
1/4 cup chopped celery
2 radishes, sliced
1 tablespoon finely chopped onion

Cook macaroni according to package directions, omitting salt. Drain and allow to cool.

Mix mayonnaise, yogurt, sugar, vinegar and pepper together to make a dressing.

Toss macaroni, dressing and remaining ingredients together. Chill and serve cold.

NUTRIENT ANALYSIS

CALORIES	201 KCAL
PROTEIN	5 GM
CARBOHYDRATE	31 GM
TOTAL FAT	6 GM
SATURATED	1 GM
POLYUNSATURATED	3 GM
MONOUNSATURATED	2 GM
CHOLESTEROL	4 MG
SODIUM	53 MG
POTASSIUM	136 MG
CALCIUM	31 MG

CREAMY COLESLAW

SERVES 4

NUTRIENT ANALYSIS	
CALORIES	60 KCAL
PROTEIN	2 GM
CARBOHYDRATE	8 GM
TOTAL FAT	2 GM
SATURATED	0 GM
POLYUNSATURATED	1 GM
MONOUNSATURATED	1 GM
CHOLESTEROL	3 MG
SODIUM	92 MG
POTASSIUM	260 MG
CALCIUM	71 MG

2½ cups shredded red cabbage
1 cup grated carrots
⅓ cup plain nonfat yogurt
2 tablespoons mayonnaise
1 teaspoon mustard
½ teaspoon sugar
2 tablespoons cider vinegar
¼ teaspoon freshly ground black pepper

Place cabbage and carrots in a large bowl. Mix and set aside.

In a small bowl, combine yogurt, mayonnaise, mustard, sugar, vinegar and pepper. Mix well. Add yogurt mixture to cabbage-carrot mixture. Stir to mix thoroughly. Chill for 1 to 2 hours.

PINEAPPLE COLESLAW

SERVES 5

2 cups shredded cabbage
1/4 cup chopped green bell pepper
1 15 1/4-ounce can crushed pineapple, canned in natural juices, drained
3 tablespoons mayonnaise
1 1/2 teaspoons white vinegar
1/4 teaspoon dill weed
1/8 teaspoon freshly ground black pepper

In a large bowl, combine cabbage, green pepper and crushed pineapple. Toss lightly.

In a separate bowl, combine remaining ingredients. Mix well. Add to cabbage mixture and blend thoroughly.

Chill well before serving.

NUTRIENT ANALYSIS

CALORIES	120 KCAL
PROTEIN	1 GM
CARBOHYDRATE	16 GM
TOTAL FAT	7 GM
SATURATED	1 GM
POLYUNSATURATED	3 GM
MONOUNSATURATED	2 GM
CHOLESTEROL	5 MG
SODIUM	53 MG
POTASSIUM	191 MG
CALCIUM	28 MG

CUCUMBER RAITA

SERVES 4

NUTRIENT ANALYSIS	
CALORIES	111 KCAL
PROTEIN	11 GM
CARBOHYDRATE	16 GM
TOTAL FAT	0 GM
SATURATED	0 GM
POLYUNSATURATED	0 GM
MONOUNSATURATED	0 GM
CHOLESTEROL	4 MG
SODIUM	141 MG
POTASSIUM	563 MG
CALCIUM	377 MG

3 cups plain nonfat yogurt
2 small cucumbers, peeled, seeded and finely diced (approximately 2 cups)
2 green onions with tops, finely chopped (approximately 4 tablespoons)
1/8 teaspoon cayenne pepper

In a bowl, whisk the yogurt until smooth. Add remaining ingredients. Stir well, cover and chill until ready to serve. Can be made up to 2 hours in advance.

WALDORF SALAD

SERVES 6

NUTRIENT ANALYSIS	
CALORIES	160 KCAL
PROTEIN	3 GM
CARBOHYDRATE	19 GM
TOTAL FAT	9 GM
SATURATED	1 GM
POLYUNSATURATED	5 GM
MONOUNSATURATED	2 GM
CHOLESTEROL	5 MG
SODIUM	75 MG
POTASSIUM	257 MG
CALCIUM	96 MG

3 tablespoons reduced-calorie mayonnaise
1 cup plain nonfat yogurt
2 tablespoons cider vinegar
4 medium apples, unpeeled, cored and diced
1/4 cup diced celery
1/4 cup chopped walnuts

In a medium bowl, combine mayonnaise, yogurt and vinegar. Mix until blended. Add apples, celery and walnuts and mix until well combined. Chill thoroughly before serving.

AMBROSIA

SERVES 6

1/4 recipe (1/2 cup) Mock Sour Cream (see recipe, page 178)
1/4 cup powdered sugar
1/4 teaspoon vanilla
1 15-ounce can pineapple chunks, canned in natural juices, drained
1 11-ounce can mandarin orange segments, canned in light syrup, drained
1/2 cup miniature marshmallows
6 lettuce leaves

Mix Mock Sour Cream, powdered sugar and vanilla. Add fruit and marshmallows and toss together lightly. Chill for at least 1 hour.

Serve on salad plates lined with lettuce leaves.

NUTRIENT ANALYSIS

CALORIES	129 KCAL
PROTEIN	6 GM
CARBOHYDRATE	27 GM
TOTAL FAT	0 GM
SATURATED	0 GM
POLYUNSATURATED	0 GM
MONOUNSATURATED	0 GM
CHOLESTEROL	2 MG
SODIUM	13 MG
POTASSIUM	212 MG
CALCIUM	42 MG

ORANGE-GRAPEFRUIT SALAD

SERVES 4

NUTRIENT ANALYSIS	
CALORIES	154 KCAL
PROTEIN	7 GM
CARBOHYDRATE	25 GM
TOTAL FAT	5 GM
SATURATED	1 GM
POLYUNSATURATED	3 GM
MONOUNSATURATED	1 GM
CHOLESTEROL	0 MG
SODIUM	51 MG
POTASSIUM	1111 MG
CALCIUM	136 MG

1 large orange, preferably navel, peeled and sectioned
1 large grapefruit, peeled and sectioned
1 green onion and top, chopped
1 tablespoon acceptable vegetable oil
1 tablespoon white vinegar
4 large lettuce leaves

In a medium bowl, combine orange and grapefruit sections with onions. Cover and chill.

When ready to serve, mix oil and vinegar together with a fork and toss lightly with fruit.

Divide fruit mixture into 4 portions and serve on lettuce leaves.

CHICKEN SALAD

SERVES 6

2 cups unsalted, cooked and diced chicken
½ cup chopped celery
½ cup chopped fresh parsley
½ cup chopped fresh scallions
⅛ teaspoon dry mustard powder
¼ teaspoon freshly ground black pepper
1 teaspoon fresh lemon juice
½ cup mayonnaise

In a large bowl, toss chicken with celery, parsley and scallions. Combine dry mustard, pepper, lemon juice and mayonnaise and mix well. Pour over chicken mixture and stir until well mixed. Cover and chill.

Use as a sandwich filling or serve on lettuce leaves for a main dish salad. Garnish with any of the following: grapes, cut in half and seeded; pineapple chunks; fresh tomato wedges; toasted, unsalted almonds or pecans.

TURKEY SALAD

Use turkey in place of chicken.

CHICKEN SALAD NUTRIENT ANALYSIS

CALORIES	223 KCAL
PROTEIN	14 GM
CARBOHYDRATE	2 GM
TOTAL FAT	18 GM
SATURATED	3 GM
POLYUNSATURATED	8 GM
MONOUNSATURATED	5 GM
CHOLESTEROL	50 MG
SODIUM	153 MG
POTASSIUM	213 MG
CALCIUM	29 MG

TURKEY SALAD NUTRIENT ANALYSIS

CALORIES	223 KCAL
PROTEIN	14 GM
CARBOHYDRATE	2 GM
TOTAL FAT	18 GM
SATURATED	3 GM
POLYUNSATURATED	8 GM
MONOUNSATURATED	5 GM
CHOLESTEROL	50 MG
SODIUM	153 MG
POTASSIUM	213 MG
CALCIUM	29 MG

HAWAIIAN CHICKEN SALAD

SERVES 6

NUTRIENT ANALYSIS	
CALORIES	167 KCAL
PROTEIN	15 GM
CARBOHYDRATE	6 GM
TOTAL FAT	9 GM
SATURATED	2 GM
POLYUNSATURATED	4 GM
MONOUNSATURATED	3 GM
CHOLESTEROL	42 MG
SODIUM	86 MG
POTASSIUM	184 MG
CALCIUM	15 MG

2 cups unsalted, cooked and diced chicken
1 8-ounce can crushed pineapple, canned in natural juices, drained
2 tablespoons finely chopped green bell pepper
1/4 cup mayonnaise

In a medium bowl, mix all ingredients together. Cover and chill.

Serve on bread as sandwiches or on lettuce leaves for a main-dish salad.

TUNA SALAD

SERVES 3

NUTRIENT ANALYSIS	
CALORIES	174 KCAL
PROTEIN	17 GM
CARBOHYDRATE	1 GM
TOTAL FAT	11 GM
SATURATED	2 GM
POLYUNSATURATED	6 GM
MONOUNSATURATED	3 GM
CHOLESTEROL	30 MG
SODIUM	106 MG
POTASSIUM	204 MG
CALCIUM	12 MG

1 6 1/2-ounce can unsalted tuna, in spring water, drained, rinsed and flaked
1/2 cup chopped, unpeeled cucumber
3 tablespoons mayonnaise
1/8 teaspoon onion powder
1/8 teaspoon dry mustard powder

In a medium bowl, combine flaked tuna with cucumber. In a small bowl, combine mayonnaise, onion powder and mustard and mix well. Pour over tuna mixture and toss until well mixed. Chill.

Use as a sandwich filling or serve on lettuce leaves for a main-dish salad.

SEAFOOD SALAD

SERVES 8

1/2 pound imitation crab
1/2 pound fresh cooked crabmeat
4 ounces cooked shrimp, without shells
1/4 cup reduced-calorie mayonnaise
1/4 cup low-fat sour cream
1/3 cup chopped green bell pepper
1/4 cup chopped green onion
2 tablespoons fresh dill weed
2 tablespoons fresh lemon juice
1/4 cup chopped fresh parsley
2 cloves garlic, minced
1/4 teaspoon cayenne pepper
1/4 teaspoon freshly ground black pepper
1/4 teaspoon hot pepper sauce

Dice imitation crab, crabmeat and shrimp and place in a medium bowl. Set aside. In a small bowl, combine remaining ingredients and mix thoroughly. Add to diced seafood. Stir to mix thoroughly. Cover and refrigerate for 30 to 60 minutes. Serve cold.

NUTRIENT ANALYSIS

CALORIES	108 KCAL
PROTEIN	14 GM
CARBOHYDRATE	5 GM
TOTAL FAT	4 GM
SATURATED	1 GM
POLYUNSATURATED	1 GM
MONOUNSATURATED	1 GM
CHOLESTEROL	67 MG
SODIUM	406 MG
POTASSIUM	236 MG
CALCIUM	84 MG

Salad Dressings

Basic Salad Dressing I

Basic Salad Dressing II

Tomato French Dressing

Italian Dressing

Russian Dressing

Thousand Island Dressing

Yogurt Dressing

Vinaigrette Dressing

Reduced-Calorie Ranch Dressing

Orange-Yogurt Dressing

Lemon-Poppy Seed Dressing

Tofu Mayonnaise

The taste of homemade salad dressing prepared with fresh herbs, spices and oils is a little bit of heaven—vastly better than that of even the best commercially prepared dressings.

When salad dressing ingredients are at their freshest and most piquant, what they do to a colorful variety of greens and vegetables —or fruit—is nothing short of amazing. Spicy Russian Dressing is a wonderful example. So is Lemon-Poppy Seed Dressing, with its crunchy texture and tangy taste. You'll even find that the make-your-own mayonnaise recipe here, Tofu Mayonnaise, is much smoother and richer than what you're used to.

Now, most people think that making their own salad dressing is complicated and time-consuming. Not true: You can make almost any salad dressing in this book in under five minutes.

Is it worth it? You bet! You can control your fat and salt intake and enjoy herbs and spices at their flavor-packed best. You can also avoid chemical stabilizers and other additives so often found in commercial brands of dressing.

And here's another place you can be really creative: Use oil bases such as corn, olive and sesame. Flavor a polyunsaturated oil with apple cider vinegar, garlic and mustard. Other possible bases for salad dressings include low-fat or nonfat yogurt, tahini and other nut and seed butters, or hummus, made from chick-peas. Flavored vinegars, from balsamic to raspberry to tarragon, can also change a salad dressing dramatically. The creations you like best can make thoughtful, tasty gifts for friends when presented in a pretty stoppered cruet. (Be sure to use only sterilized glass bottles or cruets for gifts or storing dressing.)

For a delicious taste treat, try using homemade dressings as marinades for vegetables and meats. Instead of basting a roast chicken with pan drippings, try using one of these salad dressings. You'll be glad you did.

BASIC SALAD DRESSING I

MAKES 1 CUP
SERVES 16; 1 TABLESPOON PER SERVING

NUTRIENT ANALYSIS	
CALORIES	31 KCAL
PROTEIN	0 GM
CARBOHYDRATE	0 GM
TOTAL FAT	3 GM
SATURATED	1 GM
POLYUNSATURATED	1 GM
MONOUNSATURATED	2 GM
CHOLESTEROL	0 MG
SODIUM	4 MG
POTASSIUM	5 MG
CALCIUM	1 MG

1/4 cup cider vinegar
1/4 cup acceptable vegetable oil
1/2 cup water
1 teaspoon Dijon mustard
1 clove garlic, minced
1/4 teaspoon freshly ground black pepper
1/4 teaspoon sugar

In a jar with a tight-fitting lid, combine all ingredients. Shake well and refrigerate.

Note: Basic Salad Dressing I has a more robust flavor, while Basic Salad Dressing II has a more delicate citrus flavor.

BASIC SALAD DRESSING II

MAKES 1 CUP
SERVES 16; 1 TABLESPOON PER SERVING

¼ cup red wine vinegar
¼ cup acceptable vegetable oil
½ cup water
¼ teaspoon freshly ground black pepper
¼ teaspoon garlic powder
¼ teaspoon sugar
1 teaspoon fresh lemon juice

In a jar with a tight-fitting lid, combine all ingredients. Shake well and refrigerate.

NUTRIENT ANALYSIS

CALORIES	31 KCAL
PROTEIN	0 GM
CARBOHYDRATE	0 GM
TOTAL FAT	3 GM
SATURATED	1 GM
POLYUNSATURATED	1 GM
MONOUNSATURATED	2 GM
CHOLESTEROL	0 MG
SODIUM	0 MG
POTASSIUM	5 MG
CALCIUM	0 MG

TOMATO FRENCH DRESSING

MAKES 1¼ CUPS
SERVES 20; 1 TABLESPOON PER SERVING

1 recipe Basic Salad Dressing I or II (see page 74 and above)
2 tablespoons no-salt-added tomato paste
2 teaspoons sugar
1 tablespoon minced onion

In a jar with a tight-fitting lid, combine all ingredients. Shake well and refrigerate.

NUTRIENT ANALYSIS

CALORIES	34 KCAL
PROTEIN	0 GM
CARBOHYDRATE	1 GM
TOTAL FAT	3 GM
SATURATED	1 GM
POLYUNSATURATED	1 GM
MONOUNSATURATED	2 GM
CHOLESTEROL	0 MG
SODIUM	5 MG
POTASSIUM	21 MG
CALCIUM	2 MG

ITALIAN DRESSING

MAKES 1¼ CUPS
SERVES 20; 1 TABLESPOON PER SERVING

NUTRIENT ANALYSIS	
CALORIES	32 KCAL
PROTEIN	0 GM
CARBOHYDRATE	1 GM
TOTAL FAT	3 GM
SATURATED	1 GM
POLYUNSATURATED	1 GM
MONOUNSATURATED	2 GM
CHOLESTEROL	0 MG
SODIUM	4 MG
POTASSIUM	8 MG
CALCIUM	2 MG

1 recipe Basic Salad Dressing I or II (see pages 74 and 75)
½ teaspoon basil, crumbled
½ teaspoon oregano, crumbled

In a jar with a tight-fitting lid, combine all ingredients. Shake well and refrigerate.

RUSSIAN DRESSING

MAKES 1¼ CUPS
SERVES 20; 1 TABLESPOON PER SERVING

NUTRIENT ANALYSIS	
CALORIES	33 KCAL
PROTEIN	0 GM
CARBOHYDRATE	1 GM
TOTAL FAT	3 GM
SATURATED	1 GM
POLYUNSATURATED	1 GM
MONOUNSATURATED	2 GM
CHOLESTEROL	0 MG
SODIUM	5 MG
POTASSIUM	21 MG
CALCIUM	2 MG

1 recipe Basic Salad Dressing I or II (see pages 74 and 75)
2 tablespoons no-salt-added tomato paste
1 tablespoon finely chopped green bell pepper
¼ teaspoon Chili Powder (see page 37)
⅛ teaspoon onion powder
Dash hot pepper sauce

In a jar with a tight-fitting lid, combine all ingredients. Shake well and refrigerate.

THOUSAND ISLAND DRESSING

MAKES 1¼ CUPS
SERVES 20; 1 TABLESPOON PER SERVING

½ cup plain nonfat yogurt
2 tablespoons reduced-calorie mayonnaise
½ cup Chili Sauce (see recipe, page 183)
1 tablespoon finely chopped green bell pepper
1 tablespoon finely chopped celery
¼ teaspoon onion powder
Dash freshly ground black pepper
1 hard-cooked egg white, finely chopped

In a jar with a tight-fitting lid, combine all ingredients. Shake well and refrigerate.

NUTRIENT ANALYSIS

CALORIES	17 KCAL
PROTEIN	1 GM
CARBOHYDRATE	2 GM
TOTAL FAT	1 GM
SATURATED	0 GM
POLYUNSATURATED	0 GM
MONOUNSATURATED	0 GM
CHOLESTEROL	1 MG
SODIUM	19 MG
POTASSIUM	53 MG
CALCIUM	15 MG

YOGURT DRESSING

MAKES 1 CUP
SERVES 16; 1 TABLESPOON PER SERVING

1 cup plain nonfat yogurt
2 tablespoons low-fat sour cream
2 tablespoons honey
½ teaspoon paprika
¼ teaspoon cayenne pepper

Place all ingredients in a small bowl. Stir with a wire whisk until mixed thoroughly. Cover and refrigerate.

NUTRIENT ANALYSIS

CALORIES	19 KCAL
PROTEIN	1 GM
CARBOHYDRATE	4 GM
TOTAL FAT	0 GM
SATURATED	0 GM
POLYUNSATURATED	0 GM
MONOUNSATURATED	0 GM
CHOLESTEROL	1 MG
SODIUM	14 MG
POTASSIUM	50 MG
CALCIUM	38 MG

VINAIGRETTE DRESSING

MAKES 1 CUP
SERVES 16; 1 TABLESPOON PER SERVING

NUTRIENT ANALYSIS	
CALORIES	42 KCAL
PROTEIN	0 GM
CARBOHYDRATE	0 GM
TOTAL FAT	5 GM
SATURATED	1 GM
POLYUNSATURATED	3 GM
MONOUNSATURATED	1 GM
CHOLESTEROL	0 MG
SODIUM	4 MG
POTASSIUM	11 MG
CALCIUM	3 MG

1/3 cup acceptable vegetable oil
2 tablespoons fresh lemon juice
2 tablespoons tarragon vinegar
1 teaspoon chopped fresh parsley or 1/2 teaspoon dry parsley flakes
1/2 teaspoon freshly ground black pepper
1/4 teaspoon dry mustard powder
1/8 teaspoon garlic powder
1 hard-cooked egg white, finely chopped (optional)
1 tablespoon plain low-fat yogurt (optional)

In a jar with a tight-fitting lid, combine all ingredients. Shake well and refrigerate. Serve with cooked or raw chilled vegetables or with fresh tomato slices.

REDUCED-CALORIE RANCH DRESSING

MAKES 1½ CUPS
SERVES 24; 1 TABLESPOON PER SERVING

1 cup low-fat buttermilk
½ cup plain low-fat yogurt
1 tablespoon Dijon mustard
2 teaspoons minced onion
1 tablespoon fresh dill
1 tablespoon chopped fresh parsley
½ teaspoon garlic powder
¼ teaspoon freshly ground black pepper

In a jar with a tight-fitting lid, combine all ingredients. Shake well to blend. Refrigerate for at least 2 hours, allowing flavors to blend.

NUTRIENT ANALYSIS

CALORIES	8 KCAL
PROTEIN	1 GM
CARBOHYDRATE	1 GM
TOTAL FAT	0 GM
SATURATED	0 GM
POLYUNSATURATED	0 GM
MONOUNSATURATED	0 GM
CHOLESTEROL	1 MG
SODIUM	23 MG
POTASSIUM	36 MG
CALCIUM	25 MG

ORANGE-YOGURT DRESSING

MAKES 1¼ CUPS
SERVES 20; 1 TABLESPOON PER SERVING

NUTRIENT ANALYSIS	
CALORIES	9 KCAL
PROTEIN	1 GM
CARBOHYDRATE	2 GM
TOTAL FAT	0 GM
SATURATED	0 GM
POLYUNSATURATED	0 GM
MONOUNSATURATED	0 GM
CHOLESTEROL	0 MG
SODIUM	9 MG
POTASSIUM	37 MG
CALCIUM	25 MG

1 cup plain nonfat yogurt
¼ cup orange juice
1 teaspoon honey

In a small bowl, mix all ingredients until well blended. Cover and refrigerate.

LEMON-POPPY SEED DRESSING

MAKES 1 CUP
SERVES 16; 1 TABLESPOON PER SERVING

NUTRIENT ANALYSIS	
CALORIES	54 KCAL
PROTEIN	0 GM
CARBOHYDRATE	10 GM
TOTAL FAT	2 GM
SATURATED	0 GM
POLYUNSATURATED	1 GM
MONOUNSATURATED	0 GM
CHOLESTEROL	0 MG
SODIUM	2 MG
POTASSIUM	11 MG
CALCIUM	4 MG

½ cup frozen lemonade concentrate, undiluted
⅓ cup honey
2 tablespoons acceptable vegetable oil
1 teaspoon poppy seeds

Combine all ingredients in a small mixing bowl. Beat with rotary beater until smooth. Serve over fruit salad.

TOFU MAYONNAISE

MAKES 3/4 CUP
SERVES 12; 1 TABLESPOON PER SERVING

1/2 pound firm tofu
1/2 teaspoon dry mustard
1/8 teaspoon cayenne pepper
2 tablespoons fresh lemon juice
3 tablespoons acceptable vegetable oil
2 tablespoons water

In a food processor or blender, process tofu, mustard, cayenne pepper and lemon juice until mixed. With machine still running, add oil very slowly and then add water. Blend until smooth. Stop the machine a few times during processing and scrape the sides.

Keeps up to 3 months when refrigerated in an airtight container.

NUTRIENT ANALYSIS

CALORIES	45 KCAL
PROTEIN	2 GM
CARBOHYDRATE	1 GM
TOTAL FAT	4 GM
SATURATED	1 GM
POLYUNSATURATED	2 GM
MONOUNSATURATED	2 GM
CHOLESTEROL	0 MG
SODIUM	2 MG
POTASSIUM	26 MG
CALCIUM	20 MG

Fish

Herbed Fillet of Sole

Fish Fillets Supreme

Rolled Fish Fillets

Oven-Fried Fish

Crispy Baked Fish

Southern Catfish Fillets

Fish Steaks with Thyme

Poached Salmon Steaks

Tuna-Macaroni Casserole

Tuna Oriental

Fresh, fabulous fish!

It's everything you could want in an entrée: low in calories, low in fat, low in salt, but high in taste.

Most fish contains about two-thirds the calories of an equal serving of red meat. For instance, a 3½-ounce broiled hamburger has about 290 calories; an equal serving of swordfish has just 154.

Fish is also higher in protein and lower in fat than red meat. A 3½-ounce serving of flounder gives you 30 grams of protein and 8 grams of fat for a very reasonable 202 calories. A similar-size serving of beef rump supplies somewhat less protein (24 grams) and three times the amount of fat (27 grams) for 347 calories.

It's not only the amount of fat that's different in fish, it's also the *kind* of fat. Beef contains saturated fat and cholesterol, while most of the fat in fish is unsaturated, with only a small amount of cholesterol. Certain kinds of fish contain a special kind of fat called Omega-3 fatty acids, which research suggests may have a protective effect on the heart. Fish rich in Omega-3 fatty acids include salmon, mackerel, trout, haddock and albacore tuna.

And what about salt? More good news: Even saltwater fish is low in salt but packed to the gills with vitamins and minerals. Best of all, fish is one of the easiest foods to prepare—simply broil it in just a little margarine—and one that truly needs "only a little lemon juice" to be delectable.

Just remember when shopping to opt for fresh rather than frozen fish because fish is usually frozen in brine. And anyway, the fresher the fish, the better it tastes.

So dive into this chapter. You'll net exciting and healthful fish dishes like Herbed Fillet of Sole, Southern Catfish Fillets, Tuna Oriental, and Poached Salmon Steaks—don't let them get away.

HERBED FILLET OF SOLE

SERVES 4

NUTRIENT ANALYSIS	
CALORIES	147 KCAL
PROTEIN	19 GM
CARBOHYDRATE	1 GM
TOTAL FAT	7 GM
SATURATED	2 GM
POLYUNSATURATED	2 GM
MONOUNSATURATED	3 GM
CHOLESTEROL	53 MG
SODIUM	88 MG
POTASSIUM	293 MG
CALCIUM	18 MG

1/3 cup fresh lemon juice
1/4 teaspoon dry mustard powder
1/2 teaspoon tarragon
2 tablespoons acceptable margarine, softened
1 pound fillet of sole

Preheat broiler.

Combine lemon juice, mustard and tarragon. Set aside.

Spread margarine in a flat baking dish and add fish. Brush fish with seasoned lemon juice. Broil 2 to 3 inches from the heat 5 to 8 minutes for thin fillets (10 to 12 minutes for thicker fillets). Brush once or twice with lemon juice mixture during broiling.

Fish is done when it is firm and flakes easily with a fork. Do not overcook.

FISH FILLETS SUPREME

SERVES 6

1½ cups water
2 tablespoons fresh lemon juice
1½ pounds cod fillets
Vegetable oil spray
⅛ teaspoon freshly ground black pepper
2 large fresh tomatoes, sliced ¼ inch thick
½ medium green bell pepper, finely chopped
2 tablespoons finely chopped onion
¼ cup dry bread crumbs
½ teaspoon basil
1 tablespoon acceptable vegetable oil

Combine water and lemon juice. Pour over fish fillets and let stand 30 minutes. Drain fillets.

Preheat oven to 350° F.

Spray an ovenproof pan lightly with vegetable oil spray. Place fish in prepared pan. Season with black pepper. Place tomato slices over fish and sprinkle with green pepper and onion.

Combine bread crumbs, basil and oil. Blend well. Spread seasoned crumb mixture evenly over tomatoes.

Bake uncovered 25 minutes or until fish is firm and flakes easily with a fork. Do not overcook.

NUTRIENT ANALYSIS

CALORIES	156 KCAL
PROTEIN	23 GM
CARBOHYDRATE	7 GM
TOTAL FAT	4 GM
SATURATED	1 GM
POLYUNSATURATED	2 GM
MONOUNSATURATED	1 GM
CHOLESTEROL	60 MG
SODIUM	130 MG
POTASSIUM	463 MG
CALCIUM	30 MG

ROLLED FISH FILLETS

SERVES 8

NUTRIENT ANALYSIS	
CALORIES	138 KCAL
PROTEIN	24 GM
CARBOHYDRATE	0 GM
TOTAL FAT	4 GM
SATURATED	1 GM
POLYUNSATURATED	1 GM
MONOUNSATURATED	1 GM
CHOLESTEROL	66 MG
SODIUM	32 MG
POTASSIUM	581 MG
CALCIUM	79 MG

2 pounds fish fillets
3 tablespoons fresh lemon juice
1½ cups water or more
1 bay leaf

Dip fish fillets in lemon juice. Drain. Beginning with the narrow end, roll each fillet as for jelly roll and secure with a toothpick.

Place water in large saucepan. (Water should be 2 inches deep.) Add bay leaf and bring to a boil. Carefully place rolled fillets in boiling water, cover and reduce heat. Simmer 5 minutes or until fish is firm and flakes easily with a fork.

Carefully transfer fillets to a heated serving platter. Remove toothpicks.

For an elegant entree, serve with Yogurt-Dill Sauce (see page 189) or chopped toasted almonds.

OVEN-FRIED FISH

SERVES 4

Vegetable oil spray
2 tablespoons acceptable margarine, melted
1 tablespoon fresh lemon juice
1/4 teaspoon freshly ground black pepper
1/4 teaspoon paprika
1/4 teaspoon basil
1/8 teaspoon garlic powder
1 pound fillet of flounder or other fish
1/4 cup dry bread crumbs

Lightly spray a shallow baking dish with vegetable oil spray. Preheat oven to 475° F.

Combine margarine, lemon juice, pepper, paprika, basil and garlic powder. Mix well. Dip fish in margarine-herb mixture and roll in bread crumbs.

Arrange fish in a single layer in a baking dish. Spoon remaining margarine mixture over fish. Bake uncovered 15 minutes or until fish flakes easily with a fork. Do not overcook.

NUTRIENT ANALYSIS

CALORIES	173 KCAL
PROTEIN	21 GM
CARBOHYDRATE	5 GM
TOTAL FAT	7 GM
SATURATED	2 GM
POLYUNSATURATED	2 GM
MONOUNSATURATED	3 GM
CHOLESTEROL	56 MG
SODIUM	135 MG
POTASSIUM	306 MG
CALCIUM	27 MG

CRISPY BAKED FISH

SERVES 4

NUTRIENT ANALYSIS	
CALORIES	296 KCAL
PROTEIN	33 GM
CARBOHYDRATE	20 GM
TOTAL FAT	8 GM
SATURATED	2 GM
POLYUNSATURATED	3 GM
MONOUNSATURATED	3 GM
CHOLESTEROL	86 MG
SODIUM	270 MG
POTASSIUM	796 MG
CALCIUM	137 MG

Vegetable oil spray
1 cup whole-wheat bread crumbs
½ teaspoon freshly ground black pepper
4 tablespoons fresh minced parsley
2 tablespoons reduced-calorie mayonnaise
1 tablespoon water
2 drops hot pepper sauce
1¼ pounds fish fillets
4 lemon wedges

Preheat oven to 350° F. Lightly spray a baking sheet with vegetable oil spray. Set aside.

Place bread crumbs in the work bowl of a food processor fitted with a metal blade. Process until very fine. Sprinkle crumbs onto an ungreased baking sheet and bake 5 to 7 minutes, or until lightly browned.

Combine prepared bread crumbs, black pepper and parsley in a shallow pan and set aside.

Raise oven temperature to 450° F.

Combine mayonnaise, water and hot pepper sauce in a shallow bowl and mix well.

Dip fish in mayonnaise mixture and then dredge in bread crumbs.

Place fish on prepared baking sheet. Bake 17 to 18 minutes, or until fish flakes easily.

Serve with lemon wedges.

SOUTHERN CATFISH FILLETS

SERVES 4

Vegetable oil spray
4 5-ounce catfish fillets
1/2 teaspoon freshly ground black pepper
1 cup low-fat milk
4 drops hot pepper sauce
1 cup cornmeal
1/4 cup fresh minced parsley
1/4 teaspoon cayenne pepper
Lemon wedges (optional)

Preheat oven to 450° F. Lightly spray a baking dish with vegetable oil spray.

Sprinkle fillets with black pepper. Set aside.

In a shallow dish, combine milk and hot pepper sauce. In another dish, combine cornmeal, parsley and cayenne pepper. Dip fillets in milk mixture and then roll in cornmeal mixture. Place fillets in prepared baking dish and bake 15 to 17 minutes, or until done.

Serve with lemon wedges if desired.

NUTRIENT ANALYSIS

CALORIES	332 KCAL
PROTEIN	35 GM
CARBOHYDRATE	30 GM
TOTAL FAT	7 GM
SATURATED	2 GM
POLYUNSATURATED	2 GM
MONOUNSATURATED	2 GM
CHOLESTEROL	89 MG
SODIUM	74 MG
POTASSIUM	890 MG
CALCIUM	182 MG

FISH STEAKS WITH THYME

SERVES 4

NUTRIENT ANALYSIS*	
CALORIES	241 KCAL
PROTEIN	27 GM
CARBOHYDRATE	0 GM
TOTAL FAT	14 GM
SATURATED	2 GM
POLYUNSATURATED	5 GM
MONOUNSATURATED	6 GM
CHOLESTEROL	75 MG
SODIUM	36 MG
POTASSIUM	655 MG
CALCIUM	96 MG

*USING SWORDFISH.

Vegetable oil spray
1¼ pounds fish steaks, such as swordfish, tuna or mako shark
2 tablespoons acceptable vegetable oil
1 teaspoon dried thyme leaves
½ teaspoon freshly ground black pepper
1 tablespoon acceptable margarine, melted

Lightly spray top of grill with vegetable oil spray. Preheat grill.

Rub fish steaks with oil, thyme and pepper. Cover and let sit in refrigerator 30 to 60 minutes.

Remove fish steaks from refrigerator and place on heated grill at least 6 inches from the coals or fire. Cook 2 to 3 minutes on each side.

For an attractive crosshatch pattern, grill fish 1 to 1½ minutes and then rotate fish ¼ of a turn. Grill another 1 to 1½ minutes and flip to other side. Grill 1 to 1½ minutes and then rotate fish ¼ of a turn.

Remove from grill and brush with melted margarine.

POACHED SALMON STEAKS

SERVES 4

1 pound salmon steaks
3/4 cup water
3/4 cup dry white table wine
1 medium onion, chopped
1 bay leaf
1/4 teaspoon freshly ground black pepper
1/8 teaspoon ground cloves
1/8 teaspoon thyme

Place salmon in a large nonstick skillet. Add remaining ingredients. If necessary, add additional water so fish is barely covered with liquid. Simmer over low heat 15 to 20 minutes or until salmon is firm and flakes easily with a fork.

Drain liquid and serve fish with Yogurt-Dill Sauce (see page 189).

NUTRIENT ANALYSIS

CALORIES	166 KCAL
PROTEIN	22 GM
CARBOHYDRATE	3 GM
TOTAL FAT	4 GM
SATURATED	1 GM
POLYUNSATURATED	1 GM
MONOUNSATURATED	1 GM
CHOLESTEROL	61 MG
SODIUM	33 MG
POTASSIUM	610 MG
CALCIUM	84 MG

TUNA-MACARONI CASSEROLE

SERVES 4

NUTRIENT ANALYSIS	
CALORIES	334 KCAL
PROTEIN	22 GM
CARBOHYDRATE	38 GM
TOTAL FAT	10 GM
SATURATED	2 GM
POLYUNSATURATED	4 GM
MONOUNSATURATED	4 GM
CHOLESTEROL	20 MG
SODIUM	153 MG
POTASSIUM	414 MG
CALCIUM	112 MG

1 cup uncooked macaroni
Vegetable oil spray
1 tablespoon acceptable vegetable oil
2 tablespoons chopped onion
1 tablespoon all-purpose flour
1/4 teaspoon curry powder
1/4 teaspoon onion powder
1/8 teaspoon freshly ground black pepper
1 tablespoon finely chopped fresh parsley or 1/2 tablespoon dry parsley flakes
1 cup skim milk
1/2 cup no-salt-added canned tomatoes, drained and chopped
1 6 1/2-ounce can unsalted tuna packed in spring water, drained, rinsed and flaked
2 tablespoons acceptable margarine, melted
1/4 cup dry bread crumbs

Cook macaroni as directed on package, omitting salt. Drain and set aside.

Preheat oven to 350° F. Lightly spray a 1 1/2-quart ovenproof casserole dish with vegetable oil spray.

Heat oil in a saucepan. Add chopped onion and sauté until tender. Add flour, curry and onion powders, pepper and parsley. Mix thoroughly. Gradually stir in milk, blending well. Cook, stirring constantly, until mixture comes to a boil. Remove from heat.

Add macaroni, tomatoes and tuna. Pour into prepared pan.

In a small bowl, combine melted marga-

TUNA-MACARONI CASSEROLE

rine and bread crumbs. Sprinkle evenly over top of tuna-macaroni mixture. Bake 30 to 35 minutes or until sauce is bubbly.

TUNA ORIENTAL

SERVES 3

½ green bell pepper, cut in ¼-inch strips
1 small onion, thinly sliced
2 teaspoons acceptable vegetable oil
⅓ cup pineapple juice
1½ teaspoons cornstarch
⅔ cup pineapple chunks, canned in natural juices, drained
1 tablespoon sugar
1 tablespoon cider vinegar
1 6½-ounce can unsalted tuna packed in spring water, drained, rinsed and flaked
⅛ teaspoon freshly ground black pepper
Dash hot pepper sauce

Sauté green pepper and onion in oil, leaving slightly crisp.

Mix pineapple juice with cornstarch and add to green pepper and onion mixture. Cook, stirring gently, until thickened. Add remaining ingredients. Cook 5 minutes, stirring occasionally.

This dish is good served over rice.

NUTRIENT ANALYSIS

CALORIES	180 KCAL
PROTEIN	17 GM
CARBOHYDRATE	21 GM
TOTAL FAT	4 GM
SATURATED	1 GM
POLYUNSATURATED	2 GM
MONOUNSATURATED	1 GM
CHOLESTEROL	22 MG
SODIUM	31 MG
POTASSIUM	343 MG
CALCIUM	26 MG

Poultry

Golden Baked Chicken

Lemon-Baked Chicken

Roast Chicken

Oven-Fried Chicken

Chicken À l'Orange

Chicken Dijon

Chicken with Yogurt-Cilantro Sauce

Chicken Paprikash

Chicken Primavera

Chicken Marengo

Arroz con Pollo (Chicken with Rice)

Chicken Cacciatore

Chicken Enchiladas

Chicken Tuscany

Chicken with Ginger and Snow Peas

Lemon-Barbecued Chicken

Roast Turkey

Turkey Stew

Turkey with Rosemary

Turkey Sausage Patties

In many ways, poultry is a cook's best friend. It's high in protein, low in fat, flavorful, versatile and inexpensive. What more can you ask from any food?

Chicken, turkey and other poultry contain protein and B vitamins with fewer calories per serving than red meat. Their gentle flavors lend themselves well to a wide variety of cooking techniques, and offer cooks a good excuse to innovate. Virtually every cuisine in the world has a poultry specialty.

From the delicately tart taste of Lemon-Baked Chicken to the ultra-spicy kick of Chicken Cacciatore, you'll find a variety of dishes here to please a variety of palates.

But don't stop there. As long as you're careful of added salt and fat, go ahead and create your own poultry dishes with spices from Africa, Israel, Indonesia and Mexico. With cayenne pepper, curry, turmeric or cumin, and so many other popular spices, you can create almost infinite taste sensations.

If you want to save money preparing these recipes, buy whole chickens and cut them up yourself—you can save as much as 30 percent on the cost. Plus, you'll have the necks, backs and bones at hand for making your own low-sodium broth.

As for turkey, well, at holiday time—or any time—everyone loves a stuffed turkey. To keep it moist, stuff it with moisture-producing materials instead of bread stuffing, which tends to soak up fats and moisture. For example, coarsely chop a bunch of parsley, a couple of leeks, an onion, a few stalks of celery, a couple of apples and an orange with peel, then pack the cavity with this mixture of fruits and vegetables. (Discard them when cooking is finished.) This lends flavor as well as moistness to the meat.

Wrap the bird in foil and baste with a flavorful, low-sodium broth every 45 minutes. You can still have bread stuffing: Just prepare it on the side so you can control the amount of fat and salt it contains.

Poultry dishes are among America's family favorites. Try these recipes and you'll see why.

GOLDEN BAKED CHICKEN

SERVES 4

NUTRIENT ANALYSIS	
CALORIES	316 KCAL
PROTEIN	38 GM
CARBOHYDRATE	1 GM
TOTAL FAT	17 GM
SATURATED	4 GM
POLYUNSATURATED	5 GM
MONOUNSATURATED	6 GM
CHOLESTEROL	109 MG
SODIUM	108 MG
POTASSIUM	371 MG
CALCIUM	31 MG

2½-pound frying chicken, cut in pieces, skinned, all visible fat removed
3 tablespoons acceptable margarine, melted
2 tablespoons fresh lemon juice
½ teaspoon paprika
⅛ teaspoon freshly ground black pepper
⅛ teaspoon garlic powder

Preheat oven to 375° F.

Rinse chicken and pat dry.

Place chicken on a rack in a shallow baking dish. Combine remaining ingredients and brush about half of mixture on chicken. Brush chicken with remaining margarine mixture again once or twice during baking. Bake 1 hour.

LEMON-BAKED CHICKEN

SERVES 4

Vegetable oil spray
2½-pound frying chicken, cut in pieces, skinned, all visible fat removed
2 tablespoons acceptable vegetable oil
¼ cup fresh lemon juice
2 teaspoons oregano or tarragon (optional)
⅛ teaspoon garlic powder
2 tablespoons chopped fresh parsley
¼ teaspoon paprika

Preheat oven to 350° F. Lightly spray an ovenproof casserole dish with vegetable oil spray.

Rinse chicken and pat dry. Place chicken pieces in prepared casserole.

In a small bowl, combine oil, lemon juice, oregano or tarragon and garlic powder. Brush about half of mixture on chicken. Cover and bake 35 minutes.

Remove cover. Brush with remainder of oil-lemon mixture. Continue baking, uncovered, 20 minutes longer or until tender.

Sprinkle with parsley and paprika before serving.

NUTRIENT ANALYSIS

CALORIES	304 KCAL
PROTEIN	38 GM
CARBOHYDRATE	2 GM
TOTAL FAT	15 GM
SATURATED	4 GM
POLYUNSATURATED	5 GM
MONOUNSATURATED	6 GM
CHOLESTEROL	109 MG
SODIUM	107 MG
POTASSIUM	393 MG
CALCIUM	43 MG

ROAST CHICKEN

SERVES 6

NUTRIENT ANALYSIS	
CALORIES	194 KCAL
PROTEIN	31 GM
CARBOHYDRATE	0 GM
TOTAL FAT	7 GM
SATURATED	2 GM
POLYUNSATURATED	2 GM
MONOUNSATURATED	2 GM
CHOLESTEROL	89 MG
SODIUM	84 MG
POTASSIUM	291 MG
CALCIUM	23 MG

1 4- to 4½-pound chicken
½ teaspoon poultry seasoning
¼ teaspoon freshly ground black pepper
¼ teaspoon paprika
1 lemon

Preheat oven to 350° F.

Remove parts from inside cavity of chicken and discard. Rinse chicken and pat dry. Sprinkle seasonings over chicken, and place whole lemon inside cavity.

Place chicken on a roasting rack, breast side up, in a deep roasting pan. Bake 1¼ to 1½ hours.

Chicken is done if clear juices run from the thigh when pierced with a fork or when thermometer inserted in the thigh registers 180° to 185° F.

Serve on a heated platter and remove skin after carving.

For a delicious flavor combination, serve this with Mushroom and Herb Dressing (page 164). The dressing may be stuffed into the chicken before roasting or cooked in a casserole dish alongside the roasting pan.

OVEN-FRIED CHICKEN

SERVES 6

1 chicken (2½ to 3 pounds) cut into serving pieces, skinned, all visible fat removed
½ cup plain nonfat yogurt
2 cloves garlic, minced
2 cups whole-wheat bread crumbs
¼ cup minced fresh parsley sprigs
1 teaspoon basil
1 teaspoon oregano
4 tablespoons grated Parmesan cheese
¼ teaspoon freshly ground black pepper
1 tablespoon acceptable margarine

Preheat oven to 350° F.

Rinse chicken and pat dry. Set aside.

In a medium bowl, combine yogurt and garlic. Set aside. In a medium bowl, toss bread crumbs with parsley, basil, oregano, cheese and pepper. Dip each piece of chicken in the yogurt mixture and then roll it in the crumb mixture.

In a large nonstick skillet, heat margarine over medium-high heat. Add chicken pieces and cook about 5 minutes on each side, or until evenly browned.

Transfer chicken pieces to a 13×9-inch baking dish. Bake 30 to 35 minutes.

NUTRIENT ANALYSIS

CALORIES	368 KCAL
PROTEIN	37 GM
CARBOHYDRATE	27 GM
TOTAL FAT	11 GM
SATURATED	3 GM
POLYUNSATURATED	3 GM
MONOUNSATURATED	4 GM
CHOLESTEROL	92 MG
SODIUM	407 MG
POTASSIUM	419 MG
CALCIUM	164 MG

CHICKEN À L'ORANGE

SERVES 4

NUTRIENT ANALYSIS	
CALORIES	481 KCAL
PROTEIN	37 GM
CARBOHYDRATE	30 GM
TOTAL FAT	23 GM
SATURATED	5 GM
POLYUNSATURATED	7 GM
MONOUNSATURATED	9 GM
CHOLESTEROL	106 MG
SODIUM	98 MG
POTASSIUM	576 MG
CALCIUM	49 MG

2½-pound frying chicken, cut in pieces, skinned, all visible fat removed
½ cup all-purpose flour
2 teaspoons freshly grated orange peel
1 teaspoon paprika
½ teaspoon freshly ground black pepper
1 tablespoon acceptable vegetable oil
½ cup water
1½ cups orange juice
2 tablespoons firmly packed brown sugar
¼ teaspoon ground ginger
⅛ teaspoon ground cinnamon
¼ cup finely chopped pecans

Rinse chicken and pat dry. Set aside.

Combine flour, orange peel, paprika and pepper. Set aside 2 tablespoons flour mixture and coat chicken with remainder.

Brown chicken in oil in a large, heavy nonstick skillet over medium-high heat. Pour off fat. Add water. Cover and simmer over low heat 30 minutes or until tender.

Remove chicken to a warm platter.

Pour drippings from pan, reserving 2 tablespoons and discarding remainder. Return reserved 2 tablespoons of drippings to skillet over medium-high heat. Add reserved seasoned flour mixture. Blend well. Add orange juice, brown sugar, ginger and cinnamon. Cook, stirring constantly, until thickened.

Serve chicken topped with orange sauce and pecans.

CHICKEN DIJON

SERVES 6

1½ pounds boneless chicken breasts, skinned, all visible fat removed
2 tablespoons acceptable margarine
2 tablespoons flour
1 cup skim milk
¼ teaspoon freshly ground black pepper
1 to 2 teaspoons Dijon mustard
¼ cup low-sodium chicken broth
1 clove garlic, cut in half
¼ teaspoon freshly ground black pepper
1 medium zucchini, sliced
2 medium carrots, sliced
½ medium red bell pepper, cut into strips
1 tablespoon chopped fresh parsley

NUTRIENT ANALYSIS	
CALORIES	208 KCAL
PROTEIN	27 GM
CARBOHYDRATE	8 GM
TOTAL FAT	7 GM
SATURATED	2 GM
POLYUNSATURATED	2 GM
MONOUNSATURATED	3 GM
CHOLESTEROL	63 MG
SODIUM	112 MG
POTASSIUM	445 MG
CALCIUM	80 MG

Rinse chicken and pat dry. Set aside.

In a small saucepan, melt margarine over medium heat. Add flour, stirring constantly. Cook 1 to 2 minutes. Add milk, stirring constantly. Raise heat and bring mixture to a boil, then reduce heat immediately so liquid simmers. Stir in ¼ teaspoon pepper, and mustard. Add enough chicken broth to thin sauce to desired consistency.

Rub chicken with garlic clove and sprinkle with ¼ teaspoon pepper. Poach or steam breasts 12 to 15 minutes, or until meat is white throughout.

Steam vegetables until tender-crisp. Place around chicken pieces. Pour sauce over chicken and sprinkle chopped parsley on top.

CHICKEN WITH YOGURT-CILANTRO SAUCE

SERVES 4

NUTRIENT ANALYSIS	
CALORIES	249 KCAL
PROTEIN	32 GM
CARBOHYDRATE	4 GM
TOTAL FAT	11 GM
SATURATED	2 GM
POLYUNSATURATED	1 GM
MONOUNSATURATED	6 GM
CHOLESTEROL	76 MG
SODIUM	92 MG
POTASSIUM	363 MG
CALCIUM	77 MG

4 boneless chicken breasts, skinned, all visible fat removed
2 tablespoons olive oil
2 tablespoons lime juice
1/4 teaspoon freshly ground black pepper
4 ounces plain nonfat yogurt
1 tablespoon minced cilantro
1 tablespoon minced mint
1/2 teaspoon cumin
4 wedges fresh lime

Rinse chicken and pat dry. Set aside.

In a shallow dish, combine oil, lime juice and black pepper. Place chicken breasts in dish and turn until well coated. Cover and refrigerate at least 2 hours.

To make the sauce, combine yogurt, cilantro, mint and cumin in a small bowl. Set aside.

Preheat broiler or grill.

Remove chicken breasts from refrigerator 20 to 30 minutes before cooking. Cook by broiling or grilling 4 to 5 minutes on each side.

Serve sauce over chicken breasts and garnish with lime wedges.

CHICKEN PAPRIKASH

SERVES 6

Vegetable oil spray
1 3- to 3½-pound chicken
2 tablespoons acceptable margarine
1 medium red onion, sliced
2 tablespoons sweet Hungarian paprika
1 fresh tomato, peeled and chopped
½ cup low-sodium chicken broth
2 tablespoons flour
½ cup plain nonfat yogurt
2 tablespoons low-fat sour cream

Preheat oven to 350° F. Lightly spray baking dish with vegetable oil spray.

Rinse chicken and cut into serving pieces. Remove skin and visible fat. Melt margarine in a large nonstick skillet over medium heat. Brown chicken lightly on all sides. Remove chicken and set aside.

Add onion and paprika to skillet and cook 1 minute. Add tomato and chicken broth and cook for another 2 to 3 minutes. Return chicken to pan. Reduce heat, cover and simmer 30 to 40 minutes. Remove chicken.

Sprinkle flour into skillet and cook 2 to 3 minutes. In a small bowl, whisk yogurt and sour cream together. Add to skillet and then remove skillet from heat. Pour sauce over chicken pieces and serve hot.

NUTRIENT ANALYSIS

CALORIES	226 KCAL
PROTEIN	26 GM
CARBOHYDRATE	8 GM
TOTAL FAT	10 GM
SATURATED	3 GM
POLYUNSATURATED	3 GM
MONOUNSATURATED	3 GM
CHOLESTEROL	68 MG
SODIUM	93 MG
POTASSIUM	443 MG
CALCIUM	88 MG

CHICKEN PRIMAVERA

SERVES 6

NUTRIENT ANALYSIS	
CALORIES	456 KCAL
PROTEIN	28 GM
CARBOHYDRATE	75 GM
TOTAL FAT	4 GM
SATURATED	1 GM
POLYUNSATURATED	1 GM
MONOUNSATURATED	1 GM
CHOLESTEROL	39 MG
SODIUM	79 MG
POTASSIUM	733 MG
CALCIUM	75 MG

1 16-ounce can no-salt-added tomatoes, chopped
1 medium red onion, chopped
1 medium zucchini, chopped
1 medium yellow squash, chopped
½ cup sliced fresh mushrooms
½ cup low-sodium chicken broth
1 pound fettucine noodles
2 cups diced cooked chicken
1 cup frozen peas
¼ teaspoon freshly ground black pepper
¼ teaspoon red pepper flakes

In a large saucepan over medium-high heat, combine tomatoes, onion, zucchini, squash, mushrooms and chicken broth. Bring to a boil and reduce heat. Simmer 30 minutes.

Cook fettucine noodles according to package directions, omitting salt. Drain and set aside. Keep warm.

Add chicken, peas and black and red pepper to tomato mixture. Cook another 5 to 10 minutes. Spoon sauce over warm fettucine noodles.

CHICKEN MARENGO

SERVES 6

Vegetable oil spray
1 4- to 4½-pound chicken
½ teaspoon freshly ground black pepper
2 tablespoons acceptable vegetable oil
1 medium red onion, chopped
2 cloves garlic, minced
1 large fresh tomato, peeled and chopped or 1 cup no-salt-added canned tomatoes
½ pound fresh mushrooms, sliced
½ cup low-sodium chicken broth

Preheat oven to 350° F. Lightly spray a 9×13-inch baking dish with vegetable oil spray.

Rinse chicken and cut into serving pieces. Remove skin and visible fat. Sprinkle with pepper. Place oil in a large nonstick skillet over medium-high heat. Add chicken and brown lightly on all sides. Remove chicken to prepared baking dish.

Place onion and garlic in skillet and sauté until soft. Add tomatoes, mushrooms and chicken broth and cook about 5 minutes. Pour mixture over chicken.

Place in oven and bake 30 to 40 minutes, or until chicken is done.

NUTRIENT ANALYSIS

CALORIES	259 KCAL
PROTEIN	32 GM
CARBOHYDRATE	5 GM
TOTAL FAT	12 GM
SATURATED	3 GM
POLYUNSATURATED	3 GM
MONOUNSATURATED	4 GM
CHOLESTEROL	89 MG
SODIUM	93 MG
POTASSIUM	530 MG
CALCIUM	34 MG

ARROZ CON POLLO (CHICKEN WITH RICE)

SERVES 6

NUTRIENT ANALYSIS	
CALORIES	300 KCAL
PROTEIN	28 GM
CARBOHYDRATE	27 GM
TOTAL FAT	8 GM
SATURATED	2 GM
POLYUNSATURATED	3 GM
MONOUNSATURATED	2 GM
CHOLESTEROL	62 MG
SODIUM	89 MG
POTASSIUM	370 MG
CALCIUM	36 MG

1½ pounds boneless chicken breasts, skinned, all visible fat removed
1 tablespoon acceptable margarine
2 cloves garlic, minced
¼ teaspoon freshly ground black pepper
¼ teaspoon paprika
¼ cup chopped onion
¼ cup chopped green bell pepper
1 tablespoon acceptable vegetable oil
1 cup uncooked rice
2 cups low-sodium chicken broth
½ cup chopped fresh tomatoes
⅛ teaspoon saffron or turmeric
½ cup cooked green peas

Preheat oven to 350° F.

Rinse chicken and pat dry. Set aside.

In a small saucepan over medium heat, melt margarine. Add garlic, black pepper and paprika. Mix well. Remove from heat and brush on chicken breasts.

Place chicken in an ovenproof dish and bake, uncovered, 20 to 25 minutes, or until meat has turned white throughout.

Meanwhile, in a large nonstick skillet over medium heat, sauté the onion and green pepper in oil 5 to 6 minutes or until soft. Add rice and cook another 2 to 3 minutes, stirring frequently. Add chicken broth, tomatoes and saffron or turmeric and stir to mix thoroughly. Cover and simmer over

ARROZ CON POLLO

low heat 20 to 25 minutes. Add green peas and cooked chicken and cook an additional 10 minutes. Serve immediately.

CHICKEN CACCIATORE

SERVES 6

6 split chicken breasts, skinned, all visible fat removed
2 tablespoons acceptable vegetable oil
1 clove garlic, minced
1 medium onion, chopped
2 tablespoons chopped green bell pepper
4 fresh tomatoes, peeled and chopped
1/4 cup dry white table wine
1/4 teaspoon rosemary
1 bay leaf
1/4 teaspoon basil
1/8 teaspoon freshly ground black pepper

NUTRIENT ANALYSIS	
CALORIES	232 KCAL
PROTEIN	31 GM
CARBOHYDRATE	5 GM
TOTAL FAT	9 GM
SATURATED	2 GM
POLYUNSATURATED	4 GM
MONOUNSATURATED	2 GM
CHOLESTEROL	75 MG
SODIUM	77 MG
POTASSIUM	486 MG
CALCIUM	30 MG

Rinse chicken and pat dry. Set aside.

Heat oil and garlic in a large nonstick skillet over medium-high heat. Add chicken and brown. Remove chicken and set aside. Add onion and green pepper to skillet, and sauté until tender. Pour off fat.

Return chicken to skillet. Add remaining ingredients. Cover and simmer over low heat 30 minutes, or until chicken is tender.

Remove bay leaf before serving.

May be served over rice.

CHICKEN ENCHILADAS

SERVES 4; 2 ENCHILADAS PER SERVING

NUTRIENT ANALYSIS	
CALORIES	378 KCAL
PROTEIN	33 GM
CARBOHYDRATE	27 GM
TOTAL FAT	15 GM
SATURATED	5 GM
POLYUNSATURATED	3 GM
MONOUNSATURATED	4 GM
CHOLESTEROL	68 MG
SODIUM	420 MG
POTASSIUM	436 MG
CALCIUM	238 MG

¾ pound boneless chicken breasts, skinned, all visible fat removed
¼ cup chopped onion
1 clove garlic, minced
¼ teaspoon chili powder
½ teaspoon cumin
2 tablespoons acceptable margarine
2 tablespoons flour
1½ cups skim milk
¼ teaspoon freshly ground black pepper
1 teaspoon fresh lemon juice
1 cup grated low-fat Monterey Jack cheese
8 corn tortillas
3 tablespoons chopped, canned hot chili peppers

Preheat oven to 350° F. Rinse chicken and pat dry.

Poach or steam chicken breasts 5 to 6 minutes, or until white throughout. Cool under running water and dice into ¼-inch cubes. Place in a small bowl and mix with onion, garlic, chili powder and cumin.

In a small saucepan over medium heat, melt margarine and add flour. Cook 1 to 2 minutes, stirring frequently. Whisk in skim milk, stirring constantly. Bring mixture to a boil and reduce heat. Stir in pepper, lemon juice and half of cheese. Reserve remainder of cheese.

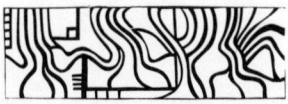

In a nonstick pan over medium heat or in a microwave oven, briefly heat each tortilla on each side until soft.

CHICKEN ENCHILADAS

Place tortillas on flat surface and add 1 to 2 tablespoons of chicken and 1 tablespoon of reserved cheese. Roll and place seam side down in a 9×13×2-inch baking dish. Repeat for each tortilla. Pour sauce over enchiladas and top with chili peppers. Bake 20 to 25 minutes.

CHICKEN TUSCANY

SERVES 4

2½-pound frying chicken, cut in pieces, skinned, all visible fat removed
2 tablespoons acceptable margarine, melted
1 teaspoon oregano
¼ teaspoon garlic powder
1 teaspoon paprika
¾ cup dry bread crumbs

Preheat oven to 350° F. Rinse chicken and pat dry. Set aside.

Place melted margarine in a shallow baking dish. In separate flat dish, mix together oregano, garlic powder, paprika and bread crumbs.

Dip chicken pieces in melted margarine, then roll each piece in seasoned crumbs, coating evenly.

Place in a shallow baking dish. Bake uncovered 1 hour, or until chicken is tender.

NUTRIENT ANALYSIS

CALORIES	364 KCAL
PROTEIN	40 GM
CARBOHYDRATE	14 GM
TOTAL FAT	15 GM
SATURATED	4 GM
POLYUNSATURATED	4 GM
MONOUNSATURATED	5 GM
CHOLESTEROL	110 MG
SODIUM	243 MG
POTASSIUM	403 MG
CALCIUM	59 MG

CHICKEN WITH GINGER AND SNOW PEAS

SERVES 6

NUTRIENT ANALYSIS	
CALORIES	174 KCAL
PROTEIN	22 GM
CARBOHYDRATE	4 GM
TOTAL FAT	7 GM
SATURATED	1 GM
POLYUNSATURATED	3 GM
MONOUNSATURATED	2 GM
CHOLESTEROL	52 MG
SODIUM	153 MG
POTASSIUM	273 MG
CALCIUM	27 MG

1¼ pounds boneless chicken breasts, skinned, all visible fat removed
6 ounces snow peas
1 tablespoon cornstarch
½ cup low-sodium chicken broth
1 teaspoon freshly ground black pepper
1 tablespoon low-sodium soy sauce
2 tablespoons acceptable vegetable oil
2 cloves garlic, minced
½ teaspoon minced fresh ginger

Rinse chicken and pat dry. Slice into thin strips. Set aside.

Remove ends from snow peas and discard. Set snow peas aside.

In a small nonplastic bowl, mix cornstarch, chicken broth, pepper and soy sauce. Set aside.

Heat oil in a wok or large, heavy nonstick skillet over high heat. Add chicken and cook 4 to 5 minutes, turning frequently. Add garlic, ginger and snow peas and cook another 2 to 3 minutes. Add soy sauce mixture and cook another 2 to 3 minutes, or until sauce thickens. If mixture begins to burn, remove wok or skillet from heat momentarily, or add a small amount of low-sodium chicken broth.

This dish is excellent served over rice.

LEMON-BARBECUED CHICKEN

SERVES 4

2½-pound frying chicken, quartered, skinned, all visible fat removed
Dash paprika
Dash cayenne pepper
¼ cup fresh lemon juice
¼ cup honey
1 tablespoon sesame seeds, toasted

Preheat broiler. Rinse chicken and pat dry.

Season chicken lightly with paprika and pepper. Combine lemon juice and honey in a small saucepan, mixing thoroughly. Heat over medium heat until warm and set aside 2 tablespoons. Coat chicken pieces with about half of the rest of the lemon-honey mixture.

Place chicken on broiler rack. Broil 4 to 5 inches from the heat for 15 minutes. Baste occasionally with remaining lemon-honey mixture. Turn pieces over, baste and broil 15 minutes longer or until tender. Combine sesame seeds and the reserved 2 tablespoons lemon-honey mixture. Spoon over chicken just before serving.

This also may be cooked on a charcoal grill.

NUTRIENT ANALYSIS

CALORIES	357 KCAL
PROTEIN	35 GM
CARBOHYDRATE	19 GM
TOTAL FAT	16 GM
SATURATED	4 GM
POLYUNSATURATED	4 GM
MONOUNSATURATED	6 GM
CHOLESTEROL	106 MG
SODIUM	99 MG
POTASSIUM	348 MG
CALCIUM	32 MG

ROAST TURKEY

SERVES 12

NUTRIENT ANALYSIS	
CALORIES	364 KCAL
PROTEIN	52 GM
CARBOHYDRATE	2 GM
TOTAL FAT	15 GM
SATURATED	4 GM
POLYUNSATURATED	4 GM
MONOUNSATURATED	5 GM
CHOLESTEROL	148 MG
SODIUM	147 MG
POTASSIUM	550 MG
CALCIUM	46 MG

1 turkey (about 12 pounds)
½ teaspoon freshly ground black pepper
½ teaspoon poultry seasoning
3 stalks celery, chopped
1 medium onion, chopped
2 carrots, chopped
⅓ cup chopped fresh parsley
¼ cup acceptable margarine, melted

Thaw turkey completely, rinse and pat dry. Remove parts from cavity of turkey. Preheat oven to 425° F.

Sprinkle pepper and poultry seasoning inside cavity of turkey. Add vegetables and parsley. Truss. Place bird on a rack in a roasting pan. Brush with melted margarine. Bake 15 minutes and reduce heat to 325° F. Cook turkey, basting often, until internal temperature reaches 185° F. when tested at the thigh. Let turkey rest 15 to 20 minutes before cutting. Discard vegetables and parsley. Carve and serve.

TURKEY STEW

SERVES 6

1¼ pounds uncooked turkey breast, skinned, all visible fat removed
¼ cup flour
3 tablespoons acceptable margarine
2 cloves garlic, minced
2 cups low-sodium chicken broth
1½ cups sliced carrots
1½ cups sliced celery
1 cup green peas
1 teaspoon fresh lemon juice
Freshly ground black pepper to taste

Rinse turkey breast and pat dry. Cut into ½-inch cubes and dredge in flour.

Melt margarine in a large pot over medium heat. Add turkey and sauté until lightly browned, about 4 to 5 minutes. Add garlic and cook 1 to 2 minutes. Add chicken broth, carrots and celery. Bring to a boil. Reduce heat and simmer 45 to 60 minutes. Add peas and cook 5 additional minutes. Add lemon juice and black pepper and serve.

NUTRIENT ANALYSIS

CALORIES	236 KCAL
PROTEIN	26 GM
CARBOHYDRATE	12 GM
TOTAL FAT	9 GM
SATURATED	2 GM
POLYUNSATURATED	2 GM
MONOUNSATURATED	3 GM
CHOLESTEROL	56 MG
SODIUM	133 MG
POTASSIUM	483 MG
CALCIUM	46 MG

TURKEY WITH ROSEMARY

SERVES 4

NUTRIENT ANALYSIS	
CALORIES	180 KCAL
PROTEIN	27 GM
CARBOHYDRATE	1 GM
TOTAL FAT	7 GM
SATURATED	1 GM
POLYUNSATURATED	1 GM
MONOUNSATURATED	3 GM
CHOLESTEROL	67 MG
SODIUM	66 MG
POTASSIUM	258 MG
CALCIUM	18 MG

1 pound turkey tenderloins
1 tablespoon olive oil
1 clove garlic, minced
1 tablespoon chopped fresh rosemary
1/4 teaspoon freshly ground black pepper
1 teaspoon fresh lemon juice
1/4 cup low-sodium chicken broth
1 tablespoon white table wine

Preheat oven to 350° F. Rinse turkey and pat dry. Set aside.

Place olive oil, garlic, rosemary, pepper and lemon juice in a shallow pan and stir until well mixed. Dip tenderloins in mixture until well coated. Place on a baking pan and bake 10 minutes. Turn and bake another 5 to 10 minutes, or until done.

Remove and slice tenderloins across grain. Place turkey slices on a warm serving platter.

Place broth and wine in a skillet over medium-high heat. Cook 2 to 3 minutes. Remove from heat and pour over turkey slices. Serve immediately.

TURKEY SAUSAGE PATTIES

SERVES 4

3/4 pound ground turkey
1/4 teaspoon freshly ground black pepper
1/4 teaspoon basil
1/4 teaspoon sage
1/4 teaspoon oregano
1/8 teaspoon allspice
1/8 teaspoon nutmeg
1/8 teaspoon dill weed
1/8 teaspoon chili powder (optional)
1/8 teaspoon hot pepper sauce (optional)
1/8 teaspoon garlic powder
1 egg white
2 tablespoons water

NUTRIENT ANALYSIS	
CALORIES	121 KCAL
PROTEIN	20 GM
CARBOHYDRATE	1 GM
TOTAL FAT	4 GM
SATURATED	1 GM
POLYUNSATURATED	1 GM
MONOUNSATURATED	1 GM
CHOLESTEROL	53 MG
SODIUM	65 MG
POTASSIUM	195 MG
CALCIUM	20 MG

Preheat broiler.

Combine all ingredients in a medium bowl and mix thoroughly. Shape into 4 patties and place on a rack in a shallow pan. Broil 2 to 4 inches from heat for 10 to 15 minutes. Turn patties and broil 5 to 10 minutes, or until done.

Serve these as breakfast patties with French Toast, Pancakes or Apple-Filled Crepes (see recipes, pages 148, 208 and 227).

Meats

Beef Bourguignon

Peppered Roast Beef

Beef Stroganoff

Lime Marinated Steak

Chili

Meat Loaf

Beef Goulash

Soft Tacos

Spaghetti with Meat Sauce

Lemon Veal with Spinach

Lamb Curry

Mediterranean Pork Chops

Hungarian Pork Chops

Can lean red meat be part of a low-sodium, low-modified-fat eating plan? You bet. It just plays a smaller role in your overall diet than perhaps you've been used to in the past.

Instead of being the centerpiece of a meal, meats are now taking a supporting role. They are often supplemented by high-fiber grains and legumes, and surrounded by salads and leafy vegetables.

Meats add potassium, B vitamins, zinc and iron to your diet. They also add saturated fat. You can limit the fat you get by looking for the leanest cuts of fresh meat and trimming all visible fat before cooking. And sodium won't be a problem if you follow the recipes here.

Meat is versatile, too. You can prepare Peppered Roast Beef as an evening meal for the family, then slice it for sandwiches for the next day's lunchbox. Mexican food need not be high in fat or salt to be delicious, as our Soft Tacos will show you.

Having a dinner party? Impress your guests and help your heart at the same time by serving our Lemon Veal with Spinach, a tangy gourmet dish. Or turn to the exotic tastes of India with our Lamb Curry.

BEEF BOURGUIGNON

SERVES 9

NUTRIENT ANALYSIS	
CALORIES	324 KCAL
PROTEIN	31 GM
CARBOHYDRATE	18 GM
TOTAL FAT	13 GM
SATURATED	4 GM
POLYUNSATURATED	2 GM
MONOUNSATURATED	5 GM
CHOLESTEROL	77 MG
SODIUM	85 MG
POTASSIUM	775 MG
CALCIUM	30 MG

2 pounds lean beef chuck roast, visible fat removed, cut into cubes
1/4 cup all-purpose flour
1/8 teaspoon freshly ground black pepper
2 tablespoons acceptable vegetable oil
1/2 cup chopped onion
1 clove garlic, minced
1/4 teaspoon thyme
1/4 teaspoon basil
1/4 teaspoon oregano
1/8 teaspoon rosemary
1/8 teaspoon marjoram
1 tablespoon chopped fresh parsley
1/2 cup dry red table wine
1 cup water
2 cups finely chopped fresh tomatoes
2 cups diced raw carrots
3 cups diced raw potatoes

Coat beef with flour and pepper. Brown meat in oil. Add onion and garlic, and cook until tender. Pour off fat. Add thyme, basil, oregano, rosemary, marjoram, parsley, wine and water.

Cover and simmer 1 hour, stirring occasionally, adding more water if necessary to keep the bottom of the pan covered.

Add tomatoes and simmer 1 additional hour. Add carrots and potatoes. Simmer 30 minutes.

PEPPERED ROAST BEEF

SERVES 18

5 pounds beef round roast, all visible fat removed
2 tablespoons acceptable vegetable oil
1 teaspoon fresh, coarsely ground black pepper
1 medium onion, sliced
1 medium carrot, sliced
1 large stalk celery, sliced
½ cup dry red table wine

Preheat oven to 350° F.

Rub meat with oil and pepper, and place in an open roasting pan. Insert meat thermometer so tip reaches center of thickest part. Arrange onion, carrot and celery slices around meat. Pour wine over meat and vegetables. Place in oven and cook uncovered 1½ hours, or until meat thermometer registers desired degree of doneness.

If more liquid is needed, baste with additional wine during the roasting period. Do not use drippings from the roast for basting.

Skim fat from pan juices or remove juices with bulb baster and discard fat. Remove meat from pan and slice thin. Spoon pan juices over meat and serve immediately.

NUTRIENT ANALYSIS

CALORIES	267 KCAL
PROTEIN	40 GM
CARBOHYDRATE	1 GM
TOTAL FAT	10 GM
SATURATED	3 GM
POLYUNSATURATED	1 GM
MONOUNSATURATED	4 GM
CHOLESTEROL	106 MG
SODIUM	82 MG
POTASSIUM	597 MG
CALCIUM	12 MG

BEEF STROGANOFF

SERVES 5

NUTRIENT ANALYSIS*	
CALORIES	331 KCAL
PROTEIN	30 GM
CARBOHYDRATE	11 GM
TOTAL FAT	18 GM
SATURATED	5 GM
POLYUNSATURATED	5 GM
MONOUNSATURATED	6 GM
CHOLESTEROL	70 MG
SODIUM	103 MG
POTASSIUM	718 MG
CALCIUM	54 MG

*USING BEEF TENDERLOIN.

1/3 cup plain low-fat yogurt
1 pound beef tenderloin or sirloin steak, 1/2 inch thick, all visible fat removed
1/8 teaspoon freshly ground black pepper
1/2 pound fresh mushrooms, sliced
1 medium onion, sliced
3 tablespoons acceptable vegetable oil
3 tablespoons all-purpose flour
2 cups low-sodium beef broth, heated
2 tablespoons no-salt-added tomato paste
1 teaspoon dry mustard powder
1/8 teaspoon oregano
1/8 teaspoon dill weed
2 tablespoons dry table sherry

Place a double-thick layer of fine-mesh cotton cheesecloth or paper coffee filters inside a colander that does not rust. Place the colander in a bowl, leaving enough space for some of the yogurt whey to drain out of the colander. Pour the yogurt into the prepared colander and refrigerate for 30 minutes.

Cut meat into thin strips about 2 inches long. Sprinkle with pepper and set aside.

In a large nonstick skillet, sauté mushrooms and onion in oil. Remove mushrooms and onion and set aside. Place meat strips in same skillet and lightly brown on all sides. Remove meat and set aside. Mix flour into oil in skillet. Add beef broth. Bring to a boil. Reduce heat and simmer, stirring constantly, until thickened. Add to-

BEEF STROGANOFF

mato paste, mustard powder, oregano, dill weed and sherry. Stir. Add beef, mushrooms and onions. Cover tightly and simmer 1 to 1½ hours, or until beef has reached desired degree of doneness. Stir in yogurt; heat for 5 minutes, but do not boil.

This dish may be served over rice or noodles.

LIME MARINATED STEAK

SERVES 4

2 tablespoons acceptable vegetable oil
½ cup fresh lime juice
½ teaspoon hot pepper sauce
½ teaspoon garlic powder
1 18-ounce boneless top round steak, visible fat removed
2 teaspoons freshly ground black pepper
Lime wedges to garnish

In a large nonplastic dish, combine oil, lime juice, hot pepper sauce and garlic powder, stirring to mix well. Add steak to marinade and turn to coat well. Cover and place in refrigerator for 6 to 8 hours, turning a few times.

Preheat grill or broiler.

Remove steak from marinade and sprinkle with black pepper. Cook 3 to 4 minutes on each side. Transfer to a cutting board and slice thinly across grain of meat. Garnish with lime wedges.

NUTRIENT ANALYSIS

CALORIES	318 KCAL
PROTEIN	41 GM
CARBOHYDRATE	3 GM
TOTAL FAT	15 GM
SATURATED	4 GM
POLYUNSATURATED	4 GM
MONOUNSATURATED	5 GM
CHOLESTEROL	107 MG
SODIUM	89 MG
POTASSIUM	613 MG
CALCIUM	16 MG

CHILI

SERVES 6

NUTRIENT ANALYSIS	
CALORIES	227 KCAL
PROTEIN	21 GM
CARBOHYDRATE	16 GM
TOTAL FAT	9 GM
SATURATED	3 GM
POLYUNSATURATED	1 GM
MONOUNSATURATED	4 GM
CHOLESTEROL	54 MG
SODIUM	71 MG
POTASSIUM	776 MG
CALCIUM	62 MG

¾ cup dried kidney beans
3 cups water
1 pound lean ground beef
½ cup chopped onion
½ green bell pepper, chopped
1 16-ounce can no-salt-added tomatoes, chopped
1 6-ounce can no-salt-added tomato paste
¾ cup water
1 tablespoon Chili Powder (see recipe, page 37)
½ teaspoon oregano
¼ teaspoon garlic powder
⅛ teaspoon freshly ground black pepper
1 bay leaf

Place beans and water in a saucepan. Bring to a boil and cook 2 minutes. Set aside for 1 hour without draining.

Return beans to heat and simmer for 1 hour or until beans are tender. Drain, rinse and set aside.

Brown ground beef, onion and green pepper together. Pour off fat. Add kidney beans and remaining ingredients. Simmer over low heat 1½ hours, stirring occasionally.

Remove bay leaf and serve hot.

MEAT LOAF

SERVES 6

½ cup skim milk
2 slices bread, broken into pieces
1 pound lean ground beef
2 egg whites, slightly beaten
½ cup chopped onion
2 teaspoons chopped celery
1 medium fresh tomato, peeled and chopped
2 tablespoons low-sodium ketchup
1 tablespoon fresh lemon juice
⅛ teaspoon freshly ground black pepper
⅛ teaspoon dry mustard powder
⅛ teaspoon sage
⅛ teaspoon garlic powder

NUTRIENT ANALYSIS	
CALORIES	198 KCAL
PROTEIN	20 GM
CARBOHYDRATE	9 GM
TOTAL FAT	9 GM
SATURATED	3 GM
POLYUNSATURATED	0 GM
MONOUNSATURATED	4 GM
CHOLESTEROL	54 MG
SODIUM	102 MG
POTASSIUM	311 MG
CALCIUM	44 MG

Preheat oven to 375° F.

Pour milk over bread and allow to stand 5 minutes. Add remaining ingredients and mix well.

Form into a loaf and place on a rack in a shallow roasting pan. Bake 1½ hours.

BEEF GOULASH

SERVES 6

NUTRIENT ANALYSIS	
CALORIES	330 KCAL
PROTEIN	23 GM
CARBOHYDRATE	39 GM
TOTAL FAT	9 GM
SATURATED	3 GM
POLYUNSATURATED	1 GM
MONOUNSATURATED	4 GM
CHOLESTEROL	54 MG
SODIUM	58 MG
POTASSIUM	823 MG
CALCIUM	42 MG

1 cup uncooked macaroni
1 pound lean ground beef
1/2 pound fresh mushrooms, sliced
1 cup chopped onion
1 clove garlic, minced
1 6-ounce can no-salt-added tomato paste
3/4 cup water
1 cup Ketchup (see recipe, page 181) or low-sodium ketchup
1 small bay leaf
1 teaspoon sugar
1/2 teaspoon freshly ground black pepper
1/4 teaspoon oregano
1/4 teaspoon basil

Cook macaroni according to package directions, omitting salt. Drain and set aside.

Brown ground beef with mushrooms, onion and garlic. Pour off fat. Add remaining ingredients. Simmer gently about 15 minutes. Add cooked, drained macaroni. Simmer 5 minutes. Remove bay leaf and serve.

SOFT TACOS

SERVES 6; 2 TACOS PER SERVING

1 pound lean ground beef
1 16-ounce can tomato puree
½ teaspoon Chili Powder (see recipe, page 37)
¼ teaspoon garlic powder
¼ teaspoon onion powder
¼ teaspoon sugar
¼ teaspoon freshly ground black pepper
12 flour tortillas
½ cup chopped green bell pepper
½ cup chopped onion
2 fresh tomatoes, chopped
½ head lettuce, shredded

NUTRIENT ANALYSIS

CALORIES	362 KCAL
PROTEIN	23 GM
CARBOHYDRATE	41 GM
TOTAL FAT	13 GM
SATURATED	5 GM
POLYUNSATURATED	1 GM
MONOUNSATURATED	6 GM
CHOLESTEROL	58 MG
SODIUM	277 MG
POTASSIUM	673 MG
CALCIUM	62 MG

Brown meat in a large nonstick skillet. Pour off fat. Add tomato puree, Chili Powder, garlic and onion powders, sugar and black pepper. Mix well. Cook uncovered over low heat 20 minutes or until thick, stirring occasionally.

Heat tortillas in a nonstick skillet over medium-high heat or in a microwave oven.

Spoon meat mixture onto hot tortillas and top with green pepper, onion, tomatoes and lettuce. Fold tortilla over filling and serve.

SPAGHETTI WITH MEAT SAUCE

SERVES 6

NUTRIENT ANALYSIS	
CALORIES	370 KCAL
PROTEIN	24 GM
CARBOHYDRATE	44 GM
TOTAL FAT	10 GM
SATURATED	3 GM
POLYUNSATURATED	1 GM
MONOUNSATURATED	4 GM
CHOLESTEROL	54 MG
SODIUM	58 MG
POTASSIUM	779 MG
CALCIUM	44 MG

1 pound lean ground beef
1 medium onion, chopped
1 clove garlic, minced
5 medium fresh tomatoes, peeled and chopped, or 1 28-ounce can no-salt-added tomatoes, chopped
1 6-ounce can no-salt-added tomato paste
½ cup dry red table wine
½ teaspoon oregano
½ teaspoon basil
½ teaspoon fennel seeds
⅛ teaspoon freshly ground black pepper
1 8-ounce package spaghetti

Brown ground beef in a large nonstick skillet. Pour off fat. Add remaining ingredients except spaghetti. Cover and simmer over low heat 1½ hours, stirring occasionally. If sauce appears too thick, add water.

Cook spaghetti according to package directions, omitting salt. Drain.

Pour sauce over spaghetti and serve.

LEMON VEAL WITH SPINACH

SERVES 6

1½ pounds lean veal, cut into cubes
3 tablespoons acceptable vegetable oil
1 large onion, chopped
¼ cup water
1 tablespoon fresh lemon juice
¼ teaspoon freshly ground black pepper
½ teaspoon crushed fennel seeds
3 green onions with tops, chopped
2 10-ounce packages frozen spinach
1 lemon, cut into 6 wedges

Brown veal in oil in a large, heavy nonstick skillet. Add chopped onion, cooking until onion is tender. Pour off fat. Add water, lemon juice, pepper and crushed fennel seeds. Cover and simmer over low heat 1 hour, or until veal is tender, stirring occasionally. (More water may be added if needed.)

Add green onions and spinach. Cover and return to simmer. Cook over low heat until spinach is tender, about 5 to 10 minutes.

Place on warm serving platter and garnish with lemon wedges.

NUTRIENT ANALYSIS

CALORIES	246 KCAL
PROTEIN	30 GM
CARBOHYDRATE	7 GM
TOTAL FAT	11 GM
SATURATED	2 GM
POLYUNSATURATED	5 GM
MONOUNSATURATED	3 GM
CHOLESTEROL	114 MG
SODIUM	120 MG
POTASSIUM	524 MG
CALCIUM	129 MG

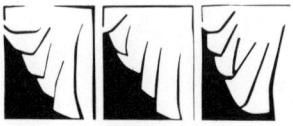

LAMB CURRY

SERVES 8

NUTRIENT ANALYSIS	
CALORIES	196 KCAL
PROTEIN	19 GM
CARBOHYDRATE	3 GM
TOTAL FAT	12 GM
SATURATED	3 GM
POLYUNSATURATED	3 GM
MONOUNSATURATED	5 GM
CHOLESTEROL	65 MG
SODIUM	65 MG
POTASSIUM	276 MG
CALCIUM	21 MG

3 tablespoons all-purpose flour
1/8 teaspoon freshly ground black pepper
2 pounds lean lamb, all visible fat removed, cut into cubes
2 tablespoons acceptable vegetable oil
1/2 cup finely chopped onion
2 teaspoons curry powder
3 cups water
2 teaspoons fresh lemon juice

Combine flour and pepper. Roll lamb in seasoned flour. Place oil in a large nonstick skillet over medium-high heat. Add lamb and brown on all sides. Pour off fat. Add onion, curry powder and water. Cover and simmer over low heat, stirring occasionally, for 1 hour or until meat is tender. Stir in lemon juice.

This dish is very good served over rice.

MEDITERRANEAN PORK CHOPS

SERVES 4

1 teaspoon acceptable vegetable oil
4 loin pork chops, very lean, 1/2 inch thick, all visible fat removed
1/2 teaspoon marjoram
1/8 teaspoon garlic powder
1/8 teaspoon onion powder
1/8 teaspoon freshly ground black pepper
1/2 cup water

Place oil in a large nonstick skillet over medium-high heat. Add pork chops and brown evenly. Pour off fat.

In a small bowl, mix seasonings together. Sprinkle over chops. Add water and cover tightly. Reduce heat and simmer over low heat 1 hour or until tender.

NUTRIENT ANALYSIS

CALORIES	172 KCAL
PROTEIN	18 GM
CARBOHYDRATE	0 GM
TOTAL FAT	10 GM
SATURATED	3 GM
POLYUNSATURATED	2 GM
MONOUNSATURATED	4 GM
CHOLESTEROL	60 MG
SODIUM	46 MG
POTASSIUM	248 MG
CALCIUM	7 MG

HUNGARIAN PORK CHOPS

SERVES 4

NUTRIENT ANALYSIS	
CALORIES	200 KCAL
PROTEIN	20 GM
CARBOHYDRATE	4 GM
TOTAL FAT	11 GM
SATURATED	4 GM
POLYUNSATURATED	2 GM
MONOUNSATURATED	5 GM
CHOLESTEROL	63 MG
SODIUM	75 MG
POTASSIUM	364 MG
CALCIUM	85 MG

⅔ cup plain low-fat yogurt
Vegetable oil spray
4 loin pork chops, very lean, ½ inch thick, all visible fat removed
1 teaspoon acceptable vegetable oil
1 teaspoon paprika
½ teaspoon caraway seeds
½ teaspoon dill weed
½ teaspoon onion powder
½ teaspoon garlic powder
½ cup water

Place a double-thick layer of fine-mesh cotton cheesecloth or paper coffee filters inside a colander that does not rust. Place the colander in a bowl, leaving enough space for some of the yogurt whey to drain out of the colander. Pour the yogurt into the prepared colander and refrigerate for 30 minutes.

Lightly spray a heavy nonstick skillet with vegetable oil spray. Place over medium-high heat. Add chops and oil and brown evenly. Pour off fat. In a small bowl, mix seasonings together. Sprinkle over chops. Add water to skillet. Reduce heat, cover tightly and simmer 1 hour or until tender. Add more water if necessary.

Remove chops and keep warm. Add yogurt to liquid in pan and stir to mix well. Heat for 5 minutes, but do not boil. Pour sauce over chops and serve.

Vegetarian Entrées

Spaghetti with Mushroom Sauce

Spaghetti Squash

Spinach Lasagna

Pizza Hero

Zucchini Frittata

Fettucine Alfredo

Vegetarian Chili

Cheese Blintzes

French Toast

No-Cholesterol Egg Substitute

Almost everyone likes an occasional meatless meal. Hearty vegetarian fare is great for weight watchers, too—and for those keeping an eye on their cholesterol levels.

You can get all the daily protein you need by combining grains, legumes and vegetables in interesting ways in casseroles, vegetable pizzas and stir-fries.

Try Spaghetti with Mushroom Sauce or Spinach Lasagna for a taste of the old country, or Fettucine Alfredo, which, despite no salt and little fat in the recipe here, is wonderful and rich-tasting.

For an out-West flavor, try Vegetarian Chili. Made with beans and bulgur wheat, it offers the hearty taste of that old Texas favorite, and you can make it as spicy as your tastebuds can stand!

Breakfast used to mean bacon and eggs, but no more. For healthful alternatives, try these new versions of two old favorites: Cheese Blintzes and French Toast. With a few slight alterations, they can be made without salt and little fat for a nutritious breakfast.

Here, too, is a recipe that's a must for every low-fat kitchen: No-Cholesterol Egg Substitute. Use it anywhere you need an egg. That includes omelettes, baking, casseroles . . . anything.

SPAGHETTI WITH MUSHROOM SAUCE

SERVES 6

NUTRIENT ANALYSIS	
CALORIES	262 KCAL
PROTEIN	8 GM
CARBOHYDRATE	44 GM
TOTAL FAT	7 GM
SATURATED	1 GM
POLYUNSATURATED	2 GM
MONOUNSATURATED	3 GM
CHOLESTEROL	0 MG
SODIUM	32 MG
POTASSIUM	581 MG
CALCIUM	49 MG

3 tablespoons acceptable margarine
1 cup sliced fresh mushrooms
1/3 cup chopped onion
1 clove garlic, minced
1 16-ounce can no-salt-added tomatoes, chopped
1 6-ounce can no-salt-added tomato paste
1/2 cup water
1 tablespoon sugar
1 bay leaf
1/4 teaspoon basil
1/4 teaspoon oregano
1/8 teaspoon freshly ground black pepper
1 8-ounce package spaghetti

Melt margarine in a large nonstick skillet over medium-high heat. Add mushrooms, onion and garlic. Sauté until onion is tender. Stir in remaining ingredients except spaghetti. Cover and simmer over low heat 2 hours, stirring occasionally. If sauce appears too thick, add additional water. Remove bay leaf.

Cook spaghetti according to package directions, omitting salt. Drain. Pour sauce over spaghetti and serve.

SPAGHETTI SQUASH

SERVES 4

1 spaghetti squash, approximately 4 pounds
1 tablespoon olive oil
1 medium onion, chopped
½ pound fresh mushrooms, sliced
⅓ cup white table wine
1 16-ounce can no-salt-added tomato sauce
1 16-ounce can no-salt-added tomatoes
2 cloves garlic, minced
¼ teaspoon freshly ground black pepper
1 cup sliced fresh carrots
2 cups cooked fresh broccoli florets
1 small zucchini, sliced
¼ cup Parmesan cheese
2 tablespoons chopped fresh parsley

NUTRIENT ANALYSIS	
CALORIES	330 KCAL
PROTEIN	12 GM
CARBOHYDRATE	59 GM
TOTAL FAT	8 GM
SATURATED	2 GM
POLYUNSATURATED	2 GM
MONOUNSATURATED	3 GM
CHOLESTEROL	4 MG
SODIUM	174 MG
POTASSIUM	1857 MG
CALCIUM	222 MG

Preheat oven to 350° F. Place whole squash in a baking dish with a little water. Pierce squash with a fork a few times. Place in oven and bake 1 hour, or until squash can easily be pierced with a fork.

Meanwhile, place oil in a large saucepan over medium heat. Add onion and cook until soft. Add mushrooms and wine and cook another 2 to 3 minutes. Add tomato sauce, tomatoes, garlic and pepper. Simmer 3 to 4 minutes. Add carrots, broccoli and zucchini and allow to simmer 5 minutes.

Halve squash lengthwise and remove seeds. Scrape the squash lengthwise with a fork so the strands resemble spaghetti. Place on serving platter and pour spaghetti sauce over the squash. Sprinkle with Parmesan cheese and parsley. Toss and serve.

SPINACH LASAGNA

SERVES 8

NUTRIENT ANALYSIS	
CALORIES	432 KCAL
PROTEIN	28 GM
CARBOHYDRATE	50 GM
TOTAL FAT	14 GM
SATURATED	5 GM
POLYUNSATURATED	3 GM
MONOUNSATURATED	5 GM
CHOLESTEROL	68 MG
SODIUM	273 MG
POTASSIUM	911 MG
CALCIUM	362 MG

Vegetable oil spray
1 pound lasagna noodles, white or spinach
¼ cup shredded part-skim mozzarella cheese
2 tablespoons Parmesan cheese
1¼ cups shredded part-skim mozzarella cheese
6 tablespoons Parmesan cheese
3 cups low-fat cottage cheese (drained)
3 cups chopped raw spinach
4 cups Tomato Sauce (see recipe, page 184)

Preheat oven to 350° F. Lightly spray a 9 × 13 × 2½-inch baking dish with vegetable oil spray. Set aside.

Place noodles in a large pan of unsalted boiling water. Cook until soft but not completely cooked. (It is best to slightly undercook noodles because they will be easier to handle during assembly, and they will continue to cook while in the oven.) Drain noodles and rinse under cold running water.

In a small bowl, combine ¼ cup mozzarella and 2 tablespoons Parmesan cheese. Stir to mix well and set aside. In a medium bowl, combine 1¼ cups mozzarella with 6 tablespoons Parmesan cheese and all of the cottage cheese and spinach. Stir to mix well and set aside.

Spread a thin layer of Tomato Sauce in the bottom of the baking dish. Add about one-third of the noodles in a single layer. Spread one-half of cottage cheese mixture on top. Add a thin coating of sauce. Add

SPINACH LASAGNA

another layer of noodles and top with cottage cheese mixture and a thin coating of sauce. Top with the remaining noodles and cover with remaining sauce and reserved mozzarella-and-Parmesan mixture.

Bake 30 to 40 minutes. Let stand 10 to 15 minutes. Cut into 8 equal portions and serve.

PIZZA HERO

SERVES 2; ½ ROLL PER SERVING

1 6-inch submarine roll
¼ cup no-salt-added spaghetti sauce
1 ounce part-skim mozzarella cheese, shredded
¼ cup sliced fresh mushrooms
4 thin slices of onion
3 green bell pepper rings

Preheat oven to 400° F.

Split roll in half lengthwise and place on baking sheet, cut sides up. Pour spaghetti sauce over roll halves and top with cheese, mushrooms, onion slices and bell pepper.

Place in oven and heat about 5 minutes, or until cheese is melted. Serve warm.

NUTRIENT ANALYSIS

CALORIES	175 KCAL
PROTEIN	8 GM
CARBOHYDRATE	25 GM
TOTAL FAT	5 GM
SATURATED	2 GM
POLYUNSATURATED	1 GM
MONOUNSATURATED	2 GM
CHOLESTEROL	8 MG
SODIUM	288 MG
POTASSIUM	290 MG
CALCIUM	136 MG

ZUCCHINI FRITTATA

SERVES 4

NUTRIENT ANALYSIS	
CALORIES	189 KCAL
PROTEIN	14 GM
CARBOHYDRATE	12 GM
TOTAL FAT	10 GM
SATURATED	4 GM
POLYUNSATURATED	1 GM
MONOUNSATURATED	4 GM
CHOLESTEROL	84 MG
SODIUM	221 MG
POTASSIUM	557 MG
CALCIUM	286 MG

1 large egg
3 large egg whites
1 tablespoon olive oil
1 medium zucchini, diced
3 medium green onions, with tops, sliced
2 cloves garlic, minced
1 16-ounce can no-salt-added tomatoes
1/2 teaspoon commercial Italian seasoning
1/4 teaspoon freshly ground black pepper
1 cup grated part-skim mozzarella cheese

Preheat oven to 350° F.

In a small bowl, whisk together egg and egg whites. Set aside.

Heat oil in a 10-inch nonstick skillet with ovenproof handle, over medium heat. Add zucchini and cook until soft, about 5 minutes. Add green onions and cook another minute. Add garlic, tomatoes, Italian seasoning and pepper and cook another 3 to 4 minutes.

Add egg mixture to vegetables and stir to mix well. Sprinkle cheese on top and place skillet in oven. Bake 5 to 6 minutes, or until mixture is firm.

Change oven setting to Broil and cook an additional 2 to 3 minutes, or until golden brown. Serve immediately.

This dish works well for dinner and for breakfast or brunch.

FETTUCINE ALFREDO

SERVES 4

1 pound fettucine noodles
2 tablespoons acceptable margarine
2 tablespoons flour
1½ cups skim milk
⅓ cup Parmesan cheese
1 teaspoon fresh lemon juice
⅛ teaspoon ground white pepper
2 tablespoons chopped fresh parsley
2 tablespoons Parmesan cheese

Cook fettucine noodles according to package directions, omitting salt. Set aside and keep warm.

Melt margarine in a medium saucepan over medium heat. Add flour. Cook 1 to 2 minutes, stirring constantly. Whisk in milk and bring to a boil. Reduce heat to low and add more milk if thinner consistency is desired. Add ⅓ cup Parmesan cheese, lemon juice and pepper.

Pour sauce over warm fettucine noodles and garnish with parsley and remaining 2 tablespoons Parmesan cheese.

NUTRIENT ANALYSIS

CALORIES	612 KCAL
PROTEIN	23 GM
CARBOHYDRATE	104 GM
TOTAL FAT	10 GM
SATURATED	3 GM
POLYUNSATURATED	2 GM
MONOUNSATURATED	4 GM
CHOLESTEROL	9 MG
SODIUM	224 MG
POTASSIUM	434 MG
CALCIUM	279 MG

VEGETARIAN CHILI

SERVES 6

NUTRIENT ANALYSIS	
CALORIES	338 KCAL
PROTEIN	11 GM
CARBOHYDRATE	58 GM
TOTAL FAT	8 GM
SATURATED	1 GM
POLYUNSATURATED	5 GM
MONOUNSATURATED	2 GM
CHOLESTEROL	0 MG
SODIUM	32 MG
POTASSIUM	571 MG
CALCIUM	77 MG

1 cup dry kidney beans
6 cups water
3 tablespoons acceptable vegetable oil
2 cups chopped onions
2 cups chopped green bell peppers
2 cloves garlic, minced
1 cup no-salt-added canned tomatoes, chopped
2 cups water
1 cup bulgur
1½ tablespoons chili powder (or to taste)
¼ teaspoon cayenne pepper
½ teaspoon freshly ground black pepper
2 tablespoons ground cumin
1 tablespoon fresh lemon juice

Soak beans overnight in 3 cups of water.

Drain beans and place them in a large saucepan. Add 3 cups of fresh water and cook, uncovered, 1½ hours, or until tender. Drain, rinse and set aside.

In a large saucepan or Dutch oven, place oil, onions, green peppers and garlic. Sauté 8 to 10 minutes, or until vegetables are soft. Add tomatoes, 2 cups of water and bulgur. Simmer 45 to 60 minutes. Add cooked kidney beans and remaining ingredients and cook an additional 10 minutes. Serve hot.

CHEESE BLINTZES

SERVES 11; 2 BLINTZES PER SERVING

2 cups (1 pound) unsalted dry-curd cottage cheese
1 egg white
1/4 cup sugar
1/2 teaspoon grated fresh lemon peel
2 tablespoons fresh lemon juice
1 recipe Crepes (page 210)
1 tablespoon acceptable margarine

To make filling, combine cottage cheese, egg white, sugar, lemon peel and lemon juice in a medium bowl and beat well.

Place 1 tablespoon of filling in center of each crepe and fold in an envelope shape.

Melt margarine in large nonstick skillet over medium heat. Add blintzes and heat for approximately 10 minutes, or until heated thoroughly.

Blintzes may be refrigerated for up to 5 hours before heating.

To serve blintzes as a breakfast entrée, top with a sprinkle of ground cinnamon and sugar or with warm applesauce and cinnamon.

NUTRIENT ANALYSIS

CALORIES	175 KCAL
PROTEIN	8 GM
CARBOHYDRATE	19 GM
TOTAL FAT	7 GM
SATURATED	2 GM
POLYUNSATURATED	2 GM
MONOUNSATURATED	3 GM
CHOLESTEROL	2 MG
SODIUM	29 MG
POTASSIUM	70 MG
CALCIUM	35 MG

FRENCH TOAST

SERVES 5

NUTRIENT ANALYSIS	
CALORIES	153 KCAL
PROTEIN	6 GM
CARBOHYDRATE	14 GM
TOTAL FAT	8 GM
SATURATED	2 GM
POLYUNSATURATED	3 GM
MONOUNSATURATED	3 GM
CHOLESTEROL	1 MG
SODIUM	180 MG
POTASSIUM	100 MG
CALCIUM	52 MG

1 recipe No-Cholesterol Egg Substitute (see recipe, page 149)
1/4 cup skim milk
1/4 teaspoon vanilla
1/8 teaspoon ground cinnamon
5 slices day-old bread
2 tablespoons acceptable margarine

In a medium shallow bowl, mix Egg Substitute, skim milk, vanilla and cinnamon. Dip bread slices in egg mixture.

Melt margarine in a large nonstick skillet over medium-high heat. Add bread slices and lightly brown.

May be served with margarine and syrup or jelly.

NO-CHOLESTEROL EGG SUBSTITUTE

SERVES 1

4 large egg whites
1 tablespoon acceptable vegetable oil
1 tablespoon nonfat dry milk powder
3 drops yellow food coloring

Place all ingredients in a medium bowl. Mix until thoroughly blended.

Use in place of 2 whole eggs in recipes. (This substitution may require some experimenting in baking since it will not work effectively in every cake and cookie recipe.)

NUTRIENT ANALYSIS

CALORIES	200 KCAL
PROTEIN	15 GM
CARBOHYDRATE	4 GM
TOTAL FAT	14 GM
SATURATED	2 GM
POLYUNSATURATED	8 GM
MONOUNSATURATED	3 GM
CHOLESTEROL	1 MG
SODIUM	224 MG
POTASSIUM	253 MG
CALCIUM	67 MG

NO-CHOLESTEROL SCRAMBLED EGGS

Add a dash of thyme and a dash of freshly ground black pepper to mixture. Spray a small nonstick skillet with vegetable oil spray. Place skillet over medium heat and add egg mixture. Stir occasionally until eggs are fully cooked. Serve immediately.

NO-CHOLESTEROL OMELET

Spray a small omelet pan or nonstick skillet with vegetable oil spray. Place over medium heat and add egg mixture. Cook until lightly browned. Turn omelet and brown other side. Place chopped fresh tomatoes or sautéed sliced mushrooms, onions, green bell pepper or chives in center of omelet and fold in half. Serve immediately.

VEGETABLES

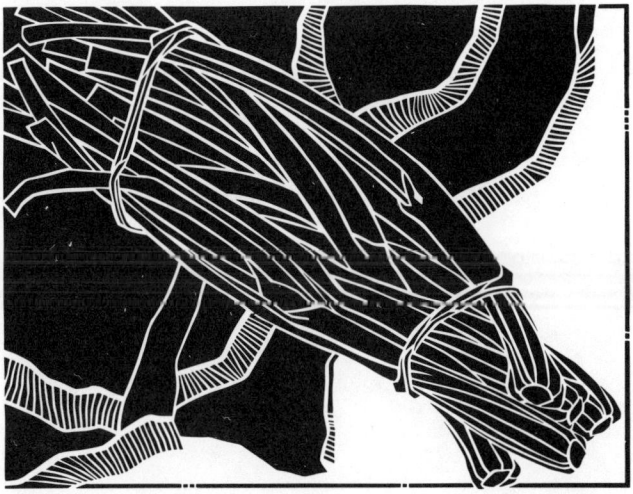

Gingered Carrots

Dilled Summer Squash

Vegetable Medley

Baked Tomatoes

Sautéed Cauliflower

Stir-Fried Cabbage with Noodles

Baked Beans

Sweet and Sour Green Beans

Green Beans and Corn

Eggplant Mexicana

Mushroom and Herb Dressing

Scalloped Potatoes

Potatoes O'Brien

Hash-Brown Potatoes

Potato Pancakes

Oven-Fried Potatoes with Oregano

Scalloped Sweet Potatoes

Sweet Potato Casserole

Seasoned Rice

Brown Rice Pilaf

Rice and Vegetable Pilaf

The 1941 edition of the *Fannie Farmer Cookbook* instructed cooks to boil green beans for at least 20 minutes. Today we laugh at the idea.

Gone are the days when vegetables were cooked until limp. Now we want vegetables tender-crisp, and often, even raw. Since overcooking can leach vegetables of vitamins and minerals, braising, steaming and stir-frying have become the cook's preferred cooking methods. And with great results!

Steaming is a particularly wonderful way to cook vegetables because it doesn't use fats or oils and leaves most of the vitamins and minerals right where you want them—in your food.

If you're skeptical that vegetables can be tasty without added fat and salt, these recipes should convince you. From crunchy, tangy Gingered Carrots to spicy Eggplant Mexicana, you'll find that flavorful vegetable dishes are easier to make than you think.

And with the hundreds of kinds of vegetables grown throughout the world, it's a cinch to come up with a new and different combination of veggies every day of the year. There's simply no excuse for having broccoli 365 days in a row!

Even the simplest vegetables have a lot to recommend them. For instance, buy summer squash when the skin is soft enough not to need peeling, then try the Dilled Summer Squash or Vegetable Medley recipes here. Unforgettable!

The humble potato is high in carbohydrates and low in fat. Each potato has a good amount of iron and potassium, some calcium, phosphorous and vitamins B_1, C and niacin. All for about 100 calories a potato. Try Hash-Brown Potatoes for breakfast, Potato Pancakes for lunch and Scalloped Potatoes for dinner.

The trick with vegetables is adding flavor without inflating the fat, sodium or calorie count. These recipes are a start. After that, use your imagination, fresh herbs and spices. You'll surprise yourself.

GINGERED CARROTS

SERVES 5

NUTRIENT ANALYSIS	
CALORIES	63 KCAL
PROTEIN	1 GM
CARBOHYDRATE	10 GM
TOTAL FAT	2 GM
SATURATED	1 GM
POLYUNSATURATED	1 GM
MONOUNSATURATED	1 GM
CHOLESTEROL	0 MG
SODIUM	33 MG
POTASSIUM	303 MG
CALCIUM	27 MG

1 pound raw carrots, peeled and cut into 1/4-inch slices
1/4 teaspoon ground ginger
1 teaspoon sugar
1 tablespoon acceptable margarine, melted
2 tablespoons finely chopped fresh parsley or 1 tablespoon dry parsley flakes

Place carrots in a saucepan. Add just enough water to cover. Boil 10 to 12 minutes or until barely tender. Drain.

Add ginger and sugar to melted margarine and pour over carrots. Stir gently.

Sprinkle with parsley and serve immediately.

DILLED SUMMER SQUASH

SERVES 4

1/4 cup water
2 medium summer squash, sliced
1 1/2 teaspoons finely chopped onion
1/2 teaspoon dill seed, crushed
1/8 teaspoon freshly ground black pepper
1 tablespoon acceptable margarine

Bring water to a boil in a medium saucepan over high heat. Add squash, onion, dill seed and pepper. Reduce heat to medium and cook 10 minutes or until squash is tender. Drain and dot with margarine. Serve immediately.

NUTRIENT ANALYSIS

CALORIES	40 KCAL
PROTEIN	1 GM
CARBOHYDRATE	3 GM
TOTAL FAT	3 GM
SATURATED	1 GM
POLYUNSATURATED	1 GM
MONOUNSATURATED	1 GM
CHOLESTEROL	0 MG
SODIUM	4 MG
POTASSIUM	247 MG
CALCIUM	16 MG

VEGETABLE MEDLEY

SERVES 4

NUTRIENT ANALYSIS	
CALORIES	92 KCAL
PROTEIN	4 GM
CARBOHYDRATE	15 GM
TOTAL FAT	3 GM
SATURATED	1 GM
POLYUNSATURATED	1 GM
MONOUNSATURATED	1 GM
CHOLESTEROL	0 MG
SODIUM	15 MG
POTASSIUM	642 MG
CALCIUM	45 MG

1 tablespoon acceptable margarine
2 medium yellow summer squash, sliced
1 medium zucchini, sliced
1 medium yellow onion, diced
3 medium fresh tomatoes, diced
1/2 cup frozen corn
1 clove garlic, minced
1/2 teaspoon oregano
1/2 teaspoon basil
1/4 teaspoon freshly ground black pepper

In a large pan over medium heat melt margarine. Add squash, zucchini and onion. Sauté 3 to 4 minutes. Add tomatoes, corn, garlic and seasonings and cook another 2 to 3 minutes. Serve immediately.

BAKED TOMATOES

SERVES 4

Vegetable oil spray
2 fresh tomatoes, cut in halves
1 tablespoon olive oil
1/2 teaspoon chopped fresh parsley or 1/4 teaspoon dried parsley flakes
1/4 teaspoon oregano
1/4 teaspoon basil

Preheat oven to 350° F. Lightly spray a 9×9-inch baking dish with vegetable oil spray.

Place tomato halves in baking dish, cut side up. Drizzle oil over tomatoes. Sprinkle remaining ingredients on top and bake 20 to 30 minutes. Serve hot.

NUTRIENT ANALYSIS

CALORIES	42 KCAL
PROTEIN	1 GM
CARBOHYDRATE	3 GM
TOTAL FAT	4 GM
SATURATED	0 GM
POLYUNSATURATED	0 GM
MONOUNSATURATED	3 GM
CHOLESTEROL	0 MG
SODIUM	5 MG
POTASSIUM	133 MG
CALCIUM	8 MG

SAUTÉED CAULIFLOWER

SERVES 4

NUTRIENT ANALYSIS	
CALORIES	33 KCAL
PROTEIN	1 GM
CARBOHYDRATE	3 GM
TOTAL FAT	2 GM
SATURATED	0 GM
POLYUNSATURATED	1 GM
MONOUNSATURATED	1 GM
CHOLESTEROL	0 MG
SODIUM	11 MG
POTASSIUM	92 MG
CALCIUM	14 MG

1 head (1 pound) fresh or 1 10-ounce package frozen cauliflower
2 teaspoons acceptable vegetable oil
1/4 teaspoon thyme
3/4 teaspoon cider vinegar
1/2 clove garlic, minced
Dash freshly ground black pepper
2 teaspoons minced fresh parsley or 1 teaspoon dried parsley flakes

Break fresh cauliflower into small florets and cook or steam in unsalted water until just tender, 10 to 12 minutes. If using frozen cauliflower, cook according to directions on package, omitting salt. Drain.

Combine oil, thyme, vinegar and garlic in a large pan or skillet. Cook over moderate heat 5 minutes. Add drained cauliflower, sprinkle with pepper and stir gently. Simmer until hot. Sprinkle with parsley and serve immediately.

STIR-FRIED CABBAGE WITH NOODLES

SERVES 6

1 cup dry noodles
3 cups finely chopped cabbage
1 tablespoon acceptable margarine
3/4 teaspoon caraway seeds
1/2 teaspoon onion powder

Cook noodles according to package directions, omitting salt.

Stir-fry chopped cabbage in margarine over medium heat until cabbage is tender but still crisp, about 5 to 8 minutes. Add drained noodles, caraway seeds and onion powder. Stir together gently. Serve immediately.

NUTRIENT ANALYSIS

CALORIES	49 KCAL
PROTEIN	1 GM
CARBOHYDRATE	6 GM
TOTAL FAT	2 GM
SATURATED	0 GM
POLYUNSATURATED	1 GM
MONOUNSATURATED	1 GM
CHOLESTEROL	6 MG
SODIUM	7 MG
POTASSIUM	97 MG
CALCIUM	20 MG

BAKED BEANS

SERVES 6

NUTRIENT ANALYSIS	
CALORIES	234 KCAL
PROTEIN	21 GM
CARBOHYDRATE	40 GM
TOTAL FAT	3 GM
SATURATED	1 GM
POLYUNSATURATED	1 GM
MONOUNSATURATED	1 GM
CHOLESTEROL	10 MG
SODIUM	37 MG
POTASSIUM	861 MG
CALCIUM	118 MG

½ pound (1 cup) dried navy beans
4 cups water
Vegetable oil spray
1 loin-end pork chop, very lean
1 cup Chili Sauce (see recipe, page 183)
¾ cup chopped onion
2 tablespoons light molasses
1 tablespoon firmly packed brown sugar
1½ teaspoons dry mustard powder
¼ teaspoon garlic powder
1 cup water

Place beans and water in a large saucepan over high heat. Bring to a boil and cook 2 minutes. Remove from heat and let stand 1 hour.

Return beans to heat and simmer 1 hour, or until beans are tender. Drain, rinse and set aside.

Preheat oven to 350° F. Lightly spray a 1½-quart casserole dish with vegetable oil spray.

Place beans in prepared casserole and set aside.

Brown pork chop in a small nonstick skillet over medium-high heat. Cut into small cubes and add to beans.

Add remaining ingredients and mix well. Cover and bake 4 hours. If needed, add additional water during cooking.

SWEET AND SOUR GREEN BEANS

SERVES 4

1 10-ounce package frozen or 1 pound fresh green beans, cut in 1-inch pieces
1 teaspoon acceptable margarine
½ teaspoon all-purpose flour
1 tablespoon water
1 tablespoon fresh lemon juice
1 tablespoon sugar
¼ teaspoon dill seeds (optional)
Dash paprika

Cook frozen green beans according to directions on package, omitting salt. If using fresh green beans, cook in ½ cup unsalted water until tender. Drain and set aside.

In a separate pan, melt margarine, stir in flour and brown lightly. Stir in remaining ingredients and cook over low heat until thickened.

Pour over drained green beans and heat 5 minutes. Serve immediately.

NUTRIENT ANALYSIS

CALORIES	48 KCAL
PROTEIN	1 GM
CARBOHYDRATE	10 GM
TOTAL FAT	1 GM
SATURATED	0 GM
POLYUNSATURATED	0 GM
MONOUNSATURATED	0 GM
CHOLESTEROL	0 MG
SODIUM	14 MG
POTASSIUM	117 MG
CALCIUM	45 MG

GREEN BEANS AND CORN

SERVES 4

GREEN BEANS AND CORN
NUTRIENT ANALYSIS

CALORIES	69 KCAL
PROTEIN	2 GM
CARBOHYDRATE	11 GM
TOTAL FAT	3 GM
SATURATED	1 GM
POLYUNSATURATED	1 GM
MONOUNSATURATED	1 GM
CHOLESTEROL	0 MG
SODIUM	7 MG
POTASSIUM	108 MG
CALCIUM	20 MG

SUCCOTASH
NUTRIENT ANALYSIS

CALORIES	104 KCAL
PROTEIN	4 GM
CARBOHYDRATE	17 GM
TOTAL FAT	3 GM
SATURATED	1 GM
POLYUNSATURATED	1 GM
MONOUNSATURATED	1 GM
CHOLESTEROL	0 MG
SODIUM	26 MG
POTASSIUM	251 MG
CALCIUM	17 MG

1 cup fresh or frozen French-style green beans
1 cup frozen whole kernel corn or fresh, cut from cob
½ cup water
3 tablespoons chopped onion
1 tablespoon acceptable margarine
½ teaspoon basil
½ teaspoon fresh lemon juice
Dash freshly ground black pepper

Cook beans and corn together in water until beans are just tender. Drain and set aside in saucepan.

In a separate pan, sauté onion in margarine until tender. Pour over beans and corn and add basil, lemon juice and pepper. Place saucepan over low heat and simmer until hot.

SUCCOTASH

Use fresh lima beans in place of green beans.

EGGPLANT MEXICANA

SERVES 6

1 medium (1 pound) eggplant, peeled and cut into cubes
4 medium fresh tomatoes, peeled and chopped, or 1 16-ounce can no-salt-added tomatoes
1 clove garlic, minced
2 tablespoons chopped onion
1/4 teaspoon Chili Powder (see recipe, page 37)
1/4 teaspoon freshly ground black pepper

Combine all ingredients in a large nonstick skillet and simmer gently 15 to 20 minutes or until eggplant is tender. Serve immediately.

NUTRIENT ANALYSIS

CALORIES	34 KCAL
PROTEIN	1 GM
CARBOHYDRATE	8 GM
TOTAL FAT	0 GM
SATURATED	0 GM
POLYUNSATURATED	0 GM
MONOUNSATURATED	0 GM
CHOLESTEROL	0 MG
SODIUM	14 MG
POTASSIUM	321 MG
CALCIUM	26 MG

MUSHROOM AND HERB DRESSING

SERVES 4

NUTRIENT ANALYSIS	
CALORIES	232 KCAL
PROTEIN	7 GM
CARBOHYDRATE	39 GM
TOTAL FAT	5 GM
SATURATED	1 GM
POLYUNSATURATED	2 GM
MONOUNSATURATED	2 GM
CHOLESTEROL	3 MG
SODIUM	374 MG
POTASSIUM	174 MG
CALCIUM	73 MG

Vegetable oil spray
1 tablespoon acceptable margarine
¼ cup chopped onions
1 cup chopped fresh mushrooms
2 cups bread crumbs
½ teaspoon thyme
½ teaspoon basil
¼ teaspoon freshly ground black pepper
¼ cup low-sodium chicken broth

Preheat oven to 350° F. Lightly spray a 1½-quart casserole with vegetable oil spray.

Melt margarine in a nonstick skillet over medium heat. Add onions and mushrooms and sauté about 5 minutes, or until soft.

In a medium bowl, combine onion-mushroom mixture, bread crumbs, thyme, basil and black pepper. Add chicken broth and mix well.

Place in prepared casserole and bake uncovered 30 minutes. Or, stuff loosely into a 4- to 4½-pound chicken, such as Roast Chicken (page 102), before roasting.

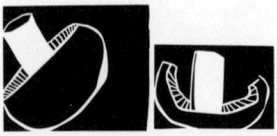

SCALLOPED POTATOES

SERVES 5

3 tablespoons acceptable margarine
2 tablespoons all-purpose flour
2 cups skim milk
1/4 teaspoon freshly ground black pepper
1/8 teaspoon onion powder
1/8 teaspoon garlic powder
Vegetable oil spray
5 medium potatoes, peeled and thinly sliced
1/2 cup chopped onion

Preheat oven to 350° F.

Melt margarine in a small saucepan. Add flour and mix well. Gradually add milk while stirring constantly. Cook over medium heat, stirring until thickened. Add pepper, onion powder and garlic powder. Stir and remove from heat.

Lightly spray a 1½-quart casserole dish with vegetable oil spray.

Place potatoes and chopped onion in bottom of casserole. Add sauce and stir lightly.

Cover and bake 30 minutes.

Stir gently and bake uncovered an additional 30 to 40 minutes, or until potatoes are tender and lightly browned. Serve hot.

NUTRIENT ANALYSIS

CALORIES	191 KCAL
PROTEIN	6 GM
CARBOHYDRATE	27 GM
TOTAL FAT	7 GM
SATURATED	2 GM
POLYUNSATURATED	2 GM
MONOUNSATURATED	3 GM
CHOLESTEROL	2 MG
SODIUM	58 MG
POTASSIUM	501 MG
CALCIUM	135 MG

POTATOES O'BRIEN

SERVES 5

NUTRIENT ANALYSIS	
CALORIES	146 KCAL
PROTEIN	2 GM
CARBOHYDRATE	22 GM
TOTAL FAT	6 GM
SATURATED	1 GM
POLYUNSATURATED	3 GM
MONOUNSATURATED	1 GM
CHOLESTEROL	0 MG
SODIUM	6 MG
POTASSIUM	393 MG
CALCIUM	19 MG

5 medium potatoes, unpeeled
2 medium onions, chopped
1 small green bell pepper, chopped
2 tablespoons acceptable vegetable oil
1/8 teaspoon freshly ground black pepper
1/8 teaspoon paprika

Boil potatoes in water 20 to 25 minutes, or until tender. Remove from heat and add cold water until potatoes are cooled slightly. Peel and cut into 1-inch cubes.

In a large nonstick skillet, sauté onions and green pepper in oil until tender. Add potatoes and sprinkle with black pepper and paprika. Cook over medium heat 10 minutes or until potatoes are browned, stirring frequently. Serve hot.

HASH-BROWN POTATOES

SERVES 6

1/4 cup acceptable vegetable oil
1/4 teaspoon freshly ground black pepper
1/8 teaspoon onion powder
1/8 teaspoon garlic powder
6 cups chopped or grated peeled potatoes
1/4 teaspoon paprika

Heat oil, pepper and onion and garlic powders in a large nonstick skillet over medium-high heat. Add potatoes and paprika. Cook until potatoes are crisp and browned, stirring frequently.

Drain on paper towels and serve immediately.

NUTRIENT ANALYSIS	
CALORIES	215 KCAL
PROTEIN	3 GM
CARBOHYDRATE	31 GM
TOTAL FAT	9 GM
SATURATED	1 GM
POLYUNSATURATED	5 GM
MONOUNSATURATED	2 GM
CHOLESTEROL	0 MG
SODIUM	8 MG
POTASSIUM	516 MG
CALCIUM	13 MG

POTATO PANCAKES

SERVES 8; 1 PANCAKE PER SERVING

POTATO PANCAKES NUTRIENT ANALYSIS	
CALORIES	108 KCAL
PROTEIN	2 GM
CARBOHYDRATE	10 GM
TOTAL FAT	7 GM
SATURATED	1 GM
POLYUNSATURATED	4 GM
MONOUNSATURATED	2 GM
CHOLESTEROL	0 MG
SODIUM	42 MG
POTASSIUM	133 MG
CALCIUM	22 MG

POTATO PANCAKES WITH APPLESAUCE AND CINNAMON NUTRIENT ANALYSIS	
CALORIES	116 KCAL
PROTEIN	2 GM
CARBOHYDRATE	12 GM
TOTAL FAT	7 GM
SATURATED	1 GM
POLYUNSATURATED	4 GM
MONOUNSATURATED	2 GM
CHOLESTEROL	0 MG
SODIUM	42 MG
POTASSIUM	145 MG
CALCIUM	26 MG

1¾ cups grated raw peeled potatoes
2 tablespoons finely chopped onion
2 egg whites
¼ cup all-purpose flour
¾ teaspoon baking powder
¼ teaspoon onion powder
¼ teaspoon garlic powder
⅛ teaspoon freshly ground black pepper
¼ cup (approximately) acceptable vegetable oil

In a large bowl, mix together potatoes and onion.

In a separate mixing bowl, beat egg whites until soft peaks form. Fold into the potato mixture.

Add remaining dry ingredients. Mix well.

Heat a small amount of oil in a large nonstick skillet over medium-high heat. Spoon ⅛ of batter into skillet and spread to ½-inch thickness. Cook until browned, turn and cook second side. Drain on paper towels. Repeat with remainder of batter, using a small amount of oil each time ⅛ of batter is added.

POTATO PANCAKES WITH APPLESAUCE AND CINNAMON

Add 1 tablespoon warm applesauce and dash of ground cinnamon to top of each pancake.

OVEN-FRIED POTATOES WITH OREGANO

SERVES 6

3 medium baking potatoes
1 tablespoon olive oil
½ teaspoon freshly ground black pepper
1 teaspoon dried oregano
2 tablespoons malt vinegar

Preheat oven to 400° F.

Scrub potatoes thoroughly. Cut each potato lengthwise into 6 wedges. Place wedges in a medium bowl and cover with cold water. Let stand 30 minutes. Drain and pat dry with paper towels.

Place potatoes and oil in a medium bowl and toss to coat evenly.

Place potatoes on baking sheet. Sprinkle with pepper and oregano. Bake 45 to 50 minutes, or until potatoes are tender. Remove from oven and sprinkle with malt vinegar.

NUTRIENT ANALYSIS

CALORIES	88 KCAL
PROTEIN	2 GM
CARBOHYDRATE	16 GM
TOTAL FAT	2 GM
SATURATED	0 GM
POLYUNSATURATED	0 GM
MONOUNSATURATED	2 GM
CHOLESTEROL	0 MG
SODIUM	5 MG
POTASSIUM	266 MG
CALCIUM	11 MG

SCALLOPED SWEET POTATOES

SERVES 6

NUTRIENT ANALYSIS	
CALORIES	168 KCAL
PROTEIN	1 GM
CARBOHYDRATE	29 GM
TOTAL FAT	6 GM
SATURATED	1 GM
POLYUNSATURATED	2 GM
MONOUNSATURATED	3 GM
CHOLESTEROL	0 MG
SODIUM	8 MG
POTASSIUM	326 MG
CALCIUM	23 MG

Vegetable oil spray
1/4 cup sugar
1/2 teaspoon ground cinnamon
3 raw medium sweet potatoes, peeled, sliced 1/4 inch thick
2 medium apples, sliced
3 tablespoons acceptable margarine

Preheat oven to 350° F. Lightly spray a 1½-quart casserole dish with vegetable oil spray.

Combine sugar and cinnamon in a small bowl and stir to mix thoroughly. Set aside. Place a layer of sweet potatoes in the casserole dish. Add a layer of apples, sprinkle with cinnamon-sugar mixture and dot with margarine. Repeat layers.

Cover and bake 1 hour. Serve hot.

SWEET POTATO CASSEROLE

SERVES 6

4 medium sweet potatoes
Vegetable oil spray
1 tablespoon acceptable margarine
1/4 cup orange juice
2 tablespoons chopped walnuts
1/4 teaspoon nutmeg

Cook whole sweet potatoes in boiling water 25 to 30 minutes or until tender. Meanwhile, preheat oven to 375° F. Lightly spray a 1-quart casserole dish with vegetable oil spray.

Remove potatoes from heat and add cold water until potatoes are cooled slightly. Peel and mash. Add remaining ingredients and mix thoroughly. Place in casserole dish and bake uncovered 25 minutes. Serve hot.

NUTRIENT ANALYSIS

CALORIES	116 KCAL
PROTEIN	2 GM
CARBOHYDRATE	20 GM
TOTAL FAT	4 GM
SATURATED	1 GM
POLYUNSATURATED	2 GM
MONOUNSATURATED	1 GM
CHOLESTEROL	0 MG
SODIUM	9 MG
POTASSIUM	393 MG
CALCIUM	25 MG

SEASONED RICE

SERVES 4

NUTRIENT ANALYSIS	
CALORIES	186 KCAL
PROTEIN	4 GM
CARBOHYDRATE	29 GM
TOTAL FAT	6 GM
SATURATED	1 GM
POLYUNSATURATED	2 GM
MONOUNSATURATED	3 GM
CHOLESTEROL	0 MG
SODIUM	24 MG
POTASSIUM	126 MG
CALCIUM	25 MG

2 tablespoons acceptable margarine
1 medium onion, finely chopped
3/4 cup uncooked long-grain rice
1 1/2 cups low-sodium chicken broth
1/4 teaspoon celery flakes
1/4 teaspoon onion powder
1/4 teaspoon dill weed
1/8 teaspoon freshly ground black pepper

Melt margarine in a nonstick skillet over medium-high heat. Add onion and rice. Brown lightly.

Add remaining ingredients and bring to a boil. Cover, reduce heat and simmer 15 to 25 minutes or until rice is tender, stirring occasionally. Serve immediately.

BROWN RICE PILAF

SERVES 4

1 tablespoon acceptable margarine
1 cup uncooked brown rice
2 cups low-sodium chicken broth
1/4 teaspoon freshly ground black pepper
2 tablespoons minced fresh parsley sprigs

Melt margarine in a 3-quart saucepan over medium heat. Add rice. Cook 3 to 4 minutes, stirring constantly. Do not brown. Add remaining ingredients and bring to a boil. Cover, reduce heat and simmer 40 to 45 minutes, or until liquid is absorbed.

NUTRIENT ANALYSIS

CALORIES	223 KCAL
PROTEIN	5 GM
CARBOHYDRATE	40 GM
TOTAL FAT	4 GM
SATURATED	1 GM
POLYUNSATURATED	1 GM
MONOUNSATURATED	2 GM
CHOLESTEROL	0 MG
SODIUM	30 MG
POTASSIUM	184 MG
CALCIUM	27 MG

RICE AND VEGETABLE PILAF

SERVES 6

NUTRIENT ANALYSIS	
CALORIES	70 KCAL
PROTEIN	2 GM
CARBOHYDRATE	15 GM
TOTAL FAT	0 GM
SATURATED	0 GM
POLYUNSATURATED	0 GM
MONOUNSATURATED	0 GM
CHOLESTEROL	0 MG
SODIUM	18 MG
POTASSIUM	175 MG
CALCIUM	21 MG

1 cup low-sodium chicken broth
1/2 cup long-grain rice
1 cup chopped fresh mushrooms
1 cup shredded carrots
1/2 cup chopped fresh parsley sprigs
1/4 cup sliced green onions, with tops
1/4 teaspoon freshly ground black pepper

In a medium saucepan over high heat, bring chicken broth to a boil. Add rice and cover. Reduce heat and simmer 20 minutes. Remove from heat and let stand 5 minutes. Stir in remaining ingredients. Return to low heat and cook another 5 minutes. Fluff with a fork and serve immediately.

SAUCES

Mock Sour Cream

Mock Whipped Cream

Mushroom Sauce

Ketchup

Hot Prepared Mustard

Horseradish Sauce

Chili Sauce

Tomato Sauce

Chunky Tomato Sauce

Barbecue Sauce

Mexican Salsa

White Sauce

Yogurt-Dill Sauce

Strawberry Sauce

Chocolate Sauce

Whether you're glazing a dessert, bringing fresh pasta to life or taking a lean cut of meat from the ordinary to the extraordinary, the hallmark of really fine cooking is a creatively prepared sauce.

Unfortunately, most of the commercial sauces we take for granted, such as ketchup, barbecue sauce, chili sauce and tomato sauce, are loaded with salt. Instead, try recipes here for these and other popular condiments. The aroma of homemade tomato sauce with fresh onion, garlic, basil, freshly squeezed lemon juice and just-ground black pepper prepares you for a taste sensation you'll love. Store-bought sauce will taste pretty tame after you try this!

For a different flavor altogether, try Yogurt-Dill Sauce. It's fabulous over fish and great as a dip for cold sliced cucumbers. And to top off a great meal, Strawberry Sauce is certain to dazzle friends and relatives. It's irresistible over Crepes, Angel Food Cake, ice milk or low-fat yogurt.

A sauce is one part of a great cuisine that is easy to experiment with: Substitute wines, spices, homemade low-sodium chicken broth, vinegar, shallots, cornstarch or plenty of fresh herbs for other ingredients wherever you see fit. Just be sure to use acceptable margarines or acceptable vegetable oils in place of butter or other animal fats, and leave out the salt. You'll find that with the creative use of herbs, spices and spirits, you'll enjoy these homemade sauces.

MOCK SOUR CREAM

MAKES 2 CUPS
SERVES 16; 2 TABLESPOONS PER SERVING

NUTRIENT ANALYSIS	
CALORIES	15 KCAL
PROTEIN	3 GM
CARBOHYDRATE	1 GM
TOTAL FAT	0 GM
SATURATED	0 GM
POLYUNSATURATED	0 GM
MONOUNSATURATED	0 GM
CHOLESTEROL	1 MG
SODIUM	6 MG
POTASSIUM	18 MG
CALCIUM	14 MG

1½ cups (12 ounces) unsalted dry-curd cottage cheese
½ cup skim milk
1 tablespoon fresh lemon juice
¼ teaspoon onion powder (optional)

Place all ingredients in a blender and combine on medium-high speed until smooth and creamy. Cover and chill.

MOCK WHIPPED CREAM

MAKES 2 CUPS
SERVES 32; 1 TABLESPOON PER SERVING

1 teaspoon unflavored gelatin
2 teaspoons cold water
3 tablespoons boiling water
½ cup ice water
½ cup nonfat dry milk
3 tablespoons sugar
3 tablespoons acceptable vegetable oil

Chill a small mixing bowl.

In another small bowl, soften gelatin with cold water. Add boiling water, stirring constantly until gelatin is completely dissolved. Cool until tepid.

Place ice water and nonfat dry milk in chilled mixing bowl. Beat at high speed of electric mixer until stiff peaks form. Continue beating and add sugar, oil and gelatin.

Place in freezer for approximately 15 minutes, then transfer to refrigerator until ready to use. Stir before using to retain creamy texture.

NUTRIENT ANALYSIS

CALORIES	20 KCAL
PROTEIN	0 GM
CARBOHYDRATE	2 GM
TOTAL FAT	1 GM
SATURATED	0 GM
POLYUNSATURATED	1 GM
MONOUNSATURATED	0 GM
CHOLESTEROL	0 MG
SODIUM	6 MG
POTASSIUM	4 MG
CALCIUM	3 MG

MUSHROOM SAUCE

MAKES 2 CUPS
SERVES 8; ¼ CUP PER SERVING

NUTRIENT ANALYSIS	
CALORIES	85 KCAL
PROTEIN	3 GM
CARBOHYDRATE	5 GM
TOTAL FAT	6 GM
SATURATED	1 GM
POLYUNSATURATED	2 GM
MONOUNSATURATED	3 GM
CHOLESTEROL	1 MG
SODIUM	35 MG
POTASSIUM	217 MG
CALCIUM	80 MG

¼ cup chopped onion
½ pound fresh mushrooms, sliced
¼ cup acceptable margarine
1 tablespoon all-purpose flour
⅛ teaspoon freshly ground black pepper
⅛ teaspoon garlic powder
2 cups skim milk
1 tablespoon dry white table wine

In a medium nonstick skillet over medium-high heat, sauté onion and mushrooms in margarine until tender. Add flour, pepper and garlic powder and mix well. Gradually add milk, stirring constantly. Cook over medium heat, stirring until thickened. Stir in wine.

Serve hot.

KETCHUP

MAKES 1 QUART
SERVES 64; 1 TABLESPOON PER SERVING

3 6-ounce cans no-salt-added tomato paste
4 cups water
½ cup chopped onion
½ cup chopped celery
½ cup cider vinegar
½ cup sugar
1 tablespoon firmly packed brown sugar
2 tablespoons acceptable margarine
1 teaspoon light molasses
⅛ teaspoon ground cloves
⅛ teaspoon ground cinnamon
⅛ teaspoon basil
⅛ teaspoon tarragon
⅛ teaspoon freshly ground black pepper
⅛ teaspoon onion powder
⅛ teaspoon garlic powder

NUTRIENT ANALYSIS	
CALORIES	18 KCAL
PROTEIN	0 GM
CARBOHYDRATE	4 GM
TOTAL FAT	0 GM
SATURATED	0 GM
POLYUNSATURATED	0 GM
MONOUNSATURATED	0 GM
CHOLESTEROL	0 MG
SODIUM	6 MG
POTASSIUM	83 MG
CALCIUM	4 MG

Place tomato paste, water, onion, celery, vinegar and sugar in a blender or the work bowl of a food processor fitted with a metal blade. Process on medium-high speed until mixture is smooth.

Place tomato mixture and remaining ingredients in a saucepan and simmer uncovered 1½ hours or until ketchup is thickened and reduced to one half original volume. Stir occasionally.

May be stored in a covered container in refrigerator for 1 month. For longer storage, freeze in small quantities for use as needed.

HOT PREPARED MUSTARD

MAKES ½ CUP
SERVES 8; 1 TABLESPOON PER SERVING

NUTRIENT ANALYSIS	
CALORIES	32 KCAL
PROTEIN	1 GM
CARBOHYDRATE	6 GM
TOTAL FAT	1 GM
SATURATED	0 GM
POLYUNSATURATED	0 GM
MONOUNSATURATED	0 GM
CHOLESTEROL	0 MG
SODIUM	1 MG
POTASSIUM	18 MG
CALCIUM	5 MG

2 tablespoons dry mustard powder
2 tablespoons sugar
¼ cup all-purpose flour
¼ teaspoon onion powder
¼ teaspoon turmeric
2 tablespoons fresh lemon juice
2 tablespoons water

Sift dry ingredients together or stir until evenly blended. Add lemon juice and water. Mix well.

Place in covered container and refrigerate.

HORSERADISH SAUCE

MAKES 1½ CUPS
SERVES 24; 1 TABLESPOON PER SERVING

NUTRIENT ANALYSIS	
CALORIES	3 KCAL
PROTEIN	0 GM
CARBOHYDRATE	1 GM
TOTAL FAT	0 GM
SATURATED	0 GM
POLYUNSATURATED	0 GM
MONOUNSATURATED	0 GM
CHOLESTEROL	0 MG
SODIUM	7 MG
POTASSIUM	26 MG
CALCIUM	5 MG

½ medium (6 ounces) horseradish root, peeled
½ cup white vinegar

Cut horseradish into cubes and place in blender. Add vinegar and process until desired consistency. Or finely grate horseradish into a medium bowl and mix with vinegar. Keep refrigerated up to a week in a covered container.

CHILI SAUCE

MAKES 3 CUPS
SERVES 48; 1 TABLESPOON PER SERVING

2 16-ounce cans no-salt-added tomato sauce
½ cup chopped onion
½ cup cider vinegar
½ cup sugar
½ cup chopped celery
½ medium green bell pepper, chopped
2 tablespoons acceptable margarine
1 tablespoon fresh lemon juice
1 teaspoon firmly packed brown sugar
1 teaspoon light molasses
¼ teaspoon hot pepper sauce
⅛ teaspoon ground cloves
⅛ teaspoon ground cinnamon
⅛ teaspoon freshly ground black pepper
⅛ teaspoon basil
⅛ teaspoon tarragon

NUTRIENT ANALYSIS	
CALORIES	20 KCAL
PROTEIN	0 GM
CARBOHYDRATE	4 GM
TOTAL FAT	1 GM
SATURATED	0 GM
POLYUNSATURATED	0 GM
MONOUNSATURATED	0 GM
CHOLESTEROL	0 MG
SODIUM	7 MG
POTASSIUM	83 MG
CALCIUM	5 MG

Place all ingredients in a 3-quart saucepan. Mix thoroughly. Bring to a boil, reduce heat and simmer uncovered 1½ hours or until sauce is thickened and reduced to one-half original volume. Stir occasionally.

May be stored in a covered container in refrigerator for 1 month. For longer storage, freeze in small quantities for use as needed.

TOMATO SAUCE

MAKES 1 QUART
SERVES 8; ½ CUP PER SERVING

NUTRIENT ANALYSIS	
CALORIES	39 KCAL
PROTEIN	2 GM
CARBOHYDRATE	9 GM
TOTAL FAT	0 GM
SATURATED	0 GM
POLYUNSATURATED	0 GM
MONOUNSATURATED	0 GM
CHOLESTEROL	0 MG
SODIUM	30 MG
POTASSIUM	412 MG
CALCIUM	18 MG

2 6-ounce cans no-salt-added tomato paste
3 cups water
¼ cup finely chopped onion
1 clove garlic, minced
2 tablespoons fresh lemon juice
Dash hot pepper sauce
¼ teaspoon basil
⅛ teaspoon freshly ground black pepper

In a medium saucepan, combine all ingredients and mix well. Place over medium-high heat and bring to a boil. Reduce heat, cover and simmer 30 minutes, stirring occasionally. Use in any recipe requiring tomato sauce.

May be stored in a covered container in refrigerator for 1 week. For longer storage, freeze in small quantities for use as needed.

CHUNKY TOMATO SAUCE

MAKES 1 CUP
SERVES 4; ¼ CUP PER SERVING

1 tablespoon chopped onion
1 tablespoon chopped green bell pepper
2 tablespoons acceptable margarine
1 tablespoon all-purpose flour
1¼ cups chopped, peeled fresh tomatoes or 1 cup canned no-salt-added tomatoes
Dash freshly ground black pepper

In a large skillet over medium-high heat, sauté onion and green pepper in margarine until tender. Stir in flour until well blended. Add chopped tomatoes and cook, stirring constantly, until tomatoes are tender and sauce is thickened. Add black pepper.

May be stored in a covered container in refrigerator for 1 week. For longer storage, freeze in small quantities for use as needed.

NUTRIENT ANALYSIS

CALORIES	69 KCAL
PROTEIN	1 GM
CARBOHYDRATE	4 GM
TOTAL FAT	6 GM
SATURATED	1 GM
POLYUNSATURATED	2 GM
MONOUNSATURATED	3 GM
CHOLESTEROL	0 MG
SODIUM	7 MG
POTASSIUM	129 MG
CALCIUM	7 MG

BARBECUE SAUCE

SERVES 64; 1 TABLESPOON PER SERVING

NUTRIENT ANALYSIS	
CALORIES	15 KCAL
PROTEIN	0 GM
CARBOHYDRATE	3 GM
TOTAL FAT	1 GM
SATURATED	0 GM
POLYUNSATURATED	0 GM
MONOUNSATURATED	0 GM
CHOLESTEROL	0 MG
SODIUM	67 MG
POTASSIUM	68 MG
CALCIUM	4 MG

2 6-ounce cans no-salt-added tomato paste
2 cups water
1/2 cup Ketchup (see recipe, page 181) or low-sodium ketchup
1/4 cup firmly packed brown sugar
2 tablespoons fresh lemon juice
1/4 cup chopped onion
1 clove garlic, minced
2 tablespoons Chili Powder (see recipe, page 37)
2 tablespoons cider vinegar
2 tablespoons acceptable vegetable oil
1 tablespoon chopped fresh parsley
1 teaspoon dry mustard powder
1 teaspoon paprika
1/8 teaspoon freshly ground black pepper
Dash hot pepper sauce (optional)

Combine all ingredients in a saucepan and mix well. Simmer uncovered over low heat 20 minutes.

May be stored in a covered container in refrigerator for 1 month. For longer storage, freeze in small quantities for use as needed.

MEXICAN SALSA

MAKES 1¼ CUPS
SERVES 5; ¼ CUP PER SERVING

5 fresh tomatoes
¼ cup minced fresh jalapeño or serrano peppers, or to taste
1 small yellow onion, diced fine
¼ cup fresh lime juice
2 cloves garlic, minced
1 6-ounce bunch cilantro, washed and chopped

Core tomatoes and blanch briefly in boiling water. Remove and run under cold water, then peel and chop fine. Add remaining ingredients and chill.

NUTRIENT ANALYSIS

CALORIES	34 KCAL
PROTEIN	2 GM
CARBOHYDRATE	8 GM
TOTAL FAT	0 GM
SATURATED	0 GM
POLYUNSATURATED	0 GM
MONOUNSATURATED	0 GM
CHOLESTEROL	0 MG
SODIUM	101 MG
POTASSIUM	308 MG
CALCIUM	16 MG

WHITE SAUCE

MAKES 1¼ CUPS
SERVES 10; 2 TABLESPOONS PER SERVING

WHITE SAUCE NUTRIENT ANALYSIS	
CALORIES	46 KCAL
PROTEIN	2 GM
CARBOHYDRATE	4 GM
TOTAL FAT	3 GM
SATURATED	0 GM
POLYUNSATURATED	1 GM
MONOUNSATURATED	1 GM
CHOLESTEROL	1 MG
SODIUM	26 MG
POTASSIUM	86 MG
CALCIUM	61 MG

2 tablespoons acceptable margarine
3 tablespoons flour
2 cups skim milk
1 teaspoon fresh lemon juice
¼ teaspoon freshly ground black pepper, or to taste

In a 1-quart saucepan heat margarine over medium heat. Add flour and cook 1 to 2 minutes, stirring frequently. Gradually add milk, stirring constantly. Add seasonings and stir until mixture thickens.

WHITE SAUCE WITH PARMESAN CHEESE NUTRIENT ANALYSIS	
CALORIES	64 KCAL
PROTEIN	4 GM
CARBOHYDRATE	4 GM
TOTAL FAT	4 GM
SATURATED	1 GM
POLYUNSATURATED	1 GM
MONOUNSATURATED	1 GM
CHOLESTEROL	4 MG
SODIUM	101 MG
POTASSIUM	90 MG
CALCIUM	117 MG

WHITE SAUCE WITH PARMESAN CHEESE

Add ½ cup Parmesan cheese for a great sauce to serve over pasta.

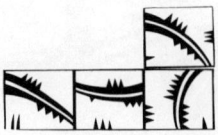

WHITE SAUCE

WHITE SAUCE WITH DIJON MUSTARD

Add 2 tablespoons Dijon mustard, or to taste.

WHITE SAUCE WITH DIJON MUSTARD NUTRIENT ANALYSIS	
CALORIES	48 KCAL
PROTEIN	2 GM
CARBOHYDRATE	4 GM
TOTAL FAT	3 GM
SATURATED	1 GM
POLYUNSATURATED	1 GM
MONOUNSATURATED	1 GM
CHOLESTEROL	1 MG
SODIUM	64 MG
POTASSIUM	90 MG
CALCIUM	64 MG

YOGURT-DILL SAUCE

MAKES 1⅛ CUPS

SERVES 18; 1 TABLESPOON PER SERVING

1 cup plain nonfat yogurt
2 tablespoons low-fat sour cream
2 teaspoons dried dill weed
1 teaspoon prepared mustard
½ teaspoon sugar
¼ teaspoon freshly ground black pepper
½ teaspoon fresh lemon juice

Place all ingredients in a small bowl. Stir to mix thoroughly. Cover and refrigerate.

Serve cold as an accompaniment for hot or chilled fish. May also be used as a dip for raw vegetables or as a dressing for sliced cucumbers.

NUTRIENT ANALYSIS	
CALORIES	11 KCAL
PROTEIN	1 GM
CARBOHYDRATE	1 GM
TOTAL FAT	0 GM
SATURATED	0 GM
POLYUNSATURATED	0 GM
MONOUNSATURATED	0 GM
CHOLESTEROL	1 MG
SODIUM	16 MG
POTASSIUM	46 MG
CALCIUM	36 MG

STRAWBERRY SAUCE

MAKES APPROXIMATELY 1 CUP
SERVES 4; APPROXIMATELY ¼ CUP PER SERVING

NUTRIENT ANALYSIS	
CALORIES	73 KCAL
PROTEIN	1 GM
CARBOHYDRATE	11 GM
TOTAL FAT	3 GM
SATURATED	1 GM
POLYUNSATURATED	1 GM
MONOUNSATURATED	1 GM
CHOLESTEROL	0 MG
SODIUM	2 MG
POTASSIUM	197 MG
CALCIUM	17 MG

1 pound fresh strawberries
1 tablespoon acceptable margarine
1 tablespoon orange juice
1 tablespoon sugar

Wash berries, remove stems and slice berries lengthwise so that slices are heart shaped.

In a nonstick pan, heat margarine and orange juice over medium setting. Add strawberries and cook for 2 to 3 minutes, stirring frequently. Add sugar and cook for 2 minutes longer. Mixture should be slightly thickened. Serve immediately.

This topping is great over plain low-fat yogurt, ice milk or angel food cake.

CHOCOLATE SAUCE

MAKES 1 CUP
SERVES 16; 1 TABLESPOON PER SERVING

3 tablespoons cocoa
½ cup sugar
⅓ cup skim milk
1 tablespoon acceptable margarine, melted
1 teaspoon vanilla

Combine cocoa and sugar in a small bowl. Set aside.

In a medium saucepan, heat milk and margarine over medium-high heat. Slowly add cocoa-sugar mixture, stirring constantly. Bring to a boil, remove from heat and add vanilla. Mixture will thicken as it cools.

This sauce is delicious over angel food cake or ice milk.

NUTRIENT ANALYSIS

CALORIES	35 KCAL
PROTEIN	0 GM
CARBOHYDRATE	7 GM
TOTAL FAT	1 GM
SATURATED	0 GM
POLYUNSATURATED	0 GM
MONOUNSATURATED	0 GM
CHOLESTEROL	0 MG
SODIUM	3 MG
POTASSIUM	29 MG
CALCIUM	8 MG

BREADS

Basic White Bread

White Bread Variations

Biscuits

Corn Muffins

Blueberry Muffins

Oat Bran and Yogurt Muffins

Banana Bread

Gingerbread

Pancakes

Crepes

Seasoned Croutons

On the following pages are recipes for delicious breads, biscuits, muffins, pancakes and more—all made from scratch. Kids will love the Gingerbread and the Blueberry Muffins. Try Oat Bran and Yogurt Muffins and Banana Bread for delicious lunchbox desserts or snacks.

Soups and salads will taste especially homemade with our Seasoned Croutons scattered on top. And for special desserts or main dishes, impress your guests with our delicate Crepes.

Fresh-baked bread is a wonderful gift for friends, family, even just for yourself. If you're baking breads without salt, however, there are a few tips you should know.

First, yeast bread made without salt will rise more quickly than normal bread dough. If you allow the dough to rise too much, your bread will be coarse and have a strong yeasty taste. You can help prevent this from happening by punching the dough lightly with two fingers periodically when it is rising in the bowl. When the indentation remains and the dough no longer springs back, it is ready to be shaped. Allow the loaves and rolls to rise only until slightly less than double in size before placing them in the oven.

Baking bread is an easy way to get children involved in healthful cooking. Let them help by measuring ingredients, shaping the loaves and forming buns with the extra dough. With luck, this early initiation will be the start of a lifelong habit.

BASIC WHITE BREAD

MAKES 2 LARGE LOAVES; 18 SLICES PER LOAF
SERVES 36; 1 SLICE PER SERVING

NUTRIENT ANALYSIS*	
CALORIES	73 KCAL
PROTEIN	2 GM
CARBOHYDRATE	14 GM
TOTAL FAT	1 GM
SATURATED	0 GM
POLYUNSATURATED	1 GM
MONOUNSATURATED	0 GM
CHOLESTEROL	0 MG
SODIUM	7 MG
POTASSIUM	39 MG
CALCIUM	17 MG

*ONE SLICE OF LOAF.

Vegetable oil spray
1 package dry yeast
1/4 cup lukewarm water
3 tablespoons sugar
2 tablespoons acceptable vegetable oil
1 3/4 cups skim milk, scalded and cooled to lukewarm
5 to 5 1/2 cups all-purpose flour

Preheat oven to 425° F. Lightly spray a large bowl and 2 9×5×3-inch loaf pans lightly with vegetable oil spray. Set aside.

Soak yeast in water for 5 minutes without stirring. In a large bowl, combine sugar, oil and milk. Add dissolved yeast. Stir in 3 cups of flour and beat until smooth. Gradually add more flour until mixture becomes stiff enough to handle. With some of remaining flour, lightly dust a clean, dry board or tabletop. Knead dough until smooth and elastic, using small amounts of remaining flour. Place kneaded dough in prepared bowl, turning dough to coat entire surface with oil. Cover loosely and let rise in a warm place until almost double in size, or when, if pressed with two fingers, an indentation remains in dough. Punch dough down, divide into 2 equal parts and let rest for 3 to 5 minutes.

Roll each piece into a 9×12-inch rectangle. Starting with the narrow side, roll up

BASIC WHITE BREAD

dough tightly. Seal ends by pinching them together, and place loaf seam side down in prepared pans. Cover loosely and let rise in warm place until sides of dough reach top of pan, 30 to 45 minutes.

Bake 25 to 30 minutes. Remove loaves from pans immediately and cool on a rack.

DINNER ROLLS

Preheat oven to 425° F. Lightly spray a baking sheet with vegetable oil spray.

Make dough as for white bread. Divide it into 2 equal parts. Roll out 1 part and divide into 12 equal sections. Shape each into a ball and place on baking sheets with sides touching for soft rolls or 1½ inches apart for crusty rolls. Let rise until almost doubled in size. Bake 15 to 20 minutes, or until brown. Remove from baking sheet and cool on a rack.

WHITE BREAD VARIATIONS

The Basic White Bread recipe (page 196) can be used as a basis for several different kinds of breads. A few variations are outlined below. Be creative and try a few of your own ideas for tasty breads.

NUTRIENT ANALYSIS	
CALORIES	77 KCAL
PROTEIN	3 GM
CARBOHYDRATE	15 GM
TOTAL FAT	1 GM
SATURATED	0 GM
POLYUNSATURATED	1 GM
MONOUNSATURATED	0 GM
CHOLESTEROL	0 MG
SODIUM	7 MG
POTASSIUM	95 MG
CALCIUM	26 MG

WHOLE-WHEAT BREAD

Use 4 cups whole-wheat or graham flour and 1 to 1½ cups all-purpose flour in place of the all-purpose flour called for in the recipe. Light molasses may be used in place of sugar.

NUTRIENT ANALYSIS	
CALORIES	67 KCAL
PROTEIN	2 GM
CARBOHYDRATE	13 GM
TOTAL FAT	1 GM
SATURATED	0 GM
POLYUNSATURATED	1 GM
MONOUNSATURATED	0 GM
CHOLESTEROL	0 MG
SODIUM	9 MG
POTASSIUM	109 MG
CALCIUM	33 MG

RYE BREAD

Use 2½ cups rye flour and 2½ to 3 cups all-purpose flour in place of the all-purpose flour called for in the recipe. Use ¼ cup dark molasses in place of sugar. If desired, 1 tablespoon caraway seeds may be added. Dough will not rise as much as white bread dough. Round loaves may be formed and baked on prepared baking sheets.

WHITE BREAD VARIATIONS

HERB BREAD

Many different seeds, herbs or herb combinations may be used with white bread recipes. Add any of the following to dough mixture with the first addition of flour: 1 teaspoon sage and 1 tablespoon caraway seeds; 1 tablespoon oregano and 1 teaspoon basil; 1 tablespoon dill seed and 2 tablespoons grated onion; or ¼ cup each finely chopped fresh chives and parsley.

NUTRIENT ANALYSIS*

CALORIES	74 KCAL
PROTEIN	2 GM
CARBOHYDRATE	14 GM
TOTAL FAT	1 GM
SATURATED	0 GM
POLYUNSATURATED	0 GM
MONOUNSATURATED	0 GM
CHOLESTEROL	0 MG
SODIUM	7 MG
POTASSIUM	42 MG
CALCIUM	18 MG

*WITH CHIVES AND PARSLEY.

RAISIN BREAD

Add 1 cup seedless raisins to white dough mixture during first addition of flour.

NUTRIENT ANALYSIS

CALORIES	86 KCAL
PROTEIN	2 GM
CARBOHYDRATE	17 GM
TOTAL FAT	1 GM
SATURATED	0 GM
POLYUNSATURATED	1 GM
MONOUNSATURATED	0 GM
CHOLESTEROL	0 MG
SODIUM	8 MG
POTASSIUM	74 MG
CALCIUM	18 MG

WHITE BREAD VARIATIONS

NUTRIENT ANALYSIS	
CALORIES	88 KCAL
PROTEIN	2 GM
CARBOHYDRATE	17 GM
TOTAL FAT	1 GM
SATURATED	0 GM
POLYUNSATURATED	1 GM
MONOUNSATURATED	0 GM
CHOLESTEROL	0 MG
SODIUM	7 MG
POTASSIUM	40 MG
CALCIUM	19 MG

CINNAMON BREAD

Prepare Basic White Bread recipe. Divide dough into 2 equal parts and roll each piece into a 9×12-inch rectangle. For each loaf, brush dough with 2 teaspoons acceptable vegetable oil and sprinkle with a mixture of ¼ cup sugar and 1 teaspoon ground cinnamon. Roll and seal as directed for Basic White Bread.

NUTRIENT ANALYSIS	
CALORIES	90 KCAL
PROTEIN	2 GM
CARBOHYDRATE	18 GM
TOTAL FAT	1 GM
SATURATED	0 GM
POLYUNSATURATED	1 GM
MONOUNSATURATED	0 GM
CHOLESTEROL	0 MG
SODIUM	8 MG
POTASSIUM	90 MG
CALCIUM	19 MG

SWEDISH BREAD

Increase sugar in Basic White Bread recipe to ⅓ cup. Add 4 shelled, pulverized cardamom seeds, ½ cup finely chopped dried apricots and ¾ cup seedless raisins to white dough mixture during first addition of flour.

WHITE BREAD VARIATIONS

CINNAMON ROLLS

Prepare Basic White Bread Recipe. Divide dough into 2 equal parts and roll into rectangles about ¼ inch thick. Mix 1 cup firmly packed brown sugar, 1 tablespoon ground cinnamon and 1 cup chopped walnuts. Brush dough with ¼ cup melted acceptable margarine and sprinkle with brown sugar mixture. Roll the dough tightly into cylinders and cut in 1-inch slices. Place cut side up with sides touching on prepared baking sheet. Allow to rise until almost doubled in size, about 35 minutes. Bake in preheated 400° F. oven 30 to 35 minutes or until golden brown. Invert on rack to cool. While warm, drizzle with a glaze made by mixing 1 cup powdered sugar, 1 teaspoon vanilla and 1 to 2 tablespoons water.

NUTRIENT ANALYSIS

CALORIES	143 KCAL
PROTEIN	3 GM
CARBOHYDRATE	24 GM
TOTAL FAT	4 GM
SATURATED	1 GM
POLYUNSATURATED	2 GM
MONOUNSATURATED	1 GM
CHOLESTEROL	0 MG
SODIUM	9 MG
POTASSIUM	78 MG
CALCIUM	28 MG

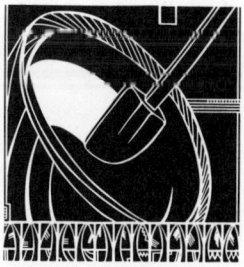

BISCUITS

SERVES 12; 1 BISCUIT PER SERVING

BISCUITS

NUTRIENT ANALYSIS

CALORIES	115 KCAL
PROTEIN	2 GM
CARBOHYDRATE	15 GM
TOTAL FAT	5 GM
SATURATED	1 GM
POLYUNSATURATED	3 GM
MONOUNSATURATED	1 GM
CHOLESTEROL	0 MG
SODIUM	80 MG
POTASSIUM	41 MG
CALCIUM	65 MG

DROP BISCUITS

NUTRIENT ANALYSIS

CALORIES	116 KCAL
PROTEIN	3 GM
CARBOHYDRATE	16 GM
TOTAL FAT	5 GM
SATURATED	1 GM
POLYUNSATURATED	3 GM
MONOUNSATURATED	1 GM
CHOLESTEROL	0 MG
SODIUM	81 MG
POTASSIUM	45 MG
CALCIUM	69 MG

2 cups all-purpose flour
1 tablespoon baking powder
¼ cup acceptable vegetable oil
⅔ cup skim milk

Preheat oven to 450° F.

In a medium bowl, combine flour and baking powder. Set aside.

In a small bowl, combine oil and milk. Pour all at once into dry ingredients. Stir until mixture clings together and forms a ball. Knead on waxed paper 18 to 20 times without using additional flour. Gently pat or roll out until dough is ½ inch thick. Cut with 2-inch round cutter and place close together with edges touching on ungreased baking sheet. Bake 12 to 15 minutes.

HERB-SEASONED BISCUITS

Add one or more of the following to the flour mixture: 1 teaspoon garlic powder; 1 teaspoon onion powder; 2 teaspoons dried parsley flakes; 2 teaspoons dill weed; ½ teaspoon sage.

DROP BISCUITS

Add 2 additional tablespoons skim milk and stir dough until well mixed. Drop by spoonfuls onto ungreased baking sheet.

CORN MUFFINS

SERVES 8; 1 LARGE MUFFIN PER SERVING

Vegetable oil spray
1 cup all-purpose flour
1 tablespoon sugar (optional)
¾ cup yellow or white cornmeal
2 teaspoons baking powder
2 egg whites, lightly beaten
1 cup skim milk
2 tablespoons acceptable vegetable oil

Preheat oven to 425° F. Lightly spray muffin tin with vegetable oil spray.

In a large bowl, sift together flour, sugar, cornmeal and baking powder. In a medium bowl, combine egg whites, milk and oil. Pour all at once into dry ingredients. Stir just enough to blend. Pour batter into prepared muffin cups until each is ⅔ full. Bake 15 to 20 minutes, or until golden brown. Allow muffins to cool 2 minutes before removing from pan.

NUTRIENT ANALYSIS

CALORIES	151 KCAL
PROTEIN	4 GM
CARBOHYDRATE	24 GM
TOTAL FAT	4 GM
SATURATED	1 GM
POLYUNSATURATED	2 GM
MONOUNSATURATED	1 GM
CHOLESTEROL	1 MG
SODIUM	101 MG
POTASSIUM	92 MG
CALCIUM	87 MG

CORN BREAD

Pour batter into an 8-inch square baking pan that has been sprayed lightly with vegetable oil spray. Bake 20 to 25 minutes, or until golden brown. Allow to cool 2 minutes before removing from pan.

BLUEBERRY MUFFINS

SERVES 12; 1 MUFFIN PER SERVING

NUTRIENT ANALYSIS	
CALORIES	136 KCAL
PROTEIN	3 GM
CARBOHYDRATE	21 GM
TOTAL FAT	5 GM
SATURATED	1 GM
POLYUNSATURATED	3 GM
MONOUNSATURATED	1 GM
CHOLESTEROL	0 MG
SODIUM	75 MG
POTASSIUM	52 MG
CALCIUM	55 MG

Vegetable oil spray
1 cup unsweetened blueberries, fresh or frozen
1¾ cups all-purpose flour
2½ teaspoons baking powder
⅓ cup sugar
2 egg whites, slightly beaten
¼ cup acceptable vegetable oil
½ cup skim milk
1 teaspoon sugar

Preheat oven to 400° F. Lightly spray a muffin tin with vegetable oil spray.

Wash and drain fresh or frozen berries. Set aside.

In a large bowl, sift flour, baking powder and ⅓ cup sugar together.

In a small bowl, combine egg whites, oil and milk. Pour all at once into dry ingredients. Stir just enough to blend. Gently stir in blueberries. Pour batter into prepared muffin tin, filling each cup ⅔ full. Sprinkle lightly with 1 teaspoon sugar and bake 20 to 25 minutes, or until browned. Allow muffins to cool 2 minutes before removing from pan.

OAT BRAN AND YOGURT MUFFINS

SERVES 24; 1 MUFFIN PER SERVING

Vegetable oil spray
2 cups whole-wheat flour
½ cup oat bran
1 cup all-purpose flour
1 teaspoon baking soda
1 tablespoon sugar
1 egg white
2 cups plain nonfat yogurt
¼ cup honey
2 tablespoons acceptable vegetable oil
1 cup raisins

Preheat oven to 425° F. Lightly spray muffin pans with vegetable oil spray.

Combine whole-wheat flour, oat bran, all-purpose flour, baking soda and sugar in a large mixing bowl. Set aside. In a medium bowl, beat together egg white, yogurt, honey and oil. Add yogurt mixture to dry ingredients and mix well. Fold in raisins.

Place mixture in muffin pans, filling each cup ⅔ full. Bake 15 to 20 minutes.

NUTRIENT ANALYSIS

CALORIES	110 KCAL
PROTEIN	4 GM
CARBOHYDRATE	22 GM
TOTAL FAT	2 GM
SATURATED	0 GM
POLYUNSATURATED	1 GM
MONOUNSATURATED	0 GM
CHOLESTEROL	0 MG
SODIUM	54 MG
POTASSIUM	161 MG
CALCIUM	49 MG

BANANA BREAD

SERVES 16; 1 SLICE PER SERVING

NUTRIENT ANALYSIS	
CALORIES	133 KCAL
PROTEIN	2 GM
CARBOHYDRATE	21 GM
TOTAL FAT	5 GM
SATURATED	1 GM
POLYUNSATURATED	3 GM
MONOUNSATURATED	1 GM
CHOLESTEROL	0 MG
SODIUM	46 MG
POTASSIUM	77 MG
CALCIUM	27 MG

Vegetable oil spray
⅓ cup acceptable vegetable oil
⅓ cup sugar
1 cup mashed ripe banana (2 to 3 medium bananas)
1¾ cups sifted all-purpose flour
¼ teaspoon cinnamon
⅛ teaspoon nutmeg
2 teaspoons baking powder
3 egg whites
⅓ cup sugar

Preheat oven to 350° F. Lightly spray a 5 × 9-inch loaf pan with vegetable oil spray.

In a large mixing bowl, beat oil and ⅓ cup sugar together. Add banana and mix well.

In a medium bowl, sift flour, spices and baking powder together. Add to batter and beat.

In a separate bowl, beat egg whites until foamy. Gradually add ⅓ cup sugar and beat until egg whites form soft peaks. Fold egg whites into the batter.

Pour into loaf pan and bake 55 minutes.

Remove from oven and allow to stand 10 minutes. Invert bread on a wire rack to cool.

GINGERBREAD

SERVES 8

½ cup low-fat milk
2 teaspoons cider vinegar
Vegetable oil spray
¾ cup light molasses
½ cup acceptable vegetable oil
1 egg white
1 cup all-purpose flour
1 cup whole-wheat flour
1 teaspoon ground ginger
½ teaspoon baking soda
½ teaspoon ground cinnamon
¼ cup raisins

NUTRIENT ANALYSIS	
CALORIES	257 KCAL
PROTEIN	5 GM
CARBOHYDRATE	45 GM
TOTAL FAT	8 GM
SATURATED	1 GM
POLYUNSATURATED	3 GM
MONOUNSATURATED	3 GM
CHOLESTEROL	1 MG
SODIUM	79 MG
POTASSIUM	462 MG
CALCIUM	118 MG

Combine milk and vinegar and allow to stand 10 minutes.

Preheat oven to 350° F. Lightly spray a 9-inch square baking pan with vegetable oil spray.

Place prepared milk, molasses, oil and egg white in a mixing bowl. Beat until blended. In a medium bowl, combine flours, ginger, baking soda and cinnamon. Add flour mixture to liquid mixture. Mix until evenly distributed. Fold in raisins.

Pour into prepared pan. Bake 30 to 35 minutes. Remove from oven and allow to cool in pan.

PANCAKES

SERVES 5; 3 4-INCH PANCAKES PER SERVING

PANCAKES
NUTRIENT ANALYSIS

CALORIES	272 KCAL
PROTEIN	7 GM
CARBOHYDRATE	35 GM
TOTAL FAT	11 GM
SATURATED	2 GM
POLYUNSATURATED	7 GM
MONOUNSATURATED	3 GM
CHOLESTEROL	1 MG
SODIUM	223 MG
POTASSIUM	166 MG
CALCIUM	208 MG

BLUEBERRY PANCAKES
NUTRIENT ANALYSIS

CALORIES	280 KCAL
PROTEIN	7 GM
CARBOHYDRATE	37 GM
TOTAL FAT	11 GM
SATURATED	2 GM
POLYUNSATURATED	7 GM
MONOUNSATURATED	3 GM
CHOLESTEROL	1 MG
SODIUM	224 MG
POTASSIUM	179 MG
CALCIUM	209 MG

1½ cups all-purpose flour
2 tablespoons sugar
1 tablespoon baking powder
¼ teaspoon ground cinnamon
1 egg white
¼ cup acceptable vegetable oil
1½ cups skim milk
½ teaspoon vanilla
Vegetable oil spray

In a large bowl, sift dry ingredients together.

In a medium bowl, beat egg white until foamy. Add oil, milk and vanilla. Mix well. Add to dry ingredients. Beat only until batter is smooth.

Lightly spray a griddle or nonstick skillet with vegetable oil spray. Preheat griddle or skillet and spoon batter in ¼-cup portions onto cooking surface. When bubbles form and begin to break, turn and brown on other side. Serve immediately, or layer between waxed paper, freeze and reheat in toaster when needed.

BLUEBERRY PANCAKES
Add ½ cup blueberries to batter.

PANCAKES

PANCAKES WITH WALNUTS

Add ¼ cup chopped walnuts to batter.

WHEAT-GERM PANCAKES

Add ½ cup toasted wheat germ to batter.

PANCAKES WITH WALNUTS NUTRIENT ANALYSIS

CALORIES	311 KCAL
PROTEIN	8 GM
CARBOHYDRATE	37 GM
TOTAL FAT	15 GM
SATURATED	2 GM
POLYUNSATURATED	9 GM
MONOUNSATURATED	4 GM
CHOLESTEROL	1 MG
SODIUM	224 MG
POTASSIUM	196 MG
CALCIUM	214 MG

WHEAT-GERM PANCAKES NUTRIENT ANALYSIS

CALORIES	315 KCAL
PROTEIN	10 GM
CARBOHYDRATE	41 GM
TOTAL FAT	13 GM
SATURATED	2 GM
POLYUNSATURATED	7 GM
MONOUNSATURATED	3 GM
CHOLESTEROL	1 MG
SODIUM	223 MG
POTASSIUM	273 MG
CALCIUM	213 MG

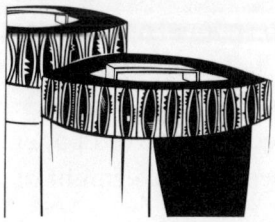

CREPES

SERVES 22; 1 6-INCH CREPE PER SERVING

NUTRIENT ANALYSIS	
CALORIES	62 KCAL
PROTEIN	1 GM
CARBOHYDRATE	7 GM
TOTAL FAT	3 GM
SATURATED	1 GM
POLYUNSATURATED	1 GM
MONOUNSATURATED	1 GM
CHOLESTEROL	0 MG
SODIUM	10 MG
POTASSIUM	27 MG
CALCIUM	13 MG

¾ cup skim milk
¾ cup cold water
2 egg whites
1½ cups sifted all-purpose flour
⅓ cup acceptable margarine, melted
2 tablespoons rum or orange liqueur (optional)
1 tablespoon sugar
4 drops yellow food coloring
Vegetable oil spray

Place all ingredients in a large mixing bowl. Beat well. Cover and refrigerate for 2 hours or overnight. Batter will be thin.

Spray a small nonstick skillet lightly with vegetable oil spray. Place over moderate heat. Pour 2 tablespoons batter in center of skillet. Tilt pan in all directions until batter covers bottom of pan. Return to heat for about 1 minute. Shake pan sharply to loosen crepe. Lift edges with a spatula and turn the crepe over when lightly browned. Brown lightly, approximately ½ minute, on the other side.

If first crepe appears too thick, beat in 2 to 3 tablespoons additional water.

Spray skillet lightly again with vegetable oil spray. Pour 2 tablespoons batter into skillet and proceed as before. Repeat process with remaining batter.

Crepes may be stacked with waxed paper between each and refrigerated overnight or

CREPES

frozen. Crepes should be at room temperature when used, for ease in rolling.

For a deliciously simple dessert, brush rolled crepes with margarine, warm in oven and serve topped with maple syrup, powdered sugar or cinnamon-sugar. (See recipes for Banana Crepes, Strawberry Crepes and Apple-Filled Crepes on pages 228, 229 and 227.)

SEASONED CROUTONS

MAKES 2 CUPS
SERVES 8; ¼ CUP PER SERVING

½ teaspoon onion powder
¼ teaspoon garlic powder
¼ teaspoon dill weed
⅛ teaspoon freshly ground black pepper
¼ cup acceptable margarine, softened
4 slices bread

Preheat oven to 300° F.

In a small bowl, add seasonings to margarine and mix well. Spread margarine mixture on one side of each slice of bread. Cut bread into ½-inch cubes. Place on a cookie sheet and bake 15 to 20 minutes, or until crisp and dry.

Cool and store in a tightly covered container. Use as a garnish for soups or salads.

NUTRIENT ANALYSIS

CALORIES	85 KCAL
PROTEIN	1 GM
CARBOHYDRATE	7 GM
TOTAL FAT	6 GM
SATURATED	1 GM
POLYUNSATURATED	2 GM
MONOUNSATURATED	3 GM
CHOLESTEROL	0 MG
SODIUM	66 MG
POTASSIUM	19 MG
CALCIUM	14 MG

DESSERTS

Applesauce Cake
Angel Food Cake
Chocolate Cake
Quick Frosting
Denver Chocolate Pudding Cake
Carrot Cake
Oatmeal Cookies
Peanut Butter Cookies
Walnut Delights
Date Rounds
Pralines
Apple-Filled Crepes
Banana Crepes
Matzo Crumb Piecrust
Piecrust
Cherry Pie
Apple Pie
Pumpkin Pie
Citrus Chiffon
Apple Crisp
Baked Pears
Orange Pudding
Raspberry Sorbet
Fresh Fruit Cobbler
Baked Custard
Vanilla Pudding
Fruit-Rice Pudding
Spiced Fruit
Brownies
Fudge

On these pages you'll find a selection of delectable goodies guaranteed to please, from Raspberry Sorbet, southern Pralines, and Fresh Fruit Cobbler, to Baked Custard and Peanut Butter Cookies. How can we do this on a low-sodium, low-fat diet? Easy. The trick is omitting most of the salt and using the right kind of fat.

Dessert is as American as . . . well, Apple Pie, which is here along with Cherry and Pumpkin, and two wonderful piecrust recipes: regular Piecrust and Matzo Crumb Piecrust.

Fruit still makes a great dessert, especially if you innovate a bit. For example, serve strawberries, pineapple chunks, grapes and melon balls on small skewers or layered in a parfait dish and chilled, with a tablespoon of liqueur on top. Need other ideas? Look for the recipes in this section for Baked Pears, Apple Crisp, Fruit-Rice Pudding and Spiced Fruit.

If ice cream is your favorite dessert, skip the saturated fat and cholesterol by substituting low-fat frozen yogurt, ice milk or sherbet. Top it off with Chocolate Sauce (page 191) for a winning finale to any meal.

Need an impressive dessert for company? Denver Chocolate Pudding Cake looks and tastes like a rich confection, but its ingredients make it a healthful treat.

Every family has a few favorite desserts that are hard to give up. Happily, maybe you don't have to. Just look closely at the ingredients list and, if possible, substitute low-sodium, low-fat ingredients for those high in sodium and fat. It can be that easy.

The very best desserts, the ones that taste great and are good for you, are the ones you make yourself. Try these and be convinced.

APPLESAUCE CAKE

SERVES 9

NUTRIENT ANALYSIS	
CALORIES	315 KCAL
PROTEIN	4 GM
CARBOHYDRATE	53 GM
TOTAL FAT	11 GM
SATURATED	2 GM
POLYUNSATURATED	3 GM
MONOUNSATURATED	5 GM
CHOLESTEROL	2 MG
SODIUM	68 MG
POTASSIUM	148 MG
CALCIUM	51 MG

Vegetable oil spray
½ cup acceptable margarine
1 cup sugar
2 egg whites
1½ cups applesauce
2 cups all-purpose flour
1½ teaspoons baking powder
1 teaspoon ground cloves
1 teaspoon nutmeg
2 teaspoons ground cinnamon
½ cup raisins

Preheat oven to 350° F. Lightly spray a 9-inch square cake pan with vegetable oil spray.

In a large mixing bowl, cream margarine with sugar until fluffy. Add egg whites and beat well. Add applesauce and beat.

In a medium bowl, sift dry ingredients together. Add to margarine mixture and mix well. Stir in raisins. Pour into prepared pan and bake 45 minutes. Serve warm.

ANGEL FOOD CAKE

SERVES 12

1 cup sifted cake flour
½ cup sugar
1¼ cups (10 to 12) egg whites, room temperature
1 teaspoon cream of tartar
½ teaspoon vanilla
½ teaspoon almond extract
¾ cup sugar

Preheat oven to 350° F.

In 2 medium bowls, sift together flour and ½ cup sugar 3 times.

In a large mixing bowl, beat egg whites until foamy. Add cream of tartar, vanilla and almond extract. Continue beating until soft, moist, glossy peaks form. Gradually add ¾ cup sugar and continue beating at high speed until volume increases and stiff peaks form. By hand, gently fold in sifted flour-sugar mixture only until all flour is moistened.

Pour into a 9-inch tube pan. Cut through batter carefully with a thin spatula to break up large air pockets. Bake 40 to 45 minutes.

Remove from oven and invert pan for 1½ hours, or until cold. Remove cake from pan before storing.

Strawberry Sauce (see recipe, page 190) makes a delicious topping for this cake.

NUTRIENT ANALYSIS

CALORIES	119 KCAL
PROTEIN	3 GM
CARBOHYDRATE	27 GM
TOTAL FAT	0 GM
SATURATED	0 GM
POLYUNSATURATED	0 GM
MONOUNSATURATED	0 GM
CHOLESTEROL	0 MG
SODIUM	56 MG
POTASSIUM	52 MG
CALCIUM	4 MG

CHOCOLATE CAKE

SERVES 16

NUTRIENT ANALYSIS*	
CALORIES	240 KCAL
PROTEIN	3 GM
CARBOHYDRATE	36 GM
TOTAL FAT	10 GM
SATURATED	2 GM
POLYUNSATURATED	5 GM
MONOUNSATURATED	2 GM
CHOLESTEROL	0 MG
SODIUM	84 MG
POTASSIUM	79 MG
CALCIUM	56 MG

*UNFROSTED.

Vegetable oil spray
2½ cups all-purpose flour
⅓ cup cocoa
3½ teaspoons baking powder
⅔ cup acceptable vegetable oil
¾ cup water
½ cup skim milk
1 teaspoon vanilla
4 egg whites
¼ teaspoon cream of tartar
1¾ cups sugar

Preheat oven to 375° F. Lightly spray a 9×13-inch cake pan or 2 layer-cake pans with vegetable oil spray. Line pan with waxed paper cut to fit the bottom.

In a large mixing bowl, sift flour, cocoa and baking powder together.

In a small bowl, mix oil, water, milk and vanilla together. Add to flour mixture and beat until well combined. Batter will resemble a thick paste.

In a medium mixing bowl, beat egg whites until foamy. Add cream of tartar and gradually add sugar, beating until egg whites form soft peaks. Fold egg whites into batter.

Pour into prepared pan and bake 35 to 40 minutes, or until toothpick inserted in center of pan comes out clean.

Remove from oven and let cool on wire rack for 5 minutes. Remove cake from pan and serve warm or cold.

CHOCOLATE CAKE

Serve this cake plain or frost with Quick Frosting (see recipe, page 219). Remember to allow cake to cool completely before frosting.

QUICK FROSTING

FROSTS 1 9×13-INCH OR 1 2-LAYER CAKE
SERVES 16

2 large egg whites
1 1/2 cups powdered sugar
1/4 teaspoon cream of tartar
1/3 cup water
1 teaspoon vanilla
1 tablespoon fresh lemon juice
1/4 teaspoon grated lemon peel

In a medium mixing bowl, combine egg whites, sugar, cream of tartar and water. Beat with electric mixer 1 minute.

Place in double boiler over boiling water and beat about 5 minutes with electric mixer. Remove from heat and stir in vanilla, lemon juice and lemon peel. Beat 1 additional minute.

This frosting is delicious on Chocolate Cake (see recipe, page 218).

NUTRIENT ANALYSIS

CALORIES	49 KCAL
PROTEIN	0 GM
CARBOHYDRATE	12 GM
TOTAL FAT	0 GM
SATURATED	0 GM
POLYUNSATURATED	0 GM
MONOUNSATURATED	0 GM
CHOLESTEROL	0 MG
SODIUM	10 MG
POTASSIUM	9 MG
CALCIUM	1 MG

DENVER CHOCOLATE PUDDING CAKE

SERVES 9

NUTRIENT ANALYSIS	
CALORIES	250 KCAL
PROTEIN	3 GM
CARBOHYDRATE	52 GM
TOTAL FAT	5 GM
SATURATED	2 GM
POLYUNSATURATED	1 GM
MONOUNSATURATED	2 GM
CHOLESTEROL	0 MG
SODIUM	77 MG
POTASSIUM	163 MG
CALCIUM	78 MG

Vegetable oil spray
1 cup all-purpose flour
¾ cup sugar
2 teaspoons baking powder
3 tablespoons acceptable margarine, melted
3 tablespoons cocoa
½ cup skim milk
½ teaspoon vanilla
½ cup firmly packed brown sugar
½ cup sugar
¼ cup cocoa
1½ cups cold water or cold coffee

Preheat oven to 350° F. Lightly spray a 9-inch square baking pan with vegetable oil spray.

In a large bowl, sift flour, ¾ cup sugar and baking powder together.

In a small bowl, combine margarine and 3 tablespoons cocoa. Add to dry ingredients.

Beat in milk and vanilla.

Pour into prepared pan. Sprinkle the brown sugar, ½ cup sugar, and ¼ cup cocoa over the top of the batter one at a time but do not mix. Pour water (or coffee) over the top. Bake 40 minutes. To serve, cut cake into 9 equal pieces. Invert each piece onto a dessert plate.

Serve plain or with Mock Whipped Cream (see recipe, page 179).

CARROT CAKE

SERVES 16

Vegetable oil spray
1/4 cup acceptable vegetable oil
1 cup honey
2 egg whites
1/2 teaspoon vanilla
2 cups shredded carrots
1 cup all-purpose flour
1 cup whole-wheat flour
1/4 cup nonfat dry milk powder
1 teaspoon ground cinnamon
1/8 teaspoon nutmeg
1 tablespoon baking powder

NUTRIENT ANALYSIS	
CALORIES	161 KCAL
PROTEIN	3 GM
CARBOHYDRATE	31 GM
TOTAL FAT	4 GM
SATURATED	1 GM
POLYUNSATURATED	1 GM
MONOUNSATURATED	2 GM
CHOLESTEROL	0 MG
SODIUM	77 MG
POTASSIUM	129 MG
CALCIUM	69 MG

Preheat oven to 350° F. Lightly spray a 9×13-inch baking dish with vegetable oil spray.

In a medium mixing bowl, combine oil and honey and beat until smooth. Beat in egg whites and vanilla. Stir in carrots. Set aside.

In a large mixing bowl, combine remaining ingredients. Add liquid mixture and mix thoroughly. Pour into prepared baking pan. Bake 25 to 30 minutes. Remove from oven and allow to cool in pan.

OATMEAL COOKIES

SERVES 30; 1 COOKIE PER SERVING

NUTRIENT ANALYSIS	
CALORIES	72 KCAL
PROTEIN	1 GM
CARBOHYDRATE	10 GM
TOTAL FAT	3 GM
SATURATED	1 GM
POLYUNSATURATED	1 GM
MONOUNSATURATED	1 GM
CHOLESTEROL	0 MG
SODIUM	27 MG
POTASSIUM	29 MG
CALCIUM	7 MG

Vegetable oil spray
½ cup acceptable margarine
½ cup firmly packed brown sugar
1 tablespoon water
¼ teaspoon vanilla
1½ cups all-purpose flour
1 cup quick-cooking oatmeal, uncooked

Preheat oven to 350° F. Lightly spray a cookie sheet with vegetable oil spray.

In a large mixing bowl, cream margarine with brown sugar. Stir in water and vanilla. Add flour, mixing well. Stir in oatmeal. Form dough into 1-inch balls and place 2 inches apart on prepared cookie sheet. Flatten with a fork that has been dipped in flour.

Bake 15 minutes, or until lightly browned. Transfer to cooling rack immediately.

PEANUT BUTTER COOKIES

SERVES 48; 1 COOKIE PER SERVING

Vegetable oil spray
½ cup acceptable margarine
½ cup sugar
½ cup firmly packed brown sugar
1 egg
1 cup unsalted peanut butter
½ teaspoon vanilla
1½ cups all-purpose flour
1¼ teaspoons baking powder

Preheat oven to 350° F. Lightly spray a cookie sheet with vegetable oil spray.

In a large mixing bowl, cream margarine and sugars. Stir in egg. Add peanut butter and vanilla and beat.

In a medium bowl, sift flour and baking powder together. Add to margarine mixture and mix well.

Form dough into 1½-inch balls and place 3 inches apart on prepared cookie sheet. Flatten with a fork. Bake 15 minutes or until done. Allow cookies to cool 2 to 3 minutes on cookie sheet before transferring to cooling rack.

NUTRIENT ANALYSIS	
CALORIES	79 KCAL
PROTEIN	2 GM
CARBOHYDRATE	8 GM
TOTAL FAT	5 GM
SATURATED	1 GM
POLYUNSATURATED	1 GM
MONOUNSATURATED	2 GM
CHOLESTEROL	6 MG
SODIUM	11 MG
POTASSIUM	52 MG
CALCIUM	10 MG

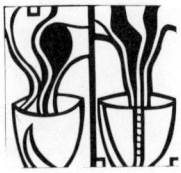

WALNUT DELIGHTS

SERVES 24; 1 COOKIE PER SERVING

NUTRIENT ANALYSIS	
CALORIES	100 KCAL
PROTEIN	2 GM
CARBOHYDRATE	8 GM
TOTAL FAT	7 GM
SATURATED	1 GM
POLYUNSATURATED	3 GM
MONOUNSATURATED	2 GM
CHOLESTEROL	0 MG
SODIUM	2 MG
POTASSIUM	34 MG
CALCIUM	7 MG

Vegetable oil spray
1½ cups all-purpose flour
2 tablespoons powdered sugar
½ cup acceptable margarine
1 cup finely chopped walnuts
1 teaspoon vanilla
3 tablespoons (approximately) cold water
⅓ cup powdered sugar

Preheat oven to 350° F. Lightly spray a cookie sheet with vegetable oil spray.

In a large bowl, sift flour and sugar together. Cut in margarine with a fork or pastry blender. Mix in walnuts, vanilla and enough cold water to make a soft dough.

Form into small rolls 1 inch long and ½ inch thick. Place 2 inches apart on prepared cookie sheet. Bake 25 to 30 minutes, or until firm. While cookies are still warm, roll them in powdered sugar.

DATE ROUNDS

SERVES 30; 1 COOKIE PER SERVING

1/2 cup acceptable margarine
1/3 cup powdered sugar
1 tablespoon skim milk
1 teaspoon vanilla
1 1/4 cups sifted all-purpose flour
2/3 cup chopped dates
1/2 cup chopped walnuts
1/3 cup powdered sugar

Preheat oven to 300° F.

In a large bowl, cream margarine with 1/3 cup powdered sugar. Add milk and vanilla and mix. Add flour and stir well. Mix in dates and nuts.

Form dough in 1-inch balls and place 2 inches apart on ungreased cookie sheet. Bake 20 to 25 minutes, or until lightly browned. While cookies are still warm, roll them in the remaining powdered sugar.

NUTRIENT ANALYSIS

CALORIES	78 KCAL
PROTEIN	1 GM
CARBOHYDRATE	9 GM
TOTAL FAT	4 GM
SATURATED	1 GM
POLYUNSATURATED	2 GM
MONOUNSATURATED	2 GM
CHOLESTEROL	0 MG
SODIUM	2 MG
POTASSIUM	43 MG
CALCIUM	6 MG

PRALINES

SERVES 72; 1 COOKIE PER SERVING

NUTRIENT ANALYSIS	
CALORIES	55 KCAL
PROTEIN	0 GM
CARBOHYDRATE	5 GM
TOTAL FAT	4 GM
SATURATED	1 GM
POLYUNSATURATED	1 GM
MONOUNSATURATED	2 GM
CHOLESTEROL	4 MG
SODIUM	3 MG
POTASSIUM	22 MG
CALCIUM	5 MG

Vegetable oil spray
1 cup acceptable margarine
1 cup firmly packed brown sugar
1 egg
1 tablespoon vanilla
1½ cups sifted all-purpose flour
1 cup chopped, toasted pecans

Preheat oven to 350° F. Lightly spray a cookie sheet with vegetable oil spray.

In a large mixing bowl, cream margarine with sugar. Add egg and vanilla and beat. Add flour and mix well. Mix in nuts.

Drop by teaspoonfuls on prepared cookie sheet. Bake 12 minutes, or until lightly browned. Remove from oven and allow to cool on rack.

APPLE-FILLED CREPES

SERVES 10; 1 CREPE PER SERVING

Vegetable oil spray
2 tablespoons acceptable margarine
5 apples, peeled and sliced (Golden Delicious apples preferred)
1/4 cup sugar
1 tablespoon fresh lemon juice
1 teaspoon grated lemon peel
1/8 teaspoon nutmeg
10 crepes (1/2 of recipe for Crepes, page 210)

Preheat oven to 325° F. Lightly spray a 9-inch square covered casserole dish with vegetable oil spray.

To make filling, melt margarine in a large nonstick skillet. Add remaining ingredients and cook until apples are tender, stirring occasionally. Remove from heat. Spoon 2/3 of apple mixture into center of crepes. Roll. Place seam side down in prepared baking dish. Spoon remaining apple mixture over top of crepes. Cover and bake 25 minutes or until hot.

To serve as a dessert, sprinkle with powdered sugar before serving. Serve for brunch with Turkey Sausage Patties (see recipe, page 119).

NUTRIENT ANALYSIS

CALORIES	138 KCAL
PROTEIN	2 GM
CARBOHYDRATE	22 GM
TOTAL FAT	5 GM
SATURATED	1 GM
POLYUNSATURATED	1 GM
MONOUNSATURATED	2 GM
CHOLESTEROL	0 MG
SODIUM	11 MG
POTASSIUM	103 MG
CALCIUM	16 MG

BANANA CREPES

SERVES 10; 1 CREPE PER SERVING

BANANA CREPES NUTRIENT ANALYSIS*

CALORIES	283 KCAL
PROTEIN	4 GM
CARBOHYDRATE	39 GM
TOTAL FAT	12 GM
SATURATED	3 GM
POLYUNSATURATED	4 GM
MONOUNSATURATED	5 GM
CHOLESTEROL	0 MG
SODIUM	27 MG
POTASSIUM	228 MG
CALCIUM	36 MG

*WITHOUT ADDED POWDERED SUGAR, YOGURT OR NUTMEG.

BANANA CREPES WITH POWDERED SUGAR NUTRIENT ANALYSIS

CALORIES	292 KCAL
PROTEIN	4 GM
CARBOHYDRATE	41 GM
TOTAL FAT	12 GM
SATURATED	3 GM
POLYUNSATURATED	4 GM
MONOUNSATURATED	5 GM
CHOLESTEROL	0 MG
SODIUM	27 MG
POTASSIUM	228 MG
CALCIUM	36 MG

1/3 cup acceptable margarine
1/2 cup orange marmalade
2 tablespoons sugar
1 tablespoon cornstarch
3 large bananas, sliced,
10 crepes (1/2 of recipe for Crepes, page 210)

To make filling, place margarine and marmalade in a medium saucepan over medium heat. Stir constantly until margarine melts.

In a small bowl, mix sugar and cornstarch together. Slowly stir into margarine mixture. Cook over medium heat, stirring constantly, until mixture is smooth and bubbly. Remove from heat. Fold in bananas.

Spoon banana mixture into center of 10 warm crepes. Roll.

BANANA CREPES WITH POWDERED SUGAR

Top each warm crepe with approximately 1 teaspoon powdered sugar.

BANANA CREPES

BANANA CREPES WITH YOGURT AND NUTMEG

Top each warm crepe with 2 tablespoons plain low-fat yogurt and ⅛ teaspoon nutmeg.

STRAWBERRY CREPES

(Omit banana filling.) Refrigerate unfilled crepes. Remove from refrigerator just before using. Place 2 tablespoons vanilla ice milk in center of each crepe and roll up. Top each crepe with ¼ cup Strawberry Sauce (see recipe, page 190).

BANANA CREPES WITH YOGURT AND NUTMEG NUTRIENT ANALYSIS

CALORIES	303 KCAL
PROTEIN	5 GM
CARBOHYDRATE	41 GM
TOTAL FAT	13 GM
SATURATED	3 GM
POLYUNSATURATED	4 GM
MONOUNSATURATED	6 GM
CHOLESTEROL	2 MG
SODIUM	49 MG
POTASSIUM	301 MG
CALCIUM	92 MG

STRAWBERRY CREPES NUTRIENT ANALYSIS

CALORIES	233 KCAL
PROTEIN	5 GM
CARBOHYDRATE	30 GM
TOTAL FAT	10 GM
SATURATED	2 GM
POLYUNSATURATED	3 GM
MONOUNSATURATED	4 GM
CHOLESTEROL	3 MG
SODIUM	37 MG
POTASSIUM	289 MG
CALCIUM	67 MG

MATZO CRUMB PIECRUST

MAKES 1 9-INCH PIE SHELL; SERVES 8

NUTRIENT ANALYSIS*	
CALORIES	136 KCAL
PROTEIN	2 GM
CARBOHYDRATE	20 GM
TOTAL FAT	6 GM
SATURATED	1 GM
POLYUNSATURATED	2 GM
MONOUNSATURATED	3 GM
CHOLESTEROL	0 MG
SODIUM	4 MG
POTASSIUM	27 MG
CALCIUM	3 MG

*FOR 1/8 OF PIE SHELL.

1 cup unsalted matzo meal
1/4 cup sugar
1/4 teaspoon ground cinnamon (optional)
1/4 cup acceptable margarine, melted

Preheat oven to 350° F.

In a small bowl, mix matzo meal and sugar together. Add cinnamon and margarine and mix thoroughly. Press firmly into a 9-inch pie plate. Bake 20 minutes, or until lightly browned.

This crust is particularly suited to a pudding or cream pie filling prepared without egg yolk, and with skim milk or nonfat dry milk, such as Citrus Chiffon (recipe, page 235).

PIECRUST

MAKES PASTRY FOR 1 2-CRUST PIE OR 2 9-INCH PIE SHELLS

2¼ cups all-purpose flour
½ teaspoon sugar
⅓ cup cold skim milk
½ cup plus 1 tablespoon acceptable vegetable oil
1 teaspoon sugar (optional)

In a medium bowl, combine flour and sugar. Stir to mix. Pour milk and oil into a measuring cup. Do not stir. Add all at once to flour. Stir with fork until well mixed. Form into a smooth ball with hands.

Roll out between 2 12-inch squares of waxed paper using short, brisk strokes until pastry reaches edge of paper. Peel off top paper. Invert crust and place on a pie plate. Carefully peel off paper and gently fit crust into pie plate.

For 2-crust pie, place fruit filling in piecrust and top with second crust; flute edges and make slits in top crust. Sprinkle crust with 1 teaspoon sugar, if desired, and bake according to filling directions.

To prebake single-crust pie shells, flute the edges and prick pastry with a fork. Preheat oven to 450° F.

Place several large raw dried beans on top of crust. Or place a sheet of waxed paper and another pie plate of the same size on top before baking. These methods will help prevent the crust from shrinking.

Bake piecrust 12 to 14 minutes, or until lightly browned.

NUTRIENT ANALYSIS*

CALORIES	258 KCAL
PROTEIN	4 GM
CARBOHYDRATE	25 GM
TOTAL FAT	16 GM
SATURATED	2 GM
POLYUNSATURATED	9 GM
MONOUNSATURATED	4 GM
CHOLESTEROL	0 MG
SODIUM	6 MG
POTASSIUM	48 MG
CALCIUM	18 MG

*FOR ⅛ OF A DOUBLE-CRUST PIE SHELL.

CHERRY PIE

MAKES 1 9-INCH PIE; SERVES 8

CHERRY PIE
NUTRIENT ANALYSIS

CALORIES	458 KCAL
PROTEIN	5 GM
CARBOHYDRATE	72 GM
TOTAL FAT	18 GM
SATURATED	2 GM
POLYUNSATURATED	10 GM
MONOUNSATURATED	5 GM
CHOLESTEROL	0 MG
SODIUM	7 MG
POTASSIUM	202 MG
CALCIUM	30 MG

1 1/3 cups sugar
1/3 cup all-purpose flour
1/2 teaspoon ground cinnamon
2 16-ounce cans sour cherries, drained
1/8 teaspoon almond extract
Piecrust (see recipe, page 231)
1 tablespoon acceptable margarine

Preheat oven to 425° F.

In a medium bowl, combine sugar, flour and cinnamon. In a small bowl, combine cherries and almond extract. Add to flour mixture.

Line pan with piecrust and fill with cherry mixture. Dot with margarine and top with second crust. Seal edges and make slits in top crust. Bake 35 to 45 minutes.

BLUEBERRY PIE
NUTRIENT ANALYSIS

CALORIES	432 KCAL
PROTEIN	5 GM
CARBOHYDRATE	66 GM
TOTAL FAT	17 GM
SATURATED	2 GM
POLYUNSATURATED	10 GM
MONOUNSATURATED	4 GM
CHOLESTEROL	0 MG
SODIUM	12 MG
POTASSIUM	136 MG
CALCIUM	26 MG

BLUEBERRY PIE

Use 4 cups fresh or frozen unsweetened blueberries in place of cherries and reduce sugar to 1 cup.

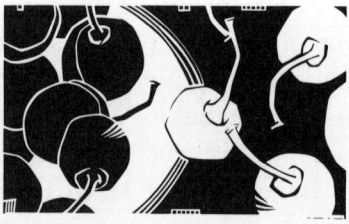

PEACH PIE

Use 2½ to 3 pounds (10 medium) peaches, peeled and sliced, in place of cherries and reduce sugar to ⅔ cup.

PEACH PIE

NUTRIENT ANALYSIS

CALORIES	405 KCAL
PROTEIN	5 GM
CARBOHYDRATE	59 GM
TOTAL FAT	17 GM
SATURATED	2 GM
POLYUNSATURATED	10 GM
MONOUNSATURATED	4 GM
CHOLESTEROL	0 MG
SODIUM	7 MG
POTASSIUM	309 MG
CALCIUM	27 MG

APPLE PIE

MAKES 1 9-INCH PIE; SERVES 8

1 cup sugar
1 teaspoon ground cinnamon
2½ pounds (8 medium) tart, firm apples, peeled, cored and sliced
Piecrust (see recipe, page 231)
1 tablespoon acceptable margarine

Preheat oven to 425° F.

In a medium bowl, combine sugar and cinnamon. Add sliced apples. Mix thoroughly.

Line pan with piecrust and fill with mixture. Dot with margarine and top with second crust. Seal edges and make slits in top crust. Bake 35 to 45 minutes.

NUTRIENT ANALYSIS

CALORIES	432 KCAL
PROTEIN	4 GM
CARBOHYDRATE	67 GM
TOTAL FAT	17 GM
SATURATED	2 GM
POLYUNSATURATED	10 GM
MONOUNSATURATED	4 GM
CHOLESTEROL	0 MG
SODIUM	7 MG
POTASSIUM	187 MG
CALCIUM	26 MG

PUMPKIN PIE

MAKES 1 9-INCH PIE; SERVES 8

NUTRIENT ANALYSIS	
CALORIES	264 KCAL
PROTEIN	8 GM
CARBOHYDRATE	41 GM
TOTAL FAT	8 GM
SATURATED	1 GM
POLYUNSATURATED	5 GM
MONOUNSATURATED	2 GM
CHOLESTEROL	2 MG
SODIUM	90 MG
POTASSIUM	396 MG
CALCIUM	195 MG

⅔ cup firmly packed brown sugar
1 teaspoon ground cinnamon
½ teaspoon ground ginger
¼ teaspoon ground cloves
1½ cups (1 16-ounce can) pumpkin
1 13-ounce can evaporated skim milk
3 egg whites, beaten until foamy
½ recipe Piecrust (see recipe, page 231), unbaked

Preheat oven to 400° F.

In a medium bowl, mix together brown sugar, spices and pumpkin. Add milk and egg whites and beat until thoroughly mixed.

Line pan with piecrust and fill with mixture. Bake 45 to 50 minutes, or until knife inserted near center of pie comes out clean.

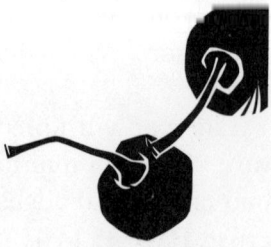

CITRUS CHIFFON

SERVES 8

1/4 cup cold water
2 teaspoons unflavored gelatin
1/2 cup hot water
1/2 cup sugar
2 teaspoons grated lemon peel
3/4 cup orange juice
2 tablespoons fresh lemon juice
1/3 cup nonfat dry milk powder

Place cold water in a medium saucepan and sprinkle gelatin over water. Allow to stand 5 minutes. Add hot water and sugar.

Place saucepan over medium-high heat and stir constantly until gelatin is dissolved.

Remove from heat. Stir in lemon peel and orange and lemon juices. Chill until thickened to the consistency of unbeaten egg white.

Sprinkle milk powder over gelatin mixture. Using an electric mixer, beat until light and fluffy. Pour into a serving bowl or a 1-quart mold and chill 8 hours or overnight. Unmold or spoon into serving dishes.

If desired, serve with fresh strawberries or orange slices.

NUTRIENT ANALYSIS

CALORIES	70 KCAL
PROTEIN	2 GM
CARBOHYDRATE	16 GM
TOTAL FAT	0 GM
SATURATED	0 GM
POLYUNSATURATED	0 GM
MONOUNSATURATED	0 GM
CHOLESTEROL	0 MG
SODIUM	17 MG
POTASSIUM	98 MG
CALCIUM	37 MG

APPLE CRISP

SERVES 8

APPLE CRISP
NUTRIENT ANALYSIS

CALORIES	219 KCAL
PROTEIN	2 GM
CARBOHYDRATE	36 GM
TOTAL FAT	8 GM
SATURATED	2 GM
POLYUNSATURATED	2 GM
MONOUNSATURATED	4 GM
CHOLESTEROL	0 MG
SODIUM	55 MG
POTASSIUM	172 MG
CALCIUM	26 MG

PEACH CRISP
NUTRIENT ANALYSIS

CALORIES	201 KCAL
PROTEIN	2 GM
CARBOHYDRATE	31 GM
TOTAL FAT	8 GM
SATURATED	2 GM
POLYUNSATURATED	2 GM
MONOUNSATURATED	4 GM
CHOLESTEROL	0 MG
SODIUM	55 MG
POTASSIUM	209 MG
CALCIUM	23 MG

Vegetable oil spray
1½ pounds (5 medium) apples, cored and sliced, unpeeled
2 tablespoons fresh lemon juice
¼ teaspoon ground cinnamon
⅔ cup all-purpose flour
½ cup firmly packed brown sugar
½ cup uncooked oatmeal
⅓ cup acceptable margarine

Preheat oven to 375° F. Lightly spray a 2-quart casserole dish with vegetable oil spray. Arrange apples in prepared dish. Sprinkle with lemon juice and cinnamon.

In a medium bowl, combine flour, brown sugar and oatmeal. Cut in margarine with a fork or pastry blender until mixture is crumbly. Spread over fruit. Bake 40 minutes or until apples are tender.

PEACH CRISP

Use 1½ pounds (6 medium) fresh peaches (pitted, peeled and sliced) in place of apples.

BLUEBERRY CRISP

Use 3 cups fresh or frozen unsweetened blueberries in place of apples.

BLUEBERRY CRISP
NUTRIENT ANALYSIS

CALORIES	211 KCAL
PROTEIN	2 GM
CARBOHYDRATE	34 GM
TOTAL FAT	8 GM
SATURATED	2 GM
POLYUNSATURATED	2 GM
MONOUNSATURATED	3 GM
CHOLESTEROL	0 MG
SODIUM	59 MG
POTASSIUM	143 MG
CALCIUM	24 MG

BAKED PEARS

SERVES 4

4 fresh pears, cut in half, peeled and cored
1/4 cup water
1/4 cup sugar
4 lemon slices
1/4 teaspoon ground ginger

Preheat oven to 350° F.

Place pears in a baking dish. Set aside.

Place water and sugar in a small saucepan over medium-high heat. Bring to a boil. Add lemon and ginger. Pour syrup mixture over pears.

Cover and bake 30 to 45 minutes or until tender. Turn once during baking period. Serve warm to accompany meat or chilled for dessert.

NUTRIENT ANALYSIS

CALORIES	146 KCAL
PROTEIN	1 GM
CARBOHYDRATE	38 GM
TOTAL FAT	1 GM
SATURATED	0 GM
POLYUNSATURATED	0 GM
MONOUNSATURATED	0 GM
CHOLESTEROL	0 MG
SODIUM	0 MG
POTASSIUM	218 MG
CALCIUM	20 MG

ORANGE PUDDING

SERVES 4

ORANGE PUDDING OR ORANGE WHIP

NUTRIENT ANALYSIS

CALORIES	96 KCAL
PROTEIN	2 GM
CARBOHYDRATE	23 GM
TOTAL FAT	0 GM
SATURATED	0 GM
POLYUNSATURATED	0 GM
MONOUNSATURATED	0 GM
CHOLESTEROL	0 MG
SODIUM	3 MG
POTASSIUM	125 MG
CALCIUM	6 MG

FRUIT PUDDING

NUTRIENT ANALYSIS

CALORIES	139 KCAL
PROTEIN	2 GM
CARBOHYDRATE	34 GM
TOTAL FAT	0 GM
SATURATED	0 GM
POLYUNSATURATED	0 GM
MONOUNSATURATED	0 GM
CHOLESTEROL	0 MG
SODIUM	7 MG
POTASSIUM	213 MG
CALCIUM	14 MG

1/4 cup cold water
1 tablespoon unflavored gelatin
3/4 cup hot water
1/3 cup sugar
1 cup orange juice
1 tablespoon fresh lemon juice
1 teaspoon grated orange rind (optional)

Place cold water in a medium saucepan and sprinkle gelatin over water. Allow to stand 5 minutes. Add hot water and sugar.

Place saucepan over medium-high heat and stir constantly until gelatin is dissolved.

Remove from heat. Stir in remaining ingredients. Pour into 4 half-cup custard cups or a 2-cup mold and chill until firm.

ORANGE WHIP

Chill gelatin until thickened to the consistency of unbeaten egg white. Beat with rotary beater or electric mixer until light and foamy. Chill until firm.

If desired, serve with orange sections or fresh berries.

FRUIT PUDDING

Chill gelatin until thickened to the consistency of unbeaten egg white. Stir in 1½ cups fresh or canned, drained, cut-up fruit. Chill until firm.

RASPBERRY SORBET

SERVES 4

1 cup sugar
1¾ cups water
3 cups fresh raspberries
2 tablespoons fresh lemon juice

In a medium saucepan over medium-high heat, combine sugar and water and bring to a boil. Boil until sugar is dissolved. Remove from heat and allow to cool.

In a blender or the work bowl of a food processor fitted with a metal blade, combine sugar-water mixture, raspberries and lemon juice. Process until pureed.

Pour mixture into a 9-inch square pan and freeze until firm.

If a smoother consistency is desired, press pureed mixture through a sieve before freezing.

NUTRIENT ANALYSIS

CALORIES	296 KCAL
PROTEIN	1 GM
CARBOHYDRATE	75 GM
TOTAL FAT	1 GM
SATURATED	0 GM
POLYUNSATURATED	0 GM
MONOUNSATURATED	0 GM
CHOLESTEROL	0 MG
SODIUM	3 MG
POTASSIUM	161 MG
CALCIUM	25 MG

FRESH FRUIT COBBLER

SERVES 6

FRESH FRUIT COBBLER NUTRIENT ANALYSIS

CALORIES	283 KCAL
PROTEIN	3 GM
CARBOHYDRATE	53 GM
TOTAL FAT	7 GM
SATURATED	1 GM
POLYUNSATURATED	4 GM
MONOUNSATURATED	2 GM
CHOLESTEROL	0 MG
SODIUM	81 MG
POTASSIUM	206 MG
CALCIUM	79 MG

CANNED FRUIT COBBLER NUTRIENT ANALYSIS*

CALORIES	287 KCAL
PROTEIN	3 GM
CARBOHYDRATE	54 GM
TOTAL FAT	7 GM
SATURATED	1 GM
POLYUNSATURATED	4 GM
MONOUNSATURATED	2 GM
CHOLESTEROL	0 MG
SODIUM	81 MG
POTASSIUM	216 MG
CALCIUM	80 MG

*USING CANNED CHERRIES.

Vegetable oil spray
3 cups fresh fruit (cherries, blueberries, blackberries, peaches or apricots)
¾ cup sugar
1 tablespoon cornstarch
1 cup boiling water
½ teaspoon ground cinnamon
1 tablespoon acceptable margarine
½ recipe Biscuits, uncooked (see recipe, page 202)

Preheat oven to 400° F. Lightly spray a shallow 1½-quart baking dish with vegetable oil spray.

Rinse fruit and drain. Peel and slice peaches or apricots. Remove pits from cherries. Set aside.

In a medium saucepan, combine sugar and cornstarch and mix well. Pour boiling water gradually into sugar mixture, stirring constantly. Place over medium-high heat. Bring to a boil and add fruit. Stir to mix well and remove from heat.

Pour into prepared baking dish. Sprinkle cinnamon over top and dot with margarine. Drop spoonfuls of biscuit dough on top of fruit. Bake 25 to 30 minutes or until biscuits are done.

CANNED FRUIT COBBLER

Use 3 cups canned fruit packed in juices, drained, in place of fresh fruit. (Canned cherries or blueberries are recommended.)

FRESH FRUIT COBBLER

Reserve juice in which fruit was packed; add cold water to make 1 cup. Stir cornstarch into cold juice until dissolved. Cook until thickened, stirring constantly, and combine with fruit. Proceed as directed above.

BAKED CUSTARD

SERVES 6

Vegetable oil spray
2½ cups skim milk
¼ cup sugar
4 egg whites
1 teaspoon vanilla
1 tablespoon table sherry
Few drops yellow food coloring
Dash nutmeg

Preheat oven to 325° F. Lightly spray 6 custard cups with vegetable oil spray.

In a large mixing bowl, combine milk, sugar, egg whites, vanilla, sherry and food coloring. Mix thoroughly. Pour into prepared custard cups. Sprinkle with nutmeg.

Place custard cups in a pan of hot water and bake 50 minutes or until knife inserted near center of custard comes out clean.

NUTRIENT ANALYSIS	
CALORIES	83 KCAL
PROTEIN	6 GM
CARBOHYDRATE	14 GM
TOTAL FAT	0 GM
SATURATED	0 GM
POLYUNSATURATED	0 GM
MONOUNSATURATED	0 GM
CHOLESTEROL	2 MG
SODIUM	87 MG
POTASSIUM	203 MG
CALCIUM	128 MG

VANILLA PUDDING

SERVES 5

VANILLA PUDDING
NUTRIENT ANALYSIS

CALORIES	166 KCAL
PROTEIN	5 GM
CARBOHYDRATE	27 GM
TOTAL FAT	5 GM
SATURATED	1 GM
POLYUNSATURATED	1 GM
MONOUNSATURATED	2 GM
CHOLESTEROL	3 MG
SODIUM	72 MG
POTASSIUM	227 MG
CALCIUM	167 MG

CHOCOLATE PUDDING
NUTRIENT ANALYSIS

CALORIES	228 KCAL
PROTEIN	5 GM
CARBOHYDRATE	41 GM
TOTAL FAT	6 GM
SATURATED	2 GM
POLYUNSATURATED	1 GM
MONOUNSATURATED	2 GM
CHOLESTEROL	3 MG
SODIUM	72 MG
POTASSIUM	291 MG
CALCIUM	173 MG

⅓ cup sugar
¼ cup cornstarch
2¾ cups skim milk
2 tablespoons acceptable margarine
1 teaspoon vanilla
3 drops yellow food coloring (optional)

Combine sugar and cornstarch in a medium saucepan and mix well. Add 1 cup of milk and stir until sugar is dissolved and cornstarch is evenly dispersed. Stir in remaining milk.

Place saucepan over medium heat. Bring to a boil, stirring constantly. Boil 1 minute. Remove from heat. Stir in margarine, vanilla and food coloring. Chill.

Vanilla pudding may be served in parfait glasses layered with fresh strawberries or other fruit or used as a filling for Matzo Crumb Piecrust (see recipe, page 230).

CHOCOLATE PUDDING

Increase sugar to ⅔ cup and add 3 tablespoons cocoa to sugar and cornstarch mixture. Omit yellow food coloring.

BUTTERSCOTCH PUDDING

Substitute brown sugar for white sugar. Increase margarine to 3 tablespoons. Omit yellow food coloring.

BUTTERSCOTCH PUDDING NUTRIENT ANALYSIS

CALORIES	174 KCAL
PROTEIN	5 GM
CARBOHYDRATE	23 GM
TOTAL FAT	7 GM
SATURATED	2 GM
POLYUNSATURATED	2 GM
MONOUNSATURATED	3 GM
CHOLESTEROL	3 MG
SODIUM	75 MG
POTASSIUM	261 MG
CALCIUM	176 MG

FRUIT-RICE PUDDING

SERVES 6

1¼ cups unsalted cooked rice
1 cup canned fruit cocktail, drained
¼ cup maple syrup
1 tablespoon powdered sugar

In a medium bowl, combine rice, fruit cocktail and maple syrup. Mix well. Spoon into sauce dishes or small parfait glasses. Sprinkle with powdered sugar and serve.

NUTRIENT ANALYSIS

CALORIES	106 KCAL
PROTEIN	1 GM
CARBOHYDRATE	26 GM
TOTAL FAT	0 GM
SATURATED	0 GM
POLYUNSATURATED	0 GM
MONOUNSATURATED	0 GM
CHOLESTEROL	0 MG
SODIUM	3 MG
POTASSIUM	75 MG
CALCIUM	22 MG

SPICED FRUIT

SERVES 8

SPICED FRUIT
NUTRIENT ANALYSIS

CALORIES	212 KCAL
PROTEIN	1 GM
CARBOHYDRATE	53 GM
TOTAL FAT	1 GM
SATURATED	0 GM
POLYUNSATURATED	0 GM
MONOUNSATURATED	0 GM
CHOLESTEROL	0 MG
SODIUM	15 MG
POTASSIUM	439 MG
CALCIUM	126 MG

SPICED FRUIT
WITH ICE MILK
NUTRIENT ANALYSIS

CALORIES	304 KCAL
PROTEIN	4 GM
CARBOHYDRATE	68 GM
TOTAL FAT	3 GM
SATURATED	2 GM
POLYUNSATURATED	0 GM
MONOUNSATURATED	1 GM
CHOLESTEROL	9 MG
SODIUM	97 MG
POTASSIUM	571 MG
CALCIUM	214 MG

1 cup firmly packed brown sugar
½ cup sauterne table wine
¼ cup cider vinegar
15 whole cloves
2 sticks cinnamon
⅛ teaspoon curry powder
8 canned peach halves, drained
8 canned pear halves, drained
16 or more honeydew melon balls, fresh or frozen, or 2 kiwi fruit, pared and sliced
8 fresh pineapple spears or 1 20-ounce can pineapple chunks, drained

In a medium saucepan over medium heat, combine brown sugar, wine, vinegar, cloves, cinnamon and curry powder. Stir frequently until thoroughly heated. Place fruits in a large bowl. Pour hot spiced syrup over fruit. Cool, then chill overnight. Remove cloves and cinnamon sticks. Serve cold.

SPICED FRUIT WITH ICE MILK

For a simple but delicious variation, spoon ½ cup ice milk into each of 8 dessert bowls. Top with equal portions of Spiced Fruit.

BROWNIES

SERVES 12; 1 BROWNIE PER SERVING

Vegetable oil spray
3/4 cup all-purpose flour
1 cup sugar
1/3 cup cocoa
1/2 teaspoon baking powder
1/2 cup acceptable margarine, melted
3 egg whites
1 teaspoon vanilla
1/2 cup chopped walnuts

Preheat oven to 350° F. Lightly spray an 8-inch square baking pan with vegetable oil spray.

Sift dry ingredients together into a medium bowl. Add margarine, egg whites and vanilla and beat. Stir in nuts. Pour into prepared baking pan. Bake 30 to 35 minutes. Cool and cut into 12 equal portions.

NUTRIENT ANALYSIS

CALORIES	201 KCAL
PROTEIN	3 GM
CARBOHYDRATE	24 GM
TOTAL FAT	11 GM
SATURATED	2 GM
POLYUNSATURATED	4 GM
MONOUNSATURATED	4 GM
CHOLESTEROL	0 MG
SODIUM	28 MG
POTASSIUM	94 MG
CALCIUM	21 MG

FUDGE

SERVES 48; 1 PIECE PER SERVING

FUDGE

NUTRIENT ANALYSIS

CALORIES	42 KCAL
PROTEIN	0 GM
CARBOHYDRATE	9 GM
TOTAL FAT	1 GM
SATURATED	0 GM
POLYUNSATURATED	0 GM
MONOUNSATURATED	0 GM
CHOLESTEROL	0 MG
SODIUM	3 MG
POTASSIUM	34 MG
CALCIUM	9 MG

NUT FUDGE

NUTRIENT ANALYSIS

CALORIES	50 KCAL
PROTEIN	0 GM
CARBOHYDRATE	9 GM
TOTAL FAT	2 GM
SATURATED	0 GM
POLYUNSATURATED	1 GM
MONOUNSATURATED	1 GM
CHOLESTEROL	0 MG
SODIUM	4 MG
POTASSIUM	40 MG
CALCIUM	10 MG

Vegetable oil spray
1 cup firmly packed brown sugar
1 cup sugar
⅓ cup cocoa
⅔ cup skim milk
3 tablespoons acceptable margarine
1 teaspoon vanilla

Lightly spray an 8-inch square baking pan with vegetable oil spray. Set aside.

Place brown sugar, sugar and cocoa in a 3-quart saucepan. Add milk and mix.

Cook over medium heat until mixture reaches 236° F. on a candy thermometer, or until a small amount of syrup dropped in cold water forms a soft ball. Remove from heat.

Add margarine but do not stir. Cool until bottom of pan is lukewarm. Add vanilla and beat with an electric mixer 5 to 10 minutes or until fudge is thick and no longer glossy. Spread in prepared pan. Cool until firm. Cut into 48 equal portions.

NUT FUDGE

After beating, stir in ½ cup chopped walnuts.

PEANUT BUTTER FUDGE

After beating, add ½ cup peanut butter. Run a table knife through the fudge to form streaks.

PEANUT BUTTER FUDGE

NUTRIENT ANALYSIS

CALORIES	58 KCAL
PROTEIN	1 GM
CARBOHYDRATE	10 GM
TOTAL FAT	2 GM
SATURATED	1 GM
POLYUNSATURATED	1 GM
MONOUNSATURATED	1 GM
CHOLESTEROL	0 MG
SODIUM	4 MG
POTASSIUM	53 MG
CALCIUM	10 MG

Appetizers and Snacks

Fresh Vegetable Platter

Stuffed Mushrooms

Sautéed Mushrooms on Toast

Dill Pickles

Bread-and-Butter Pickles

Sugared Peanuts

Spiced Nuts

Fruit-Nut Snack Mix

Party Mix

Mock Cream Cheese

California Onion Dip

Chili Dip

Snacking is an all-American pastime, whether it's munching at the movies, noshing after school or raiding the refrigerator at midnight.

Unfortunately, commercial snack foods like chips, cookies, chocolate candy, pizza and ice cream are often loaded with fat and salt. If you want nutritious snacks without all those "extras," look for fresh fruits and vegetables and snacks you can make using less fat and salt. Next time you're looking for a good TV snack, make up a Fresh Vegetable Platter with California Onion Dip or Chili Dip.

Nuts and seeds are wonderful, crunchy treats, as the Sugared Peanuts and Spiced Nuts recipes should convince you. Since these are a little higher in fat than most of the recipes in this book, you'll want to eat them only occasionally. Eat them when you aren't concerned with calories or you need a quick, high-energy snack.

With a little ingenuity, you can create delicious snacks that are low in fat and salt. Here's a starter list, but use your imagination and add to it!

- Fruit and juices
- Raw vegetables with dips
- Home-fried tortilla shells broken into chip-size pieces and served with salsa
- Soda crackers with unsalted tops
- Skim milk, low-fat yogurt, low-fat frozen yogurt, sherbet or ice milk
- Low-sodium cereal
- Bread sticks, unsalted pretzels, nuts and seeds
- Unsalted popcorn with acceptable margarine
- Specially prepared homemade cookies and cakes
- Sandwiches, canapés or tea sandwiches
- Plain hard candies

Even snacks can fit into a healthful low-sodium diet. The trick is to find the *right* snacks. These recipes will help you do just that.

FRESH VEGETABLE PLATTER

Green, red or yellow bell peppers
Carrots
Cucumbers
Zucchini
Fresh mushrooms
Radishes
Green onions
Asparagus spears
Whole green beans
Cauliflower florets
Broccoli florets
Cherry tomatoes

Rinse and dry vegetables.

Remove core and seeds from bell peppers and cut into strips. Scrub or peel carrots, cucumbers and zucchini and cut into slices or sticks. Slice mushrooms. Prepare radish roses.

Arrange these and remaining vegetables on a platter.

Serve with Chili Dip, California Onion Dip, Mock Sour Cream or Yogurt-Dill Sauce (see recipes, pages 263, 262, 178 and 189).

(Because vegetables and amounts used will vary widely according to individual preference, no nutrient analysis has been provided.)

STUFFED MUSHROOMS

SERVES 4; 4 MUSHROOMS PER SERVING

16 medium-size fresh mushrooms
1 tablespoon acceptable margarine
1 small onion, chopped
1 slice bread, torn into small pieces
1/2 cup diced cooked chicken, unsalted, skinned, all visible fat removed
2 tablespoons table sherry
1/4 teaspoon marjoram
1/8 teaspoon freshly ground black pepper
1/8 teaspoon oregano
1 tablespoon acceptable margarine, melted

NUTRIENT ANALYSIS	
CALORIES	132 KCAL
PROTEIN	8 GM
CARBOHYDRATE	9 GM
TOTAL FAT	7 GM
SATURATED	2 GM
POLYUNSATURATED	2 GM
MONOUNSATURATED	3 GM
CHOLESTEROL	14 MG
SODIUM	50 MG
POTASSIUM	360 MG
CALCIUM	20 MG

Preheat broiler.

Clean mushrooms with a vegetable brush or wipe with a damp cloth. Remove and finely chop stems. Heat 1 tablespoon margarine in a nonstick skillet over medium-high heat. Sauté chopped mushroom stems and onion until tender. Add all ingredients except remaining margarine.

Place mushroom caps, round side up, on a baking sheet. Brush with half of melted margarine. Broil 2 minutes. Remove from broiler. Invert caps and fill with chicken mixture. Brush with remaining melted margarine. Broil 3 minutes, or until mushrooms are tender and lightly browned on top. Serve as an appetizer.

SAUTÉED MUSHROOMS ON TOAST

SERVES 4; 1 SLICE PER SERVING

NUTRIENT ANALYSIS	
CALORIES	155 KCAL
PROTEIN	5 GM
CARBOHYDRATE	20 GM
TOTAL FAT	7 GM
SATURATED	2 GM
POLYUNSATURATED	2 GM
MONOUNSATURATED	3 GM
CHOLESTEROL	1 MG
SODIUM	134 MG
POTASSIUM	481 MG
CALCIUM	35 MG

1 medium onion, finely chopped
2 tablespoons acceptable margarine
1 pound fresh mushrooms, sliced
2 teaspoons fresh lemon juice
Dash freshly ground black pepper
4 slices bread, toasted

Sauté onion in margarine until tender. Add mushrooms, cover and cook over low heat 8 to 10 minutes or until mushrooms are tender. Sprinkle with lemon juice and pepper. Serve over toast. This delicious snack is good anytime.

DILL PICKLES

MAKES 1 QUART
SERVES 12; 1 PICKLE PER SERVING

12 small cucumbers
1 tablespoon dill seed or 3 heads fresh dill
1 tablespoon whole pickling spice
2 cloves garlic
⅛ teaspoon alum
2 grape leaves (optional)
2¼ cups water
1½ cups cider vinegar
1 tablespoon sugar

Rinse cucumbers thoroughly. Soak overnight in cold water. Dry cucumbers and place in a clean, hot quart jar. Add dill, pickling spice, garlic, alum and grape leaves to the jar.

In a small saucepan, heat water, vinegar and sugar over medium-high heat. Bring to a boil. Pour boiling liquid into a jar, filling jar to within ½ inch of the top. Wipe rim of jar, screw lid on tightly and place in a Dutch oven or other deep pan.

Cover jar completely with water. Bring to a boil and cook 20 minutes. (At higher altitudes longer processing is necessary.)

Store pickles 2 weeks before using.

NUTRIENT ANALYSIS

CALORIES	34 KCAL
PROTEIN	1 GM
CARBOHYDRATE	9 GM
TOTAL FAT	0 GM
SATURATED	0 GM
POLYUNSATURATED	0 GM
MONOUNSATURATED	0 GM
CHOLESTEROL	0 MG
SODIUM	8 MG
POTASSIUM	334 MG
CALCIUM	61 MG

BREAD-AND-BUTTER PICKLES

MAKES 1 QUART
SERVES 16; APPROXIMATELY ¼ CUP PER SERVING

BREAD-AND-BUTTER PICKLES NUTRIENT ANALYSIS

CALORIES	69 KCAL
PROTEIN	0 GM
CARBOHYDRATE	18 GM
TOTAL FAT	0 GM
SATURATED	0 GM
POLYUNSATURATED	0 GM
MONOUNSATURATED	0 GM
CHOLESTEROL	0 MG
SODIUM	1 MG
POTASSIUM	81 MG
CALCIUM	8 MG

PICKLE RELISH NUTRIENT ANALYSIS

CALORIES	17 KCAL
PROTEIN	0 GM
CARBOHYDRATE	5 GM
TOTAL FAT	0 GM
SATURATED	0 GM
POLYUNSATURATED	0 GM
MONOUNSATURATED	0 GM
CHOLESTEROL	0 MG
SODIUM	0 MG
POTASSIUM	23 MG
CALCIUM	2 MG

8 medium, crisp cucumbers (approximately 4 cups when sliced)
2 medium onions
1¼ cups cider vinegar
1¼ cups sugar
½ teaspoon turmeric
½ teaspoon mustard seed
¼ teaspoon celery seed

Slice thoroughly chilled cucumbers and onions, cover and place in refrigerator.

In a medium saucepan over medium-high heat, combine vinegar, sugar and spices. Heat just to boiling. Add cucumber mixture and heat 2 to 3 minutes.

Chill and serve. May be stored in a covered container in refrigerator for 1 month.

For storage without refrigeration, sterilize 2 pint jars and immediately pack hot pickles loosely to within ½ inch of top. Wipe rim of jar, screw lid on tightly and place in a Dutch oven or other deep pan. Cover jars completely with water. Bring to a boil and cook 5 minutes. (At higher altitudes, longer processing is necessary.)

PICKLE RELISH

Finely chop the cucumbers and onions and add 1 finely chopped green or red bell pepper. Cook until liquid in mixture is nearly gone and relish is thickened. Storage is the same as for Bread-and-Butter Pickles.

SUGARED PEANUTS

SERVES 10

Vegetable oil spray
2 cups unsalted, roasted peanuts
1 cup sugar
½ cup water

Preheat oven to 350° F. Lightly spray a cookie sheet with vegetable oil spray.

Mix peanuts, sugar and water together in a medium saucepan over medium heat, stirring occasionally. Cook until mixture crystallizes and coats peanuts, approximately 10 to 12 minutes. Spread on cookie sheet and bake 20 to 25 minutes, mixing occasionally. Cool and store in tightly covered container.

Because of the high fat and sugar content of this recipe, these nuts should be used only as an occasional snack. They should not be eaten in large quantities.

NUTRIENT ANALYSIS

CALORIES	244 KCAL
PROTEIN	8 GM
CARBOHYDRATE	25 GM
TOTAL FAT	14 GM
SATURATED	2 GM
POLYUNSATURATED	5 GM
MONOUNSATURATED	7 GM
CHOLESTEROL	0 MG
SODIUM	5 MG
POTASSIUM	200 MG
CALCIUM	26 MG

SPICED NUTS

SERVES 10

NUTRIENT ANALYSIS	
CALORIES	195 KCAL
PROTEIN	2 GM
CARBOHYDRATE	17 GM
TOTAL FAT	15 GM
SATURATED	1 GM
POLYUNSATURATED	4 GM
MONOUNSATURATED	9 GM
CHOLESTEROL	0 MG
SODIUM	5 MG
POTASSIUM	91 MG
CALCIUM	11 MG

Vegetable oil spray
1 egg white
⅔ cup sugar
1 teaspoon ground cinnamon
2 cups pecan halves

Preheat oven to 325° F. Lightly spray a cookie sheet with vegetable oil spray. Set aside.

Beat egg white until foamy. Gradually add sugar and cinnamon, and beat until egg white forms stiff peaks. Add pecans and stir until coated with mixture. Pour coated nuts onto prepared cookie sheet. Using a fork, arrange nuts so they are not touching. Bake 15 to 20 minutes, or until egg white is dry and slightly browned. Cool and store in a tightly covered container.

Because of the high fat and sugar content of this recipe, these nuts should be used only as an occasional snack. They should not be eaten in large quantities.

FRUIT-NUT SNACK MIX

SERVES 12; ¼ CUP PER SERVING

½ cup dried apricots, cut in quarters
½ cup dates, cut in half
¼ cup raisins
½ cup whole almonds
½ cup walnut halves
½ cup unsalted peanuts
¼ cup unsalted sunflower seeds

In a large bowl, toss ingredients together. Store in tightly covered container.

This high-energy mix is great to take on hikes and camping trips.

Note: You may substitute your favorite dried fruits or nuts in place of those listed.

NUTRIENT ANALYSIS*

CALORIES	162 KCAL
PROTEIN	5 GM
CARBOHYDRATE	15 GM
TOTAL FAT	11 GM
SATURATED	1 GM
POLYUNSATURATED	5 GM
MONOUNSATURATED	5 GM
CHOLESTEROL	0 MG
SODIUM	4 MG
POTASSIUM	280 MG
CALCIUM	35 MG

*BASED ON INGREDIENTS LISTED.

PARTY MIX

SERVES 14

NUTRIENT ANALYSIS*	
CALORIES	76 KCAL
PROTEIN	2 GM
CARBOHYDRATE	5 GM
TOTAL FAT	6 GM
SATURATED	1 GM
POLYUNSATURATED	2 GM
MONOUNSATURATED	3 GM
CHOLESTEROL	0 MG
SODIUM	4 MG
POTASSIUM	86 MG
CALCIUM	11 MG

*BASED ON INGREDIENTS LISTED.

1/4 cup acceptable margarine
1/2 teaspoon garlic powder
1/2 cup small unsalted pretzel sticks
1/2 cup puffed rice
1 cup spoon-size shredded wheat
1/2 cup unsalted peanuts

Melt margarine in a nonstick skillet over medium heat. Add garlic powder and mix well. Add remaining ingredients and toss together. Serve warm.

For a slightly different taste, use walnuts, pecans or a mixture of nuts in place of peanuts. For a sweeter taste, use 1/4 cup raisins in place of the garlic powder.

MOCK CREAM CHEESE

MAKES 1¼ CUPS
SERVES 5; ¼ CUP PER SERVING

1 cup (8 ounces) unsalted dry-curd cottage cheese
¼ cup acceptable margarine, softened
Skim milk, if needed

In a blender or the work bowl of a food processor fitted with a metal blade, combine cottage cheese and margarine. Process until thoroughly blended.

If mixture appears too thick to spread, add skim milk, 1 teaspoon at a time, until the desired consistency is reached.

Cover tightly and store in refrigerator. Use as a sandwich spread topped with marmalade, jam or honey.

NUTRIENT ANALYSIS

CALORIES	105 KCAL
PROTEIN	5 GM
CARBOHYDRATE	1 GM
TOTAL FAT	9 GM
SATURATED	2 GM
POLYUNSATURATED	3 GM
MONOUNSATURATED	4 GM
CHOLESTEROL	2 MG
SODIUM	7 MG
POTASSIUM	14 MG
CALCIUM	12 MG

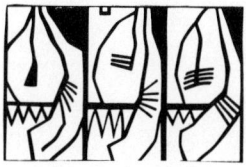

CALIFORNIA ONION DIP

SERVES 20; 1 TABLESPOON PER SERVING

NUTRIENT ANALYSIS	
CALORIES	10 KCAL
PROTEIN	1 GM
CARBOHYDRATE	1 GM
TOTAL FAT	0 GM
SATURATED	0 GM
POLYUNSATURATED	0 GM
MONOUNSATURATED	0 GM
CHOLESTEROL	1 MG
SODIUM	3 MG
POTASSIUM	17 MG
CALCIUM	8 MG

¼ cup skim milk
2 tablespoons low-sodium beef broth
1 cup (8 ounces) unsalted dry-curd cottage cheese
2 teaspoons fresh lemon juice
2 teaspoons vermouth or dry white table wine
1 teaspoon onion powder
½ teaspoon garlic powder
2 tablespoons onion flakes or ¼ cup chopped green onion

Place milk and beef broth in a blender or the work bowl of a food processor fitted with a metal blade. Process until mixed. Add remaining ingredients except onion flakes and process at high speed until smooth. Stir in onion.

Use as a dip for raw vegetables or toast strips.

CHILI DIP

SERVES 20; 1 TABLESPOON PER SERVING

1 cup Chili Sauce (see recipe, page 183)
2 tablespoons fresh lemon juice
4 drops hot pepper sauce
2 tablespoons grated fresh horseradish
½ teaspoon onion powder

Place all ingredients in a blender or the work bowl of a food processor fitted with a metal blade. Process until blended. Chill.

Use as a sauce for crabmeat or clams or as a dip for raw vegetables.

NUTRIENT ANALYSIS	
CALORIES	17 KCAL
PROTEIN	0 GM
CARBOHYDRATE	3 GM
TOTAL FAT	0 GM
SATURATED	0 GM
POLYUNSATURATED	0 GM
MONOUNSATURATED	0 GM
CHOLESTEROL	0 MG
SODIUM	9 MG
POTASSIUM	73 MG
CALCIUM	5 MG

APPENDIX

APPENDIX A

THE LOW-SODIUM DIET

The principal source of sodium in the American diet is salt, otherwise known as sodium chloride. For this reason, we entitled this book *The American Heart Association Low-Salt Cookbook.* We are, however, concerned with *all* the sodium in the diet—whether it comes from salt, monosodium glutamate, sodium bicarbonate or any other source. So we have developed a diet that we call a low-sodium diet. It is low in salt and all other forms of sodium. This diet is designed for those of you who have high blood pressure (and may also have high blood cholesterol and/or excessive weight). The recommendations in this section will help you decrease the amount of sodium in your diet, control your calorie intake and limit the amount of total fat, saturated fatty acids and dietary cholesterol you eat.

RISK FACTORS FOR HEART AND BLOOD VESSEL DISEASES

Certain risk factors increase the chance that you may develop cardiovascular disease, especially coronary heart disease and stroke. You have no control over some of them, such as a history of heart disease in the family, or being male. However, other risk factors can be controlled. Three of the most important risk factors you can control are high blood pressure, high blood cholesterol and cigarette smoking. Obesity and diabetes also increase the risk of heart disease. But no matter what your history, you may still be able to reduce your personal risk of heart disease by making healthful choices in the foods you eat, by deciding not to smoke, by maintaining a desirable body weight and by being generally active.

This section not only provides dietary treatment for high blood pressure but also includes information about dietary measures to decrease blood cholesterol levels and control body weight. Before you begin, you should know both your blood pressure and blood cholesterol levels. If you don't, have a physician measure them for you and ask him or her to explain the readings to you. If someone other than your physician takes the measurements, be sure to consult your own physician for an interpretation of the results. If your blood cholesterol levels and/or weight are high, use the information here to help lower them. If your blood cholesterol and weight are normal, use the information to help you maintain these desirable levels.

HIGH BLOOD PRESSURE (HYPERTENSION)

Blood pressure is a ratio measurement of the pressure that blood exerts against the inside of the artery wall when the heart beats, and when it is at rest. A device measures blood pressure in millimeters of mercury (mm Hg). The measurement is written as systolic blood pressure (taken while the heart is beating) over diastolic blood pressure (taken in between heartbeats). An example is 120/80 (read as "one-twenty over eighty"). Blood pressure is considered high when systolic blood pressure is 140 mm Hg or greater and/or diastolic blood pressure is 90 mm Hg or greater.

Normal Blood Pressure for Persons 18 Years of Age or Older

Less than 140/90 mm Hg

Doctors have identified two kinds of high blood pressure. The cause of *essential* or *primary hypertension,* which accounts for 90 percent of all cases, is unknown. *Secondary hypertension* occurs because of another disease or a condition such as pregnancy. It is estimated that one-fourth of all Americans have some degree of high blood pressure. Uncontrolled high blood pressure increases the risk not only for heart attack and stroke but also for kidney damage and an enlarged heart. The primary dietary factors that help lower blood pressure for many people are discussed on pages 268–273.

HIGH BLOOD CHOLESTEROL (HYPERCHOLESTEROLEMIA)

A high level of cholesterol in the blood (hypercholesterolemia) is a risk factor for heart disease. Cholesterol is measured in milligrams per deciliter of blood (mg/dl). Elevated blood cholesterol contributes to a disease process called atherosclerosis. In atherosclerosis, cholesterol and other elements in blood are deposited along the smooth inner linings of arteries to form plaque. Over time, plaque builds up and narrows the inside of the artery. If this narrowed artery becomes entirely blocked, blood cannot carry oxygen the body needs to sustain life to its cells and tissues. If the blocked artery is in the heart itself—a coronary artery—the result is a heart attack. If the blocked artery is in the neck or head, the result is a stroke.

BLOOD CHOLESTEROL CATEGORIES FOR PERSONS 20 YEARS OF AGE OR OLDER

Desirable Blood Cholesterol	Borderline-High Blood Cholesterol	High Blood Cholesterol
Less than 200 mg/dl	200 to 239 mg/dl	240 mg/dl and above

Research shows that lowering elevated blood cholesterol levels helps reduce the risk of heart disease. The primary dietary factors that help lower blood cholesterol in most people are given for your reference below.

Dietary Factors That Help Lower Blood Cholesterol

Saturated Fatty Acids—Less than 10% of calories

Dietary Cholesterol—Less than 300 mg per day

Weight Control—Achieving and maintaining desirable body weight

Several dietary factors affect both elevated blood cholesterol and high blood pressure. These are discussed in detail in the following sections.

DIETARY FACTORS AFFECTING BLOOD PRESSURE

Making the right food choices can help lower blood pressure in many people.

The three major dietary factors are:

- Restricting sodium intake
- Controlling weight
- Restricting alcohol intake

Each one can be used alone or in combination with the others to lower blood pressure in many people. Some research indicates that eating foods high in potassium helps control high blood pressure, too. Other studies are investigating the effects of other minerals (such as calcium) on blood pressure.

SODIUM

A diet high in sodium may contribute to the development of high blood pressure in some people and cause blood pressure to stay high in others. It also can limit how well certain blood pressure medications work. Some people can control their high blood pressure by reducing the amount of sodium in their diet. Other people may need medication in addition. The food plans we have developed (see pages 303–306 and 323–326) provide about 2,000 milligrams (mg) of sodium per day. If your physician recommends a higher or lower level of sodium, a registered dietitian can make the necessary changes in the eating plans for you.

Salt is the most common source of sodium. Salt, or sodium chloride, is 40 percent sodium and 60 percent chloride. Americans typically consume from 4,000 to 5,800 milligrams of sodium per day. One teaspoon of salt has 2,196 milligrams of sodium. Each of the following sources provides a portion of the sodium found in the typical American diet:

- Sodium added to food during preparation or at the table (about 18 percent)
- Sodium added to food during processing (about 67 percent)
- Sodium occurring naturally in food and water (about 15 percent)

Food Preparation. One source of sodium is salt added during food preparation (at home or in restaurants) and at the table. You were not born with the taste for salt—you acquired it. It usually takes about a month of eating less salt and high-sodium foods to reduce your desire to salt your food. You can decrease your taste for salt (and sodium) by using little or none in food preparation, by not adding it at the table and by avoiding processed foods containing large amounts of sodium. Replace salt with herbs and spices or some of the salt-free seasoning mixes on the market. Add pepper, garlic, onion and/or lemon to foods to give them a more distinct flavor and help replace the taste of salt. We've listed some of the best seasonings for various foods in our "Herb, Spice and Seasoning Guide" on pages 327–329.

Most salt substitutes are potassium chloride. Adding a small amount of salt substitute to food after cooking will make the food taste "salted." Before using any salt substitute, check with your doctor to see if it is all right for you. Products labeled "lite" salt are usually part sodium chloride (salt) and part potassium chloride. We don't recommend using "lite" salt because it adds sodium to food.

In fact, any seasoning that uses "salt" as part of the name is high in sodium. Examples are "garlic salt," "celery salt" and "onion salt." However, plain "garlic powder," "celery powder" and "onion powder" are low in sodium and make an easy substitution possible if these are flavors you love.

COMMON FOODS HIGH IN SODIUM

Anchovies	Ham, cured	Pizza
Bacon	Ketchup	Salami
Barbecue sauce	Kosher processed meat	Salt
Bologna	Meat, canned or frozen in sauce	Sauerkraut
Buttermilk	Monosodium glutamate (MSG)	Sausage
Celery salt	Mustard	Seasoned salt
Cereal, dry	Nuts, salted	Seeds, salted
Cheese	Olives, green	Soup, canned
Chips, potato* and corn*	Pastrami	Soy sauce
Crackers*	Pepperoni	Steak sauce
Cured meat	Pickles	Wieners—beef, pork and turkey
Frankfurters		Worcestershire sauce
Garlic salt		

* Unsalted varieties are available.

Note: A list of sodium-containing compounds often added to processed foods is included in the information about reading food labels (see page 278).

Sodium in Processed Foods. Processed foods, such as ham, bacon, pickles, cheese and luncheon meat, are very high in sodium. Convenience foods, including most frozen dinners and entrées, shelf-stable dinners and ready-to-eat cereals, are also high in sodium because of salt and sodium compounds used to prepare and preserve them. Ingredients used in food preparation, such as baking powder and baking soda, add to the sodium content of bakery products as well. Obviously, adding salt to any food increases its sodium content.

Sodium Naturally Occurring in Food. Sodium is present in all foods of plant and animal origin: It occurs naturally in meat, fish, poultry, dairy products, grain products, fruits and vegetables. However, the amount of sodium found in most of these foods is small.

The water supply is another source of sodium. Most adults use 2 to 2½ quarts (8 to 10 glasses) of water each day in beverages and in cooking. The sodium content of water varies, according to the supply, from 1 to 1,500 milligrams per quart. Ten glasses (2½ quarts) of water containing 1,500 milligrams of sodium per quart could total as much as 3,750 milligrams. Chemicals used in the "softening" process of most water softeners increase the sodium content of water. Your local health department can analyze your water for sodium content. If it contains more than 80 parts per million (approximately 200 milligrams sodium in 10 glasses of water), you should use distilled water or bottled water without sodium for drinking and cooking.

Be aware of all the sources of sodium you consume. The foods listed in the diets (pages 285–326) are primarily unsalted. Since the amount of sodium naturally occurring in food is low, your diet may contain less than 2,000 milligrams of sodium per day if you eat your meals at home and all the foods you eat are unsalted. For more variety, you may add a specified amount of salt or high-sodium foods to bring your level of sodium up to 2,000 milligrams. (For example, you may wish to use regular margarine instead of low-sodium margarine.) The amount of sodium you may add, based on the calorie level of your diet, is shown on pages 299 and 320. A list of typical restaurant foods and other high-sodium foods is shown on pages 282–283. It is very important that you take into account the generally high amount of sodium usually present in restaurant food.

ALCOHOL

Research shows that people who drink too much alcohol tend to have high blood pressure. To help control blood pressure, it's best to drink only in moderation or not at all. If you drink, we recommend that all alcoholic beverages provide no more than 1 to 2 fluid ounces of ethanol per day. The amounts of beer, wine and spirits equal to ½ fluid ounce of ethanol are listed on pages 297 and 318. Remember that alcohol is also a major source of calories and can contribute to obesity.

POTASSIUM

People with high blood pressure are often advised to include good sources of potassium in their diet. Some major sources of potassium are listed below.

POTASSIUM SOURCES*

Potassium	Foods
400 mg or more	Banana, 1 medium
	Cantaloupe, 1 cup, cubed
	Honeydew melon, 1 cup, cubed
	Milk, skim, 1 cup
	Nectarine, 1 large
	Orange juice, 1 cup
	Potato, 1 medium
	Prunes, 10 medium
	Prune juice, ¾ cup
	Red beans, cooked, ½ cup
	Tomato juice, salt-free, 1 cup
200 to 399 mg	Apple juice, 1 cup
	Beef, lean, cooked, 3 oz.
	Beets, cooked, ½ cup
	Blackberries, 1 cup
	Brussels sprouts, fresh, ½ cup
	Carrot, raw, 1 large
	Celery, 3 (5-in.) stalks
	Cherries, raw, 15
	Chicken, cooked, 3 oz.
	Flounder, cooked, 3 oz.
	Grapefruit, ½
	Grapefruit juice, 1 cup

Potassium	Foods
200 to 399 mg	Lentils, cooked, ½ cup Lima beans, green, ½ cup Orange, 1 medium Pork, fresh, lean, cooked, 3 oz. Salmon, pink, unsalted, canned, 3 oz. Spinach, cooked, ½ cup Strawberries, sliced, 1 cup Tomatoes, unsalted, canned, ½ cup Tuna, water-packed, unsalted, ½ cup Turkey, unprocessed, 3 oz. Watermelon, 2 cups, cubed

* For more information on potassium, see the American Heart Association's booklet "Facts About Potassium," available from your local American Heart Association.

CALCIUM

Calcium is an important nutrient for healthy bones. For the best sources of calcium, choose from the dairy products group listed on pages 290 and 291.

WEIGHT CONTROL

Reducing excess weight is associated with lowering high blood pressure. Details on weight control are on pages 276–277.

DIETARY FACTORS AFFECTING BLOOD CHOLESTEROL

The foods you eat can affect your blood cholesterol levels. If you choose foods low in saturated fatty acids, most will also be low in total fat. Research shows that a diet lower in total fat, saturated fat and dietary cholesterol will help lower blood cholesterol; so will reducing to achieve and maintain your ideal body weight. Some research studies suggest that soluble fiber in the diet also may help lower the blood cholesterol level.

FAT

The fat in food is made up of two major types of fatty acids: saturated and unsaturated. Unsaturated fatty acids may be either polyunsaturated or monounsaturated. Some fats are a concentrated source of saturated fatty acids, while others are high in polyunsaturated or monounsaturated fatty acids. All fats, however, are a mixture of saturated, polyunsaturated and monounsaturated fatty acids.

Saturated Fatty Acids. Eating foods high in saturated fatty acids tends to raise your blood cholesterol level. Saturated fatty acids are found in animal products and in some plant products.

Animal fats high in saturated fatty acids include butterfat (in butter, cheese, whole milk, cream and ice cream); fat on beef, pork and lamb; fat in chicken skin; and lard. Plant sources of saturated fatty acids are cocoa butter, coconut oil, palm kernel oil and palm oil. Commercial foods containing coconut, palm or palm kernel oil may be advertised as "cholesterol-free" if all the ingredients are from plant sources. However, if coconut, palm kernel or palm oil is a major ingredient, the product may be high in saturated fatty acids. This is important to know if you are trying to lower blood cholesterol levels. Read the nutrition section of the label and try to select foods that contain more polyunsaturated fatty acids than saturated fatty acids (monounsaturated fatty acids are not listed on food labels).

Unsaturated Fatty Acids. You can use unsaturated fatty acids to replace some of the saturated fatty acids in your diet. The two main types of unsaturated fatty acids are: polyunsaturated and monounsaturated. Polyunsaturated fats and oils help lower the level of blood cholesterol. Safflower oil is the most polyunsaturated vegetable oil, followed by sunflower oil, corn oil and soybean oil. Foods high in monounsaturated fatty acids include canola oil, olive oil, peanut oil, avocados, olives and some nuts. Some research indicates that they may be as effective as polyunsaturated oils in lowering blood cholesterol when consumed in a diet low in saturated fats.

Fish is also a source of polyunsaturated fatty acids. Some fish, including cold-water fish such as salmon, mackerel and herring, are rich in fat (fish oil), while fish from warm waters, such as red snapper and flounder, are generally low in total fat. The fat in either high or low-fat fish is low in saturated fatty acids.

When you are reading food labels, you may find hydrogenated fats and oils listed. Hydrogenation is a process that changes oils from their liquid form to a solid or semisolid form. This process makes them more saturated than they were in their original form. The greater the degree of hydrogenation, the more saturated the fat becomes. Hydrogenation is used in manufacturing margarines and shortenings. These products may be partially or almost completely hydrogenated. Some types of margarine and shortening made with partially hydrogenated unsaturated oils are acceptable to include in eating plans to lower high blood cholesterol.

The unsaturated fatty acid content of selected foods is listed in the chart below. Foods with the highest level of polyunsaturated fatty acids are listed first.

UNSATURATED FATTY ACID CONTENT OF SELECTED FOODS
(Listed in Order of Polyunsaturation)

1 Tablespoon	Polyunsaturated Fatty Acid (Grams)	Saturated Fatty Acid (Grams)	Monounsaturated Fatty Acid (Grams)
POLYUNSATURATED OILS			
Safflower oil	10.1	1.2	1.6
Sunflower oil	8.9	1.4	2.7
Corn oil	8.0	1.7	3.3
Soybean oil	7.9	2.0	3.2
MONOUNSATURATED OILS			
Canola oil	4.6	0.8	8.2
Peanut oil	4.3	2.3	6.2
Olive oil	1.1	1.8	9.9
MARGARINES, UNSALTED			
Safflower oil margarine (tub)	6.3	1.2	3.3
Corn oil margarine (tub)	4.5	2.1	4.5
Corn oil margarine (stick)	3.3	2.1	5.4
Soybean oil margarine (tub)	3.9	1.8	5.1
Soybean oil margarine (stick)	3.6	1.8	5.4
NUTS, UNSALTED			
Walnuts, black	2.9	0.3	1.0
Brazil nuts	2.1	1.4	2.0
Peanuts	1.4	0.6	2.2
Pecans	1.1	0.4	2.8
Almonds	1.0	0.4	3.0
Cashews	0.7	0.8	2.3
Pistachios	0.6	0.5	2.6
Macadamias	0.1	0.9	4.9
SEEDS, UNSALTED			
Sunflower seeds	2.9	0.5	0.9
Sesame seeds	2.0	0.6	1.7
Pumpkin/Squash seeds	1.8	0.7	1.2
SHORTENING			
Soybean and cottonseed oil	3.3	3.2	5.7

DIETARY CHOLESTEROL

Dietary cholesterol is found only in foods of animal origin, including meat, poultry, seafood and dairy products. Foods such as fruits, vegetables, grains, cereals, nuts and seeds do not contain cholesterol. Egg yolks and organ meats are very high in cholesterol. Some shellfish, such as shrimp, that are relatively high in cholesterol can be eaten occasionally within the recommended guidelines.

FIBER

Fiber is the indigestible part of food. There are two types of fiber—soluble and insoluble. Limited evidence shows that large amounts of soluble fiber can help lower blood cholesterol levels by an additional 2 percent when combined with the effects of a diet low in total fat, saturated fatty acids and dietary cholesterol as described in this section. Good sources of soluble fiber include oatmeal, oat bran and beans. Many so-called oat bran products (muffins, chips, waffles), however, actually contain very little oat bran and are high in sodium, total fat and saturated fatty acids.

Insoluble fiber, such as wheat bran, adds bulk to stools and helps with normal bowel function. Large amounts of insoluble fiber may interfere with the body's ability to absorb certain nutrients, such as calcium. Insoluble fiber does not appear to lower blood cholesterol.

WEIGHT CONTROL

Losing weight can help lower both blood pressure and blood cholesterol. To lose weight, consume fewer calories and increase your physical activity on a regular basis. Although this sounds simple, weight loss is not easy, and keeping weight off can be even more difficult than losing it.

One of the most effective methods for weight loss is reducing the amount of fat you eat. Since fat (saturated and unsaturated) is the most concentrated source of calories in your diet, reducing fat automatically decreases calories. Fat has more than twice the calories of the same amount of protein and carbohydrate. Protein and carbohydrate both have about 4 calories per gram; alcohol has 7 calories per gram; and all fats have 9 calories per gram. For example, 1 teaspoon of sugar (carbohydrate) provides 15 calories; 1 teaspoon of oil provides 40 calories—over 2½ times as many calories.

To maintain your ideal weight, eat no more calories than your body needs. As a guideline, typical calorie levels for men are 2,000 to 2,500 calories a day to maintain weight and 1,600 to 2,000 calories to lose weight. For women, typical calorie levels are 1,600 to 2,000 calories a day to maintain weight and 1,200 to 1,600 calories to lose weight.

Tips to Help You Prevent Overeating

- Select foods low in fat or fat-free.
- Eat slowly.
- Take small portions.
- Avoid second helpings.

For most people who decide to lose weight, a steady loss of 1 to 2 pounds a week is safe until the goal weight is reached. At the beginning of a weight-reduction eating plan, much of the "weight loss" is due to loss of water. Long-term success depends on two things: adopting an eating plan sufficiently low in calories to maintain the desirable lower weight; and taking part in regular physical activity. Such life-style changes help people who have lost weight keep it off.

FOOD LABELS

One of the greatest challenges of following a special eating plan is finding foods that fit your needs. You can obtain useful information by learning to read and compare food labels when you go shopping. Now that many product labels list sodium, fat and cholesterol content, shopping for low-sodium, low-fat foods is easier.

All food labels list the product's ingredients in order by weight. The ingredient present in the greatest amount is listed first. The ingredient contained in the least amount is listed last. Most packaged or prepared foods are high in sodium because their ingredients include high-sodium foods (see page 270) and/or sodium compounds (see page 278). The table on page 278 will help you identify ingredients high in sodium, saturated fatty acids and/or cholesterol. To avoid getting too much of these, limit your use of products that list one or more of the ingredients or compounds found in this table.

SODIUM, SATURATED FATTY ACIDS AND CHOLESTEROL ON FOOD LABELS

Sodium Compounds		
Baking powder	Salt	Sodium hydroxide
Baking soda	Sodium alginate	Sodium nitrite
Disodium phosphate	Sodium benzoate	Sodium propionate
Monosodium glutamate (MSG)	Sodium caseinate	Sodium sulfite

Foods High in Saturated Fatty Acids and Cholesterol		
Animal fat	Cream	Pork fat
Bacon fat	Ham fat	Turkey fat
Beef fat	Hardened fat or oil	Vegetable oil**
Butter	Hydrogenated vegetable oil*	Vegetable shortening (some types)*
Chicken fat	Lamb fat	Whole-milk solids
Cocoa butter*	Lard	
Coconut*	Palm kernel oil*	
Coconut oil*	Palm oil*	

* Source of saturated fat only.
** Could contain coconut, palm or palm kernel oil.

SODIUM LABELING

Food labels use certain terms to describe the sodium content of those products. Each has a specific meaning. Knowing what each means can help you select low-sodium food.

Food Label Terms That Indicate Reduced Sodium

- "Sodium Free" — 5 mg or less per serving
- "Low Sodium" — 35 mg or less per serving
- "Moderately Low Sodium" — 140 mg or less per serving
- "Reduced Sodium" — Usual sodium level is reduced by 75%
- "Unsalted" or "No Salt Added" — No salt added during processing

These terms refer only to sodium content and do not mean the product has less fat or saturated fatty acids. It's important to read labels carefully, since some foods low in sodium are high in fat. The following sample of nutritional information shows how to compare labels to identify a product lower in sodium, saturated fatty acids and cholesterol.

NUTRITIONAL INFORMATION: A COMPARISON OF LABELS

Nutrition Information Per Serving	Butter, Stick	Margarine, Tub	Unsalted Margarine, Tub
Serving size	1 Tbsp.	1 Tbsp.	1 Tbsp.
Calories	101	100	100
Protein, grams	0	0	0
Carbohydrate, grams	0	0	0
Fat, grams	11	11	11
Polyunsaturated, grams	1	5	5
Saturated, grams	8	2	2
Cholesterol, milligrams	33	0	0
Sodium, milligrams	120	95	4

Note: The amount of monounsaturated fat is not listed.

You can see that "unsalted" margarine has less sodium than regular margarine. Both types of margarine have less saturated fatty acid and dietary cholesterol than butter.

DINING OUT

Not surprisingly, you are more likely to find foods lower in sodium in restaurants that offer a wide variety of foods than in those that offer only a limited selection. Most restaurant food has salt and often monosodium glutamate (MSG) added to it. This is especially true if it is prepared ahead of time, frozen and reheated before serving. When you choose a restaurant that prepares food as it is ordered, you can tell the waiter to leave salt and MSG out of your portion. Naturally, you'll want to avoid using salt at the table. Also remember to avoid high-sodium condiments such as ketchup, mustard, soy sauce, steak sauce and salad dressing. A single restaurant meal may have anywhere from 1,000 to 4,000 milligrams of sodium.

The examples on page 280 compare "typical" restaurant and cafeteria menus with those that have been "modified" to be lower in fat and sodium. They illustrate how much you can decrease the sodium you are likely to consume when you dine out. Footnotes explain how the changes were made.

SAMPLE MENU—RESTAURANT MENU

Typical Menu	Sodium (mg)	Low-Fat, Low-Sodium Menu*	Sodium (mg)
Rib steak cooked with salt (6 oz.)	650	Lean steak cooked without salt (6 oz.)	120
Baked potato with butter, cheese, sour cream, bacon bits	325	Baked potato with margarine, chives	60
Tossed salad with blue cheese dressing (¼ cup)	20	Tossed salad with oil and vinegar dressing (1 Tbsp.)	20
Hot roll (1)	670	Hot roll (1)	0
Butter (1 pat)	120	Margarine (1 pat)	120
Apple pie (1 slice)	40	Sherbet (1 cup)	50
Total	400	Total	90
	2,225		460

* The waiter was asked to have the steak cooked "without salt or fat" and to serve margarine and chives on the side for the potato. Oil and vinegar (in separate bottles, not Italian dressing) were used as salad dressing. Sherbet was selected because piecrust has salt and fat.

SAMPLE MENU—CAFETERIA MENU

Typical Menu	Sodium (mg)	Low-Fat, Low-Sodium Menu*	Sodium (mg)
Baked fish with topping (5 oz.)	1,002	Baked fish, topping removed (5 oz.)	575
Mashed potatoes (½ cup)	350	No potatoes	
Green beans (½ cup)	400	Green beans (½ cup)	400
Gelatin salad with cottage cheese (½ cup)	100	Gelatin salad with fruit (½ cup)	35
Chocolate cake with frosting (1 slice)	300	Melon wedge (1)	10
Total	2,152	Total	1,020

* The topping on baked fish was removed at the table and not eaten, to decrease sodium and fat. Only one vegetable was selected, since all choices were seasoned with salt and margarine. A gelatin salad with fruit contains less sodium than one containing cottage cheese. Fruit was selected for dessert because the cake was prepared with salt and baking powder (high in sodium) and was high in fat.

If you eat out very often, you'll need to keep track of the sodium in restaurant food. This means adding up the milligrams of sodium in each food to be sure that your total does not go over 2,000 milligrams for the day. Approximate sodium values for some common restaurant foods are listed on pages 282–283.

If you do *not* eat away from home on a regular basis, you may be getting less sodium than the amount recommended by your physician. If so, you may use regular margarine instead of unsalted margarine at home. You may also be able to add other high-sodium foods, such as those listed on pages 282–283, to increase your sodium to 2,000 milligrams. A registered dietitian can help you plan your meals.

When Dining Out

- Select a restaurant where food is cooked to order.
- Request that food be prepared without salt or fat.
- Be aware of those foods that have salt added during preparation; either avoid them or select only one.
- If an entrée is served with breading, topping or sauce, remove it before eating.
- Avoid table salt and high-sodium condiments and garnishes (pickles and olives).
- Avoid salads and other foods containing cheese and cottage cheese.
- Use lemon or oil and vinegar (in separate bottles, not Italian dressing) on salad.
- Request that sauces and salad dressings be served on the side.
- Fresh or canned fruit may be eaten as an appetizer, salad or dessert.
- If fruit pie is served, decrease sodium and fat by eating only the filling and leaving the crust.
- Compensate at home for high-sodium foods eaten out by using very low-sodium foods, such as unsalted margarine, unsalted bread and unsalted cereal.

When Choosing Deli Food

- Request "fresh-cooked" turkey or lean roast beef. Most precooked deli meats have salt and sodium-containing preservatives added.
- Skip the mayonnaise, mustard and ketchup on your sandwich.
- Order lettuce, tomato and/or onion for your sandwich.
- Use thinly sliced bread or one slice of regular bread for your sandwich to decrease the sodium.
- Avoid pasta salads, which usually have salt and Italian-type dressing added.
- "Dress" a tossed green salad with oil and vinegar from separate bottles (not Italian dressing).
- Choose fruit, sherbet or frozen yogurt for dessert.

SODIUM VALUES IN RESTAURANT AND OTHER COMMERCIAL FOODS

Foods	Approximate* Sodium (mg)
ENTRÉES, SALTED WHILE COOKING	
Chicken, breast or thigh and drumstick, grilled, skin removed after cooking** (1 med.)	250
Chicken, breast or thigh and drumstick, skin removed before cooking** (1 med.)	400
Chinese stir-fried entrées (2½ cups)	1,800
Fish, broiled or grilled (5 oz.)	600
Ham, lean (fat trimmed) (5 oz.)	1,700
Spaghetti with tomato and meat sauce (2½ cups)	1,050
Spaghetti with tomato sauce (2½ cups)	1,525
Steak, grilled (fat trimmed) (6 oz.)	650
Turkey, processed, from delicatessen (1 oz.)	120
Turkey, processed and commercially packaged (1 oz.)	400
SIDE DISHES, SEASONED WITH SALT AND MARGARINE	
Mashed potatoes (no gravy) (½ cup)	350
Rice, white (½ cup)	300
Sauerkraut (½ cup)	1,000

* Values rounded off for ease in use.
** In a restaurant, removing skin after cooking removes part of the salt used in cooking.

Foods	Approximate* Sodium (mg)
Vegetables, canned (½ cup)	400
Vegetables, frozen or fresh (½ cup)	250
SALADS	
Chicken salad (½ cup)	500
Coleslaw with vinaigrette dressing (½ cup)	450
Cottage cheese (½ cup)	425
Pasta salad (½ cup)	400
Potato salad (½ cup)	600
Tuna salad (½ cup)	400
SALAD DRESSINGS, REGULAR OR LOW-CALORIE	
French dressing (1 Tbsp.)	225
Italian dressing (1 Tbsp.)	125
Ranch dressing (1 Tbsp.)	125
Thousand Island dressing (1 Tbsp.)	125
SOUPS	
Beef bouillon (1 cup)	650
Chicken with noodles (1 cup)	950
Split pea (1 cup)	1,000
CRACKERS	
Bread sticks (2 sticks, 4 x ½ in.)	120
Melba toast, rectangular (5)	250
Saltines, regular (6)	200
CEREALS	
Bran, bud type (⅓ cup)	175
Oatmeal, cooked in unsalted water (½ cup)	1
Oatmeal, instant or cooked in salted water, prepared (1 packet or approx. ¾ cup cooked)	285
Ready-to-eat flake cereals, regular (1 individual serving box)	225
CONDIMENTS	
Cocktail sauce (1 Tbsp.)	175
Ketchup (1 Tbsp.)	175
Margarine (1 pat or 1 tsp.)	35
Mayonnaise-type salad dressing (1 Tbsp.)	100
Mustard (1 Tbsp.)	200
Olives, green (10 small)	800
Olives, black or ripe (5 extra-large)	250
Pickles, dill (1 spear, 6 x ½ in.)	450
Soy sauce (1 Tbsp.)	1,025
Steak sauce (1 Tbsp.)	300
Taco sauce (1 Tbsp.)	150

* Values rounded off for ease in use.

Step-One and Step-Two Diets

The American Heart Association has two eating plans for lowering blood cholesterol: the Step-One Diet and the Step-Two Diet.

The Step-One Diet (pages 285–306) moderately decreases your intake of total fat, saturated fatty acids and cholesterol. The Step-Two Diet (pages 307–326) further restricts your intake of saturated fatty acids and cholesterol. Use it when your doctor says you need additional lowering of your blood cholesterol. The Step-One and Step-Two diets provide no more than 2,000 milligrams of sodium per day. These eating patterns can help lower blood pressure and blood cholesterol levels.

Eating plans that are reduced in calories often do not meet the Recommended Dietary Allowance (1989) for calcium and iron. When you select foods you should take special care to ensure adequate calcium and iron intake. If you follow a low-calorie eating plan for a long time, you may wish to consult your dietitian or physician about supplementing calcium and iron in your diet.

THE STEP-ONE DIET

FOOD GROUPS

In the Step-One eating plan, foods are separated into seven groups based on the amount of fat, carbohydrate, protein and calories they provide. All foods listed as appropriate are prepared without added salt. The food groups are:

1. meat, poultry and seafood
2. eggs
3. dairy products
4. fats and oils
5. breads, cereals, pasta and starchy vegetables
6. vegetables and fruits
7. optional foods—desserts, sweets and alcohol

The foods within each group contain similar amounts of nutrients (carbohydrates, protein and fat). While you're getting started, use a food scale, measuring cups and measuring spoons to help determine portion sizes.

MEAT, POULTRY AND SEAFOOD

Foods in this group average, per ounce cooked, about 22 milligrams sodium, 60 calories, 3 grams fat, 1 gram saturated fatty acids and 25 milligrams dietary cholesterol. They provide protein, phosphorus, vitamins B_6, B_{12} and other vitamins and minerals. Lean red meats in addition are good sources of iron and zinc.

We recommend eating no more than 6 ounces of cooked meat, fish or poultry each day. This will limit your intake of saturated fatty acids, dietary cholesterol and sodium. Choose from the following list.

APPROPRIATE FOODS

SEAFOOD
All fresh and frozen fish
Crab, lobster, scallops, clams and oysters
Shrimp and crayfish (moderately high in cholesterol)
Tuna and salmon (canned in water, unsalted)
Sardines (canned, unsalted—rinsed)

POULTRY (WITHOUT SKIN)
Chicken
Cornish hen
Turkey, unprocessed or fresh-cooked (not pre-basted)

VEAL (TRIMMED OF VISIBLE FAT)
All cuts are lean except for veal cutlets (ground or cubed); examples of lean veal are chops and roasts

BEEF (TRIMMED OF VISIBLE FAT)
USDA Select or Choice grades of lean beaf, such as round steak, sirloin tip, tenderloin and extra-lean ground beef

PORK (TRIMMED OF VISIBLE FAT)
Fresh pork, such as tenderloin and loin chops

LAMB (TRIMMED OF VISIBLE FAT)
Lamb chops
Lamb cubes for stew

WILD GAME
Venison
Rabbit
Squirrel
Pheasant (without skin)
Wild duck (without skin)

SODIUM, FAT AND CHOLESTEROL INFORMATION

When selecting meat, poultry and seafood, be careful to choose those most appropriate for your dietary plan. These hints will help you do just that.

- Cured, processed and pickled foods are high in sodium. Examples include ham, Canadian bacon, turkey ham, pickled herring, processed turkey, processed beef and processed chicken.
- Many processed meats, such as luncheon meat, wieners and sausage, are high in sodium and saturated fatty acids.
- Pre-basted turkeys have fat and salt added. Ask your butcher to special-order an "unbasted" or fresh turkey for you.

- Most deli-type precooked turkey and roast beef have salt or sodium compounds added.
- Most canned meats, such as tuna, salmon and chicken, are packed with broth or added salt. Purchase unsalted canned meats or rinse regular canned meats with cold water to help decrease the sodium.
- Many precooked frozen and canned entrées are prepared with salt.
- "Prime" grade, heavily marbled and fatty meats are high in saturated fatty acids.
- Liver, brains, heart, kidney and sweetbreads are high in cholesterol and should be limited.
- Shellfish contains less fat than does meat or poultry. Although shrimp and crayfish are relatively high in cholesterol, they can be eaten occasionally. Imitation shellfish (surimi) is high in sodium.

PORTION SIZE (COOKED MEAT)*	
CHICKEN	
½ breast	3 oz.
1 leg and thigh	3 oz.
FRESH PORK	
1 medium chop	3 oz.
LAMB	
2 small chops	3 oz.
BEEF	
1 small hamburger patty	3 oz.
1 piece cooked lean meat, about the size of a deck of cards	3 oz.
¾ cup diced meat	3 oz.
FISH	
¾ cup flaked	3 oz.

* Meat loses about 25% of its weight during cooking (for example, 4 oz. raw will be about 3 oz. cooked). Eat no more than 6 oz. cooked weight daily.

ABOUT FOOD PREPARATION

The way you prepare your food is important to the success of your eating plan. Use this information to learn the best ways possible.

- Rinse frozen fish packed in a salt or brine solution with water before using.
- Trim all visible fat from meat and remove skin from poultry before cooking.

- Buy only the leanest ground beef, pork and turkey (no more than 15 percent fat). Pour off fat after browning. Ground meat is generally higher in fat than nonground meat.
- After cooking meat for a stew or soup, allow it to cool so the fat can rise to the top. Then remove the fat before adding vegetables and other ingredients.
- Preparing meat, poultry or seafood by frying, basting or sautéing adds extra fat. Remember to count this in your daily fat allowance.
- Dried beans, peas, lentils and soybean curd (tofu) are good sources of protein when eaten with low-fat dairy products. Small amounts of meat, fish or poultry can be combined with rice or pasta for a hearty entrée.

EGGS

Eggs are a good source of protein, phosphorus, vitamins A, D, B_6, B_{12} and other vitamins and minerals. Egg yolks are high in cholesterol, whereas egg whites contain no cholesterol. The Step-One Diet allows up to 3 egg yolks per week. One large whole egg has about 70 milligrams sodium, 79 calories, 6 grams fat, 2 grams saturated fatty acids and 213 to 220 milligrams cholesterol. You may supplement your diet with cholesterol-free egg substitutes. Check the label to see if salt has been added and how much sodium is provided by one serving. The chart at the bottom of the opposite page shows how much egg you normally get in various foods. It's easy to underestimate the amount you eat, especially when eggs are "hidden" in cakes, cookies or baked goods.

WHEN USING EGGS

Eggs can be part of a low-sodium, low-modified-fat, low-cholesterol diet. Just remember to eat no more than 3 yolks per week. Here are some tips to help you meet that goal.

- Prepare scrambled eggs, omelettes and the like so that only one or two egg yolks per serving are used. Add a few egg whites to the mixing bowl to make more generous portions.
- Many recipes contain egg yolk. Use the chart on page 289 to find out the approximate whole-egg content of various prepared foods.
- Substitute egg whites in recipes calling for whole eggs. For exam-

ple, you may use two egg whites instead of each whole egg in muffins, cookies, puddings and pie fillings.

- The following chart shows that egg substitutes without added salt, egg whites and whole eggs have similar sodium content:

Food	Amount	Sodium
Whole egg	1 egg	70 mg
Egg substitute	¼ cup	80 to 120 mg
Egg whites	2	100 mg

- Egg substitute with cheese is high in sodium and fat.
- To prepare omelettes with egg substitute or egg, use low-sodium ingredients such as green onions, mushrooms, fresh tomatoes or green bell pepper to add flavor.

HOW EGGS ADD UP

Egg-Containing Foods	Approx. Portion of Whole Egg
BEVERAGES	
Eggnog (approximately ½ cup)	¼
BREADS	
Cornbread (1/9 of 9-in. square pan)	¼
Muffin (1)	1/10
Pancakes, 4-in. (2)	¼
DESSERTS	
Baked custard or crème brûlée (6-oz. custard cup)	½
Chocolate, lemon meringue or pumpkin pie (⅛ of 9-in. pie)	⅓
Pound cake (1/12 of loaf)	¼
Sponge cake (1/12 of 9-in. square cake)	½
Tapioca pudding (½ cup)	⅓
Yellow or chocolate 2-layer cake (1/16 of 9-in. cake)	⅛
MAIN DISHES	
Cheese soufflé (1 cup)	½
Chicken salad (½ cup)	⅓
Corn pudding (½ cup)	½
Egg salad	1 to 2
Omelette (depends on size)	1 to 3
SALAD DRESSINGS	
Mayonnaise (¼ cup)	¼
Thousand Island (¼ cup)	⅓

DAIRY PRODUCTS

The low-fat dairy products listed below average about 115 milligrams sodium, 90 calories, 3 grams fat, 2 grams saturated fatty acids and 11 milligrams cholesterol per portion. Milk and milk products are the major source of calcium in the American diet. They also provide riboflavin, protein and vitamins A, B_6 and B_{12}. Low-fat or skim-milk products that have been fortified with vitamins A and D have essentially the same nutrients as whole-milk products, but they have less fat and fewer calories. Skim milk and nonfat yogurt, however, actually have more protein and calcium than do whole milk and whole-milk yogurt.

PORTION SIZE	
MILK AND YOGURT	
Skim or 1% milk	1 cup
Nonfat or low-fat plain yogurt	1 cup
CHEESE	
Unsalted low-fat or dry-curd cottage cheese	½ cup
Mozzarella cheese, part-skim	1 oz.
Ricotta cheese, part-skim	1 oz.
Low-fat cheese; no more than 150 mg sodium and 5 grams fat per oz. (¼ cup, diced)	1 oz.
Dry, grated cheese, such as dry Parmesan (1 Tbsp.)	¼ oz.
FROZEN DESSERTS	
Frozen low-fat yogurt	½ cup
Ice milk	½ cup
Sherbet (See "Optional Foods," page 297)	

SODIUM, FAT AND CHOLESTEROL INFORMATION

Because of the wide variation among the many dairy products available, reading labels on these items is very important. These tips will help you select foods appropriate for your diet.

- Regular cheese, low-fat cheese and cottage cheese are high in sodium.
- Natural cheese is lower in sodium than processed cheese.
- Some supermarkets carry cheese reduced in both fat and sodium.
- Select low-fat cheese with no more than 5 grams fat per ounce and no more than 150 milligrams sodium per ounce.

- Cream substitutes—nondairy coffee creamers, sour cream substitutes and whipped toppings—often contain coconut, palm or palm kernel oil and are therefore high in saturated fatty acids. Read labels carefully.

ADDITIONAL FACTS ABOUT CALCIUM

(The recommended amount of calcium is 800 milligrams or more per day for adults.)

		Calcium mg.
1 cup	Skim milk	302
	1%, low-fat milk	300
	2%, low-fat milk	297
	3.3%, whole milk	291
	Yogurt, plain, skim	452
	Yogurt, plain, low-fat	414
	Yogurt, fruit flavor, low-fat	344
	Yogurt, plain, whole	274
½ cup	Cottage cheese, low-fat, 1% fat, unsalted	69
	Cottage cheese, low-fat, 2% fat, unsalted	78
	Cottage cheese, creamed, unsalted	63
	Ice milk, vanilla, soft serve, 2.6% fat	137
	Ice milk, vanilla, hard, 4.3% fat	88
	Sherbet, orange, 2% fat	52
	Frozen yogurt, fruit varieties	162
1 oz.	Cheese, mozzarella, part-skim	183
	Cheese, low-fat (low-sodium)	186

FATS AND OILS

All the foods in the "Fats and Oils" food group are high in fat and calories. Some are high in vitamins A or E. One portion of the "Fats and Oils" group averages about 1 milligram sodium, 5 grams fat, 1 gram saturated fatty acids, 45 calories and negligible cholesterol.

SODIUM, FAT AND CHOLESTEROL INFORMATION

Cocoa butter, coconut, coconut oil, palm kernel oil and palm oil contain more saturated than unsaturated fatty acids. Look for the listing of these fats when you read package labels. Select only those foods that contain 2 grams or less of saturated fat per tablespoon. (You

PORTION SIZE	
VEGETABLE OILS	
Safflower, corn, sunflower, soybean, olive, canola, peanut	1 tsp.
MARGARINE, UNSALTED	
Margarine containing 2 grams or less of saturated fat per tablespoon	1 tsp.
Diet margarine	2 tsp.
NUTS AND SEEDS, UNSALTED	
Chopped nuts, except coconut	1 Tbsp.
Seeds, any variety (without shells)	1 Tbsp.
SALAD DRESSINGS	
French, Italian, Thousand Island or mayonnaise-type salad dressing, unsalted	1 Tbsp.
Mayonnaise	2 tsp.
SHORTENING	
Soybean and cottonseed oil	1 tsp.
OTHER FATS	
Peanut butter, unsalted	2 tsp.
Avocado	⅛ medium

might wish to refer to the list on page 278 for review.) Currently, information about monounsaturated fatty acids is not listed on the nutrition label.

ABOUT USING FATS AND OILS

Follow these guidelines for selecting appropriate fats and oils for this diet.

- Use unsalted margarine at home if you eat one or more meals away from home daily. This will help make up for the high sodium content of restaurant food. If you don't eat out regularly, you may use regular margarine instead of unsalted margarine at home.
- To help you select appropriate margarines and shortenings, read the labels. As a general guide, select margarine that has 2 grams or less of saturated fat per tablespoon. Limit your use of shortening because it's higher in saturated fatty acids than are margarine and oil.
- Diet margarine has about twice as much sodium as does regular tub margarine.

- Many oil-free salad dressings are high in sodium, but oil-free, low-sodium varieties are available. Some low-sodium, low-fat salad dressings can be purchased in individual packets to use when eating out.

BREADS, CEREALS, PASTA AND STARCHY VEGETABLES

Foods in this group contain an average of 92 milligrams sodium, 80 calories, 1 gram of fat and negligible saturated fatty acids and cholesterol per portion. We have included low-fat, unsalted soups in this group. Whole-grain or enriched breads and cereals provide B vitamins and iron. They also provide protein, and they are a major source of this nutrient in vegetarian diets. Whole-grain products also contribute magnesium, folacin and fiber.

SODIUM, FAT AND CHOLESTEROL INFORMATION

The following information will help you select and prepare appropriate foods from this group.

- If you eat more than one meal away from home daily, use unsalted bread with your meals at home. This helps make up for the high sodium content of restaurant food. If you do not eat out regularly, you can use regular bread instead of unsalted bread.
- Regular canned or dehydrated varieties of soup are high in sodium. A low-sodium soup should have no more than 2 grams of fat per cup.
- If you use skim or 1 percent milk to prepare soup, count ½ cup milk per 1 cup soup as part of the dairy allowance.
- Cream soup in restaurants is usually prepared with salt and whole milk or cream.
- Most ready-to-eat cereals are high in sodium. Read the labels to find low-sodium varieties, such as shredded wheat, puffed rice and puffed wheat.
- Cook hot cereal, pasta, rice and vegetables without salt added to the water.
- Individually portioned instant hot cereals, rice mixes and pasta mixes are high in sodium.

PORTION SIZE	
BREADS	
Bagel	½
Bread sticks, unsalted, 4 in. long, ½ in. diameter	2
Bread, white, whole wheat, rye, oatmeal, pumpernickel	1 slice
Croutons, plain bread crumbs	1 cup
English muffin	½
Hamburger or hot dog bun	½
Pita, 6 in. diameter	½
Roll, plain (1 oz.)	1
Tortilla, corn, 6 in. diameter	1
CEREALS, PASTA AND RICE	
Shredded wheat	1 biscuit or ½ cup
Flake-type cereal, ready-to-eat, unsalted	1 cup
Puffed cereal, unsalted	1½ cups
Cooked cereal, bulgur, grits (cooked in unsalted water)	½ cup
Pasta (cooked in unsalted water)	½ cup
Rice (cooked in unsalted water)	⅓ cup
CRACKERS	
Animal crackers	8
Graham crackers, 2½ in. square	3
Matzo, 4 x 6 in.	¾ oz.
Melba toast, unsalted	5 slices
Popcorn (popped, no salt or fat added)	3 cups
Pretzels, unsalted	¾ oz.
Saltine-type crackers, unsalted tops	6
STARCHY VEGETABLES (FRESH, FROZEN OR CANNED WITHOUT SALT)	
Baked beans	¼ cup
Corn	½ cup
Corn on cob, 6 in. long	1
Dried beans, peas, lentils	⅓ cup
Green peas	½ cup
Lima beans	½ cup
Potato, baked (3 oz.)	1
Potato, mashed, no salt added	½ cup
Squash, acorn or butternut	¾ cup
Sweet potato or yam	⅓ cup
COMMERCIAL SOUPS, UNSALTED, PREPARED WITH WATER*	
Bouillon, broth, consommé	As desired
Chicken noodle, gazpacho, minestrone, onion, tomato, vegetarian	1 cup
Beef noodle, chicken rice, chunky-style turkey noodle, oyster stew, split pea (may use milk allowance)	¾ cup

* Homemade soups low in fat may be counted as the same amount of a similar commercial soup.

QUICK BREADS** (1 SERVING = 1 BREAD + 1 FAT)	
Banana bread (16 slices per loaf)	1 slice
Biscuit (2 in. diameter)	1
Cornbread muffin	1
Pancake (4 in. diameter)	1
Waffle (9 in. diameter)	¼

** Prepared with low-sodium baking powder, skim milk, unsaturated oil, unsalted margarine, egg substitute or egg white. Omit salt from the recipe. If you use a whole egg, count it as part of the egg allowance.

Note: Most commercial biscuits, muffins, pancakes and croissants are high in sodium and are not made with the recommended fats.

ABOUT FOOD PREPARATION

The following tips will help you prepare foods in this group.

- Homemade biscuits, muffins, cornbread, banana bread, soft rolls, pancakes, French toast and waffles should be prepared with the egg yolk allowance (no more than 3 per week), egg substitute or egg whites; skim or 1 percent milk; and unsaturated oil or unsalted margarine. Omit salt, baking powder and baking soda from the recipe and replace them with low-sodium baking powder. You may need to use more of the low-sodium baking powder than the regular to get the same effect in a recipe; read the label.
- Check the dietetic or "special" foods section of your supermarket for low-sodium mixes for pancakes and other products.
- You can stretch your meat allowance by combining meat, poultry or seafood with rice, pasta or vegetables.

VEGETABLES AND FRUITS

An average portion of vegetables has about 13 milligrams sodium and 25 calories. An average portion of fruit has about 1 milligram sodium and 60 calories. Nearly all vegetables and fruits are low in fat, and none contain cholesterol.

Vegetables and fruits are important sources of vitamins A and C and fiber. Dark green and deep yellow vegetables are good sources of vitamin A. Most dark green vegetables, if not overcooked, are important sources of vitamin C, as are citrus fruits (oranges, grapefruit, tangerines and lemons), melons, berries and tomatoes. Dark green vegetables are also valued for riboflavin, folacin, iron and magnesium. Certain greens—collards, kale, mustard, turnip and dandelion—provide calcium.

PORTION SIZE	
VEGETABLES	
Most vegetables	½ cup raw or cooked
Raw cabbage, Chinese cabbage, celery, cucumbers, mushrooms, green onions, peppers, radishes and zucchini	Quantities as desired (negligible fat and calories)
SALAD GREENS	
Endive, escarole, lettuce, romaine and spinach	Quantities as desired (negligible fat and calories)
FRUIT AND JUICE	
Fruit	½ cup or 1 medium-size piece of fruit
Fruit juice	½ cup

WHEN USING VEGETABLES AND FRUITS

When selecting and preparing foods from this group, use this information to help you get the nutrition you want without the extra sodium and fat.

- Fresh, frozen and unsalted canned vegetables are low in sodium. Select those that don't have seasoning or sauce added.
- Regular canned vegetables, tomato sauce, tomato paste, tomato puree, tomato juice and vegetable juice cocktail are high in sodium. Use the unsalted variety.
- Sauerkraut, pickles and pickled vegetables are high in sodium.
- Vegetables and fruits have no fat, except for avocados and olives. (You'll find these listed under "Fats and Oils—Portion Size" on page 292.)
- Vegetables prepared with butter, cream or cheese are high in fat.
- Fried vegetables have several times more fat and calories than vegetables prepared without fat.
- Fresh fruits and fruits canned in water are lower in calories than fruits canned in juice or in syrup. To reduce calories, drain fruits canned in syrup.

OPTIONAL FOODS—DESSERTS, SWEETS AND ALCOHOL

Each of the homemade desserts (cakes, cookies and pies) listed below has about 22 milligrams sodium, 285 calories and 6 to 10 grams fat. The amounts listed count as *two* portions of Optional Foods.

Each of the "sweets" on this list contains about 22 milligrams sodium, 75 calories and 0 to 1 grams fat. Each counts as *one* portion of Optional Foods.

One portion of any alcoholic beverage listed below contains 9 milligrams sodium, ½ ounce ethanol and 90 to 150 calories. Count each one as *one* portion of Optional Foods.

	PORTION SIZE
DESSERTS*	
2-layer cake, frosted (1/12 of cake)	1 slice
Sheet cake, frosted (2¼ × 2½ × 1½-in. piece or 1/20 of 9 × 13-in. cake)	1 piece
Cupcake, frosted (average size)	1
Oatmeal raisin cookies	4
Double-crust fruit pie (⅛ of 9-in. pie)	1 slice
SWEETS	
Carbonated beverage (sweetened)**	6 fl. oz.
Lemonade (sweetened)	6 fl. oz.
Candy made primarily with sugar (e.g., candy corn, gum drops, mints and hard candy)	¾ oz.
Angel food cake (1/24 of cake)	1 slice
Gingersnaps	2
Fruit ice	⅓ cup
Sherbet	⅓ cup
Fruit-flavored gelatin (sweetened)	½ cup
Sugar, syrup, honey, jam, preserves or marmalade	1½ Tbsp.
Fig bar	1
ALCOHOLIC BEVERAGES	
Beer	12 fl. oz.
80-proof spirits (bourbon, gin, rum, Scotch, tequila, vodka, whiskey)	1½ fl. oz.
Wine, red or white	4 fl. oz.

* Homemade, prepared according to the first tip listed on page 298.
** Be sure the beverage is low in sodium—read the label.

ABOUT DESSERTS, SWEETS AND SNACKS

Use the following information to help you select and prepare foods appropriate for your dietary plan.

- Desserts (cakes, pies, cookies and puddings) may be made with low-sodium baking powder, unsalted margarine or unsaturated oil, skim or 1 percent milk, allowed eggs, egg substitute or egg whites. Omit salt from recipe. If you use a whole egg, count it as part of the egg allowance.
- Many snack products, such as chips and rich crackers, are high in sodium and saturated fatty acids. However, some chips are cooked in unsaturated oil and are not salted. Choose only those labeled as "no salt added" and that contain more polyunsaturated than saturated fatty acids.
- A few kinds of cookies are low in fat, such as fig bars and gingersnaps. Plain angel food cake has no fat. If you are uncertain, read the label and choose only those with 2 grams of fat or less per portion.

FREE FOODS

One portion of these foods and drinks contains fewer than 20 calories and no fat. You don't need to limit those items that have no portion size specified.

	PORTION SIZE
DRINKS	
Bouillon or broth without fat, low-sodium	
Carbonated water	
Cocoa powder, unsweetened	1 Tbsp.
Coffee/tea	
Diet carbonated drinks*	1 per day
Drink mixes, sugar-free	
Tonic water, sugar-free	
SWEET SUBSTITUTES*	
Candy, hard, sugar-free	
Gelatin, sugar-free	
Gum, sugar-free	
Jam/jelly, sugar-free	2 tsp.
Pancake syrup, sugar-free	
Sugar substitutes (saccharin or aspartame)	
FRUITS	
Cranberries, unsweetened	½ cup
Rhubarb, unsweetened	½ cup

* Sweet substitutes are listed for the benefit of those following diabetic diets.

CONDIMENTS	
Horseradish, freshly grated	
Ketchup, low-sodium	1 Tbsp.
Mustard, low-sodium	
Pickles, dill, unsweetened, low-sodium	
Salad dressing, oil-free, low-sodium	
Vinegar	

SAMPLE EATING PLANS: STEP-ONE DIET*

	Daily Portions			
Food Group	**2,500 Calories**	**2,000 Calories**	**1,600 Calories**	**1,200 Calories**
Meat, Poultry and Seafood (unsalted)	6 oz.	6 oz.	6 oz.	6 oz.
Eggs, whole (unsalted)	3/week	3/week	3/week	3/week
Dairy Products (unsalted)	4	3	3	2
Fats and Oils (unsalted)	8	6	3	3
Breads, Cereals, Pasta and Starchy Vegetables (unsalted)	10	7	4	3
Vegetables (unsalted)	4	4	4	4
Fruits	5	3	3	3
Optional Foods (unsalted)	2	2	2	0
Sodium from Food Groups, mg	1,639	1,244	965	731
Sodium from Water, mg	200	200	200	200
Additional Sodium,** mg	+150	+550	+800	+1,050
Total sodium	1,989 mg	1,994 mg	1,965 mg	1,981 mg

* Your physician or dietitian can recommend an appropriate calorie plan. Sample eating plans for the Step-Two Diet are on pages 307–326.

**Additional Sodium: A specific amount of sodium can be added to each of the eating plans. This "additional sodium" can be in the form of:

- Salt added at the table or in food preparation (home only)
  ¼ tsp. salt = 500 mg sodium
  ½ tsp. salt = 1,000 mg sodium
- Restaurant foods, see pages 282–283

EATING PLANS FOR CALORIE LEVELS HIGHER THAN 2,500 CALORIES

If you eat more than 2,500 calories a day, you can easily get more than 2,000 milligrams of sodium daily. If so, limit your intake of sodium by using all unsalted products, including unsalted bread and bread products. Be careful also to limit the sodium in the food you eat away from home.

YOUR DAILY EATING PLAN IN PORTIONS

Planning your meals to lower total fat, saturated fatty acids, dietary cholesterol and sodium will be easier if you plot them on a chart. The chart on page 301 shows a sample eating plan for a person on the Step-One Diet at 2,000 calories per day and about 2,000 milligrams of sodium. Spreading the allowable portions listed on page 299 over all meals and snacks during the day, the chart reflects the daily number of portions allowed for each food group. Use the blank form on page 302 to chart your daily eating plan.

The sample menus that follow the chart are examples of how the Step-One eating plan may be used. They include a variety of foods that can be eaten at home or in restaurants.

YOUR DAILY EATING PLAN IN PORTIONS*—STEP-ONE DIET

Calories 2,000 **Fat <30%** **Saturated fat <10%** **Cholesterol <300 mg** **Sodium 2,000 mg**

	Meat, Poultry & Seafood	Eggs	Dairy Products	Fats & Oils	Bread, Cereal & Starchy Vegetables	Vegetables	Fruit	Optional
Breakfast			1	1	2		1	
Snack								
Lunch	2 oz.		1	2	2	2	1	
Snack								
Dinner	4 oz.		1	3	2	2		2
Bedtime Snack					1		1	

* A blank form is provided on page 302 for your use. < = Less than.

Your Daily Eating Plan in Portions—Step-One Diet

Calories _____ **Fat** _____ **Saturated fat** _____ **Cholesterol** _____ **Sodium** _____

	Meat, Poultry & Seafood	Eggs	Dairy Products	Fats & Oils	Bread, Cereal & Starchy Vegetables	Vegetables	Fruit	Optional
Breakfast								
Snack								
Lunch								
Snack								
Dinner								
Bedtime Snack								

SAMPLE MENU FOR THE STEP-ONE DIET—2,500 CALORIES

	Food Group Portions
BREAKFAST	
Orange Juice (1 cup)	2 Fruits
Shredded Wheat Cereal (1 cup) with	2 Breads
Sliced Banana (½)	1 Fruit
Milk, 1% (1 cup)	1 Dairy
Whole-Wheat Toast (2 slices)	2 Breads
Margarine, unsalted (2 tsp.)	2 Fats
LUNCH	
Hamburger Sandwich	
Lean Ground Beef, broiled (3 oz.)	3 Meats
Mozzarella Cheese, part-skim (1 oz.)	1 Dairy
Hamburger Bun (1)	2 Breads
Lettuce (1 leaf)	Free
Tomato (2 slices)	Free
Ketchup, regular* (1 Tbsp.)	Free
Tossed Salad	
Lettuce (1 cup)	Free
Tomato Wedges (1 tomato)	1 Vegetable
Grated Carrots (½ cup)	1 Vegetable
French Dressing, unsalted (2 Tbsp.)	2 Fats
Fresh Grapes (15)	1 Fruit
Milk, 1% (1 cup)	1 Dairy
DINNER	
Broiled Salmon (3 oz.) with	3 Meats
Margarine, unsalted (1 tsp.), and	1 Fat
Lemon (2 wedges)	Free
Steamed White Rice (⅔ cup) with	2 Breads
Margarine, unsalted (1 tsp.)	1 Fat
Steamed Snow Peas with Tomato Wedges and Onion (1 cup)	2 Vegetables
Cantaloupe, cubed (1 cup)	1 Fruit
French Bread (2 slices)	2 Breads
Margarine, unsalted (2 tsp.)	2 Fats
Milk, 1% (1 cup)	1 Dairy
Chocolate Cake with Quick Frosting (1/16 of cake)	2 Optional

* *Additional Sodium:* 150 mg allowed
Added: 1 Tbsp. regular Ketchup (175 mg sodium)

Nutrient Analysis:
1,979 mg Sodium (includes 200 mg sodium from water)
2,512 Calories, distributed as follows:

19% Protein	28% Fat	210 mg Cholesterol
55% Carbohydrate	8% Saturated Fatty Acids	

(The amount of cholesterol is less than 300 mg because no eggs were included in this menu.)

SAMPLE MENU FOR THE STEP-ONE DIET—2,000 CALORIES

	Food Group Portions
BREAKFAST	
Cranberry Juice Cocktail (1 cup)	3 Fruits
Poached Egg (1)	1 Egg
Bagel (1)	2 Breads
Margarine, unsalted (2 tsp.)	2 Fats
Milk, 1% (1 cup)	1 Dairy
LUNCH	
Roast Beef Sandwich	
Roast Beef (3 oz.)	3 Meats
Whole-Wheat Bread (2 slices)	2 Breads
Mayonnaise (2 tsp.)	1 Fat
Lettuce (1 leaf)	Free
Split Pea Soup, unsalted (¾ cup)	1 Bread
Relishes	
Sliced Tomato (1 tomato)	1 Vegetable
Cauliflower Florets (3)	1 Vegetable
Milk, 1% (1 cup)	1 Dairy
Chocolate Ice Milk (½ cup)	1 Dairy
DINNER (AT RESTAURANT)	
Grilled Chicken Breast * (3 oz.)	3 Meats
Baked Potato (1 medium) with	1 Bread
Margarine, regular * (1 tsp.), and	1 Fat
Chives (1 Tbsp.)	Free
Broccoli and Carrots * (½ cup)	1 Vegetable
Margarine, regular (1 tsp.), used in preparation of vegetables	1 Fat
Tossed Salad	
Lettuce (1 cup)	Free
Tomato Wedges (1 tomato)	1 Vegetable
Vinegar	Free
Dinner Roll (1)	1 Bread
Margarine, regular * (1 tsp.)	1 Fat
Orange Sherbet (⅔ cup)	2 Optional

* *Additional Sodium:* 550 mg allowed
Added: 3 oz. Chicken Breast prepared with salt, skin removed after cooking (250 mg sodium)
2 tsp. regular Margarine (70 mg sodium)
½ cup frozen Broccoli and Carrots prepared with salt (250 mg sodium)

Nutrient Analysis:
1,997 mg Sodium (includes 200 mg sodium from water)
1,990 Calories, distributed as follows:

21% Protein	27% Fat	451 mg Cholesterol
53% Carbohydrate	9% Saturated Fatty Acids	

(The amount of cholesterol is greater than 300 mg because an egg is included in this menu.)

SAMPLE MENU FOR THE STEP-ONE DIET—1,600 CALORIES

	Food Group Portions
BREAKFAST	
Fresh Grapefruit (½)	1 Fruit
Corn Flakes, regular* (1 cup) with	1 Bread
Sliced Nectarine (1)	1 Fruit
Milk, 1% (1 cup)	1 Dairy
LUNCH	
Broiled Chicken Thigh (2 oz.)	2 Meats
Corn on the Cob (6 in.)	1 Bread
Margarine, regular* (1 tsp.), on corn	1 Fat
Tossed Salad	
Lettuce (1 cup)	Free
Tomato Wedges (1 tomato)	1 Vegetable
Cucumber Slices (6)	Free
Vinegar	Free
Melba Toast, unsalted (5 slices)	1 Bread
Strawberry Frozen Yogurt (½ cup)	1 Dairy
DINNER	
Swiss Steak	
Round Steak (4 oz.)	4 Meats
Tomatoes, canned, unsalted (½ cup)	1 Vegetable
Green Pepper Strips (½ pepper)	Free
Onion, diced (2 Tbsp.)	Free
Steamed Broccoli (2 spears)	1 Vegetable
Carrot-Raisin Salad	
Raw Carrots, grated (½ cup)	1 Vegetable
Raisins (2 Tbsp.)	1 Fruit
Mayonnaise (2 tsp.)	1 Fat
Whole-Wheat Dinner Roll (1)	1 Bread
Margarine, regular* (1 tsp.)	1 Fat
Milk, 1% (1 cup)	1 Dairy
Angel Food Cake (1/12 of cake)	2 Optional

* *Additional Sodium:* 800 mg allowed
Added: 1 cup regular Corn Flakes (225 mg sodium)
2 tsp. regular Margarine (70 mg sodium)
¼ tsp. salt (500 mg sodium) in food preparation or at the table

Nutrient Analysis:
2,003 mg Sodium (includes 200 mg sodium from water)
1,576 Calories, distributed as follows:

23% Protein	26% Fat	177 mg Cholesterol
54% Carbohydrate	9% Saturated Fatty Acids	

(The amount of cholesterol is less than 300 mg because no eggs were included in this menu.)

SAMPLE MENU FOR THE STEP-ONE DIET—1,200 CALORIES

	Food Group Portions
BREAKFAST	
Fresh Strawberries (1¼ cup)	1 Fruit
Plain Low-fat Yogurt (1 cup)	1 Dairy
Raisin Bread Toast (1 slice)	1 Bread
Margarine, regular* (1 tsp.)	1 Fat
LUNCH (AT DELICATESSEN)	
Turkey Sandwich	
Turkey Breast, processed* (2 oz.)	2 Meats
Whole-Wheat Bread (2 slices)	2 Breads
Mayonnaise (2 tsp.)	1 Fat
Lettuce (1 leaf)	Free
Tomato (2 slices)	Free
Relishes	
Cherry Tomatoes (4)	1 Vegetable
Carrot Sticks (4)	1 Vegetable
Dill Pickle Spear* (6 in.)	Free
Fresh Bartlett Pear (1)	1 Fruit
DINNER	
Broiled Sirloin Steak (4 oz.)	4 Meats
Steak Sauce* (1 Tbsp.)	Free
Steamed Asparagus (6 spears)	1 Vegetable
Steamed Yellow Squash (½ cup)	1 Vegetable
Margarine, regular* (1 tsp.), on vegetables	1 Fat
Fresh Fruit Salad (Apples, Oranges, Grapes) (1 cup)	1 Fruit
Vanilla Frozen Yogurt (½ cup)	1 Dairy

* *Additional Sodium:* 1,050 mg allowed
Added: 2 tsp. regular Margarine (70 mg sodium)
2 oz. processed Turkey Breast (450 mg sodium)
1 6-in. long Dill Pickle Spear (450 mg sodium)
1 Tbsp. Steak Sauce (300 mg sodium)

Nutrient Analysis:
2,016 mg Sodium (includes 200 mg sodium from water)
1,229 Calories, distributed as follows:

25% Protein	29% Fat	142 mg Cholesterol
49% Carbohydrate	10% Saturated Fatty Acids	

(The amount of cholesterol is less than 300 mg because no eggs were included in this menu.)

THE STEP-TWO DIET

The Step-Two Diet is usually recommended for people who need to make additional changes in their eating plan to reach the blood cholesterol goal recommended by their physician. Since all of the foods suggested are prepared without salt, the Step-Two Diet is also low in sodium.

FOOD GROUPS

In this eating plan, as in the Step-One Diet, foods are grouped into seven categories according to the fat, carbohydrate, protein and calories they provide. The food groups are:

1. meat, poultry and seafood
2. eggs
3. dairy products
4. fats and oils
5. breads, cereals, pasta and starchy vegetables
6. vegetables and fruits
7. optional foods—desserts, sweets and alcohol

In three of these food groups (numbered above as 5, 6 and 7) the information is basically the same as it is in the Step-One Diet. The general changes you'll need to make in the other four food groups in the Step-Two Diet are:

1. meat, poultry and seafood: Choose the very leanest.
2. eggs: Limit egg yolks to one per week.
3. dairy products: Select nonfat products, skim milk and cheese with 2 grams of fat or less per ounce.
4. fats and oils: Use margarine and oils instead of shortening.

MEAT, POULTRY AND SEAFOOD

Since only the leanest foods in this group are included, 1-ounce portions average 22 milligrams sodium, 55 calories, 2 grams fat, 0.8 gram saturated fatty acids and 25 milligrams dietary cholesterol. To reduce the amount of saturated fatty acids and cholesterol in the meat group, this eating plan allows only the leanest cuts. Limit or avoid shrimp and organ meats because of their cholesterol content.

Eat no more than 6 ounces of very lean cooked meat, fish or poultry each day.

APPROPRIATE FOODS

SEAFOOD
All fresh and frozen fish
Crab, lobster, scallops, clams and oysters
Tuna or salmon (canned in water, unsalted)

POULTRY (WITHOUT SKIN)
Chicken
Cornish hen
Turkey, unprocessed or fresh-cooked (not pre-basted)

VEAL (TRIMMED OF VISIBLE FAT)
All cuts are lean except for veal cutlets.

BEEF (TRIMMED OF VISIBLE FAT)
USDA Select or Choice grades of lean beef,* such as round steak, sirloin tip and tenderloin

PORK (TRIMMED OF VISIBLE FAT)
Fresh pork, such as tenderloin and loin chops

LAMB (TRIMMED OF VISIBLE FAT)
Lamb chops
Lamb cubes for stew

WILD GAME
Venison
Rabbit
Squirrel
Pheasant (without skin)
Wild duck (without skin)

* To assure the leanest ground meat, select a lean cut such as round steak and have it ground.

SODIUM, FAT AND CHOLESTEROL INFORMATION

When selecting meat, poultry, and seafood, be careful to choose those most appropriate for your dietary plan. These hints will help you.

- Cured, processed and pickled foods are high in sodium. Examples include ham, Canadian bacon, turkey ham, pickled herring, processed turkey, processed beef and processed chicken.
- Many processed meats, such as luncheon meat, wieners and sausage, are high in sodium and saturated fatty acids.
- Pre-basted turkeys have fat and salt added. Ask your butcher to special-order an "unbasted" or fresh turkey for you.
- Most deli-type precooked turkey and roast beef have salt or sodium compounds added.
- Most canned meats, such as tuna, salmon and chicken, are packed with broth or added salt. Purchase unsalted canned meats or rinse regular canned meats with cold water to help decrease the sodium.
- Many precooked frozen and canned entrées are prepared with salt.
- "Prime" grade, heavily marbled and fatty meats are high in saturated fatty acids.
- Regular ground meat (even extra lean) has more fat than allowed in the Step-Two Diet. Select a lean meat cut, such as round steak, and have it trimmed and ground.
- Avoid all organ meats, since they are high in cholesterol.
- Shrimp and crayfish have about twice as much cholesterol as beef and chicken and should be avoided in the Step-Two Diet. Imitation shellfish (surimi) is high in sodium.

PORTION SIZE (COOKED MEAT)*	
CHICKEN	
½ breast	3 oz.
1 leg and thigh	3 oz.
FRESH PORK	
1 medium chop	3 oz.
LAMB	
2 small chops	3 oz.
BEEF	
1 piece cooked lean meat, about the size of a deck of cards	3 oz.
¾ cup diced meat	3 oz.
FISH	
¾ cup flaked	3 oz.

* Meat loses about 25% of its weight during cooking (for example, 4 oz. raw will be about 3 oz. cooked). Eat no more than 6 oz. cooked daily.

ABOUT FOOD PREPARATION

The way you prepare your food is important to the success of your eating plan. Use this information to learn the best ways possible.

- Rinse frozen fish packed in a salt or brine solution with water before using.
- Trim all visible fat from meat and remove skin from poultry before cooking.
- After cooking meat for a stew or soup, allow it to cool so the fat can rise to the top. Then remove the fat before adding vegetables and other ingredients.
- Preparing meat, poultry or seafood by frying, basting or sautéing adds extra fat. Remember to count this in your daily fat allowance.
- Dried beans, peas, lentils and soybean curd (tofu) are good sources of protein when eaten with low-fat dairy products. Small amounts of meat, fish or poultry can be combined with rice or pasta for a hearty entrée.

EGGS

To further reduce the amount of cholesterol and saturated fatty acids in your diet, limit egg yolks to 3 per week. One large whole egg contains 70 milligrams sodium, 79 calories, 5 grams fat, 2 grams saturated fatty acids and 213 to 220 milligrams cholesterol. If you like, supplement your diet with cholesterol-free egg substitutes. However, be sure to read the egg-substitute label to see if salt has been added to the product.

WHEN USING EGGS

Eggs can be part of a low-sodium, low-modified-fat, low-cholesterol diet. Just remember to eat no more than 3 yolks per week. Here are some tips to help you meet that goal.

- Prepare scrambled eggs, omelettes and the like so that only one egg yolk per portion is used. Add a few egg whites to the mixing bowl to make more generous servings.
- Many recipes contain egg yolk. To find out the approximate whole egg content of various prepared foods, see the chart on page 289.
- Substitute egg whites in recipes calling for whole eggs. For exam-

ple, you may use two egg whites instead of each whole egg in muffins, cookies, puddings and pie fillings.

- The following chart shows that egg substitutes without added salt, egg whites and whole eggs have similar sodium content.

Food	Amount	Sodium
Whole egg	1 egg	70 mg
Egg substitute	¼ cup	80 to 120 mg
Egg whites	2	100 mg

- Egg substitute with cheese is high in sodium and fat.
- To prepare omelettes with egg substitute or egg, use low-sodium ingredients such as green onions, mushrooms, fresh tomatoes or green bell pepper to add flavor.

DAIRY PRODUCTS

The dairy products in the Step-Two Diet contain less fat than those in Step-One, since the allowed amounts of fat and saturated fatty acids are lower. An average portion from this group has 117 milligrams sodium, 80 calories, 2 grams fat, 1 gram saturated fatty acids and 9 milligrams cholesterol. To further reduce the amount of saturated fatty acids you get from this food group, choose only skim milk, nonfat dairy products and cheese with 2 grams of fat or less per ounce.

PORTION SIZE	
MILK AND YOGURT	
Skim milk*	1 cup
Nonfat or low-fat plain yogurt	1 cup
CHEESE	
Unsalted low-fat or dry-curd cottage cheese	½ cup
Low-fat cheese; no more than 200 mg sodium and 2 grams fat per oz.	1 oz.
FROZEN DESSERTS	
Frozen low-fat yogurt	½ cup
Sherbet (See "Optional Foods," page 297)	

* 1% milk has 2.2 grams fat per cup more than skim milk. If skim milk is unacceptable to you, adjust the eating plan to allow 1% milk.

SODIUM, FAT AND CHOLESTEROL INFORMATION

Because of the wide variation among the many dairy products available, reading labels on these items is very important. These tips will help you select foods appropriate for your diet.

- Regular cheese, low-fat cheese and cottage cheese are high in sodium. Natural cheese is lower in sodium than processed cheese. Some supermarkets carry cheese reduced in both fat and sodium.
- Read the labels carefully because some low-fat dairy products are high in sodium, and some low-sodium products are high in fat.
- Select low-fat cheese with no more than 2 grams fat per ounce and no more than 150 milligrams sodium per ounce.
- Cream substitutes—nondairy coffee creamers, sour cream substitutes and whipped toppings—often contain coconut, palm or palm kernel oil and are therefore high in saturated fatty acids. Read labels carefully.

FATS AND OILS

An average portion from this group contains about 1 milligram sodium, 45 calories, 5 grams fat and less than 1 gram saturated fatty acids. To reduce saturated fatty acids, substitute margarine (stick or tub) for shortening.

SODIUM, FAT AND CHOLESTEROL INFORMATION

Cocoa butter, coconut, coconut oil, palm oil and palm kernel oil contain more saturated than unsaturated fatty acids. Look for these fats when you read package labels. Select only foods that contain 2 grams or less of saturated fat per tablespoon. (You might wish to refer to the list on page 278 for review.) Currently, information about monounsaturated fatty acids is not listed on the nutrition label.

ABOUT USING FATS AND OILS

Follow these guidelines for selecting appropriate fats and oils for this diet.

- If you eat one or more meals in restaurants every day, use unsalted margarine at home. This will help compensate for the high sodium content of restaurant food. If you don't eat out regularly, you may use regular margarine instead of unsalted margarine at home.

- To help you select appropriate margarines, read the labels. Try to select margarine that contains 2 grams or less of saturated fat per tablespoon. On the Step-Two Diet, avoid shortening, since it's higher in saturated fatty acids than are margarine and oil.
- Diet margarine has about twice as much sodium as does regular tub margarine.
- Many oil-free salad dressings are high in sodium, but oil-free, low-sodium varieties are available. Some low-sodium, low-fat salad dressings can be purchased in individual packets to use when eating out.

	PORTION SIZE
VEGETABLE OILS	
Safflower, corn, sunflower, soybean, olive, canola, peanut	1 tsp.
MARGARINE, UNSALTED	
Margarine containing 2 grams or less of saturated fat per tablespoon	1 tsp.
Diet margarine	2 tsp.
NUTS AND SEEDS, UNSALTED	
Chopped nuts, except coconut	1 Tbsp.
Seeds, any variety (without shells)	1 Tbsp.
SALAD DRESSINGS	
French, Italian, Thousand Island or mayonnaise-type salad dressing, unsalted	1 Tbsp.
Mayonnaise	2 tsp.
OTHER FATS	
Peanut butter, unsalted	2 tsp.
Avocado	⅛ medium

BREAD, CEREALS, PASTA AND STARCHY VEGETABLES

Foods in this group contain an average of 92 milligrams sodium, 80 calories, 1 gram of fat and negligible saturated fatty acid and cholesterol per portion. We have included low-fat, unsalted soups in this group. Whole-grain or enriched breads and cereals provide B vitamins and iron. They also provide protein and are a major source of this nutrient in vegetarian diets. Whole-grain products also contribute magnesium, folacin and fiber.

PORTION SIZE	
BREADS	
Bagel	½
Bread sticks, unsalted, 4 in. long, ½ in. diameter	2
Bread, white, whole-wheat, rye, oatmeal, pumpernickel	1 slice
Croutons, plain bread cubes	1 cup
English muffin	½
Hamburger or hot dog bun	½
Pita, 6 in. diameter	½
Roll, plain (1 oz.)	1
Tortilla, corn, 6 in. diameter	1
CEREALS, PASTA AND RICE	
Shredded wheat	1 biscuit or ½ cup
Flake-type cereal, ready-to-eat, unsalted	1 cup
Puffed cereal, unsalted	1½ cups
Cooked cereal, bulgur, grits (cooked in unsalted water)	½ cup
Pasta (cooked in unsalted water)	½ cup
Rice (cooked in unsalted water)	⅓ cup
CRACKERS	
Animal crackers	8
Graham crackers, 2½ in. square	3
Matzo, 4 x 6 in.	¾ oz.
Melba toast, unsalted	5 slices
Popcorn (popped, no salt or fat added)	3 cups
Pretzels, unsalted	¾ oz.
Saltine-type crackers, unsalted tops	6
STARCHY VEGETABLES (FRESH, FROZEN OR CANNED WITHOUT SALT)	
Baked beans	¼ cup
Corn	½ cup
Corn on cob, 6 in. long	1
Dried beans, peas, lentils	⅓ cup
Green peas	½ cup
Lima beans	½ cup
Potato, baked (3 oz.)	1
Potato, mashed, no salt added	½ cup
Squash, acorn or butternut	¾ cup
Sweet potato or yam	⅓ cup
COMMERCIAL SOUPS, UNSALTED, PREPARED WITH WATER*	
Bouillon, broth, consommé	As desired
Chicken noodle, gazpacho, minestrone, onion, tomato, vegetarian	1 cup
Beef noodle, chicken rice, chunky-style turkey noodle, oyster stew, split pea (may use milk allowance)	¾ cup

* Homemade soups low in fat may be counted as the same amount of a similar commercial soup.

QUICK BREADS** (1 SERVING = 1 BREAD + 1 FAT)	
Banana bread (16 slices per loaf)	1 slice
Biscuit (2 in. diameter)	1
Cornbread muffin	1
Pancake (4 in. diameter)	1
Waffle (9 in. diameter)	¼

** Prepared with low-sodium baking powder, skim milk, unsaturated oil, unsalted margarine, egg substitute or egg white. Omit salt from the recipe. If you use a whole egg, count it as part of the egg allowance.

Note: Most commercial biscuits, muffins, pancakes and croissants are high in sodium and are not made with the recommended fats.

SODIUM, FAT AND CHOLESTEROL INFORMATION

The following information will help you select and prepare appropriate foods from this group.

- If you eat more than one meal away from home daily, use unsalted bread at home. This helps make up for the high sodium content of restaurant food.
- Regular canned or dehydrated varieties of soup are high in sodium. A low-sodium soup should have no more than 2 grams of fat per cup.
- If you use skim milk to prepare soup, count ½ cup milk per 1 cup soup as part of the dairy allowance.
- Cream soup in restaurants is usually prepared with salt and whole milk or cream.
- Most ready-to-eat cereals are high in sodium. Read the labels to find low-sodium varieties, such as shredded wheat, puffed rice and puffed wheat.
- Cook hot cereal, pasta, rice and vegetables without salt added to the water.
- Individually portioned instant hot cereals, rice mixes and pasta mixes are high in sodium.

ABOUT FOOD PREPARATION

The following tips will help you prepare foods in this group.

- Homemade biscuits, muffins, cornbread, banana bread, soft rolls, pancakes, French toast and waffles should be prepared with the egg yolk allowance (3 per week), egg substitute or egg whites; skim milk; and unsaturated oil or unsalted margarine. Omit salt, baking powder and baking soda from the recipe and replace them with low-sodium baking powder. You may need to use more of the low-sodium baking powder than the regular to get the same effect in a recipe; read the label.

- Check the dietetic or "special" foods section of your supermarket for low-sodium mixes for pancakes and other products.
- You can stretch your meat allowance by combining meat, poultry or seafood with rice, pasta or vegetables.

VEGETABLES AND FRUITS

An average portion of vegetables has about 13 milligrams sodium and 25 calories. An average portion of fruit has about 1 milligram sodium and 60 calories. Nearly all vegetables and fruits are low in fat, and none contain cholesterol.

Vegetables and fruits are important sources of vitamins A and C and fiber. Dark green and deep yellow vegetables are good sources of vitamin A. Most dark green vegetables, if not overcooked, are important sources of vitamin C, as are citrus fruits (oranges, grapefruit, tangerines and lemons), melons, berries and tomatoes. Dark green vegetables are also valued for riboflavin, folacin, iron and magnesium. Certain greens—collards, kale, mustard, turnip and dandelion—provide calcium.

PORTION SIZE	
VEGETABLES	
Most vegetables	½ cup raw or cooked
Raw cabbage, Chinese cabbage, celery, cucumbers, mushrooms, green onions, peppers, radishes and zucchini	Quantities as desired (negligible fat and calories)
SALAD GREENS	
Endive, escarole, lettuce, romaine and spinach	Quantities as desired (negligible fat and calories)
FRUIT AND JUICE	
Fruit	½ cup or 1 medium-size piece of fresh fruit
Fruit juice	½ cup

WHEN USING VEGETABLES AND FRUITS

When selecting and preparing foods from this group, use this information to help you get the nutrition you want.

- Fresh, frozen and unsalted canned vegetables are low in sodium. Select those that don't have seasoning or sauce added.
- Regular canned vegetables, tomato sauce, tomato paste, tomato puree, tomato juice and vegetable juice cocktail are high in sodium. Use the unsalted variety.
- Sauerkraut, pickles and pickled vegetables are high in sodium.
- Vegetables and fruits have no fat, except for avocados and olives. (These are listed under "Fats and Oils—Portion Size" on page 292.)
- Vegetables prepared with butter, cream or cheese are high in fat.
- Fried vegetables have several times more fat and calories than vegetables prepared without fat.
- Fresh fruits and fruits canned in water are lower in calories than fruits canned in juice or in syrup. Drain fruits canned in syrup.

OPTIONAL FOODS—DESSERTS, SWEETS AND ALCOHOL

Each homemade dessert (cakes, cookies and pies) listed on page 318 has about 22 milligrams sodium, 285 calories and 6 to 10 grams fat. The amounts listed count as *two* portions of Optional Foods.

Each of the "sweets" on this list contains about 22 milligrams of sodium, 75 calories and 0 to 1 gram of fat. Each count as *one* portion of Optional Foods.

One portion of any alcoholic beverage listed on the following page contains 9 milligrams sodium, ½ ounce ethanol and 90 to 150 calories. Count each as *one* portion of Optional Foods.

ABOUT DESSERTS, SWEETS AND SNACKS

This information can help you select and prepare these foods.

- Desserts (cakes, pies, cookies and puddings) may be made with low-sodium baking powder, unsalted margarine or unsaturated oil, skim milk, allowed eggs, egg substitute or egg whites. Omit salt from recipe. If you use a whole egg, count it as part of the egg allowance.

PORTION SIZE	
DESSERTS*	
2-layer cake, frosted (1/12 of cake)	1 slice
Sheet cake, frosted (2¼ × 2½ × 1½-in. piece or 1/20 of 9 × 13-in. cake)	1 piece
Cupcake, frosted (average size)	1
Oatmeal raisin cookies	4
Double-crust fruit pie (⅛ of 9-in. pie)	1 slice
SWEETS	
Carbonated beverage (sweetened)**	6 fl. oz.
Lemonade (sweetened)	6 fl. oz.
Candy made primarily with sugar (e.g., candy corn, gum drops, mints and hard candy)	¾ oz.
Angel food cake (1/24 of cake)	1 slice
Gingersnaps	2
Fruit ice	⅓ cup
Sherbet	⅓ cup
Fruit-flavored gelatin (sweetened)	½ cup
Sugar, syrup, honey, jam, preserves or marmalade	1½ Tbsp.
Fig bar	1
ALCOHOLIC BEVERAGES	
Beer	12 fl. oz.
80-proof spirits (bourbon, gin, rum, Scotch, tequila, vodka, whiskey)	1½ fl. oz.
Wine, red or white	4 fl. oz.

* Homemade, prepared according to the first tip listed on page 317.
** Be sure the beverage is low in sodium—read the label.

- Many snack products, such as chips and rich crackers, are high in sodium and saturated fatty acids. However, some chips are cooked in unsaturated oil and are not salted. Choose only those labeled as "no salt added" and that contain more polyunsaturated than saturated fatty acids.
- A few types of cookies are low in fat, such as fig bars and gingersnaps. Plain angel food cake has no fat. If you are uncertain, read the label and choose only those with 2 grams of fat or less per portion.

FREE FOODS

One portion of these foods and drinks contains less than 20 calories and no fat. You don't need to limit those items that have no portion size specified.

PORTION SIZE	
DRINKS	
Bouillon or broth without fat, low-sodium	
Diet carbonated drinks *	1 per day
Carbonated water	
Cocoa powder, unsweetened	1 Tbsp.
Coffee/tea	
Drink mixes, sugar-free	
Tonic water, sugar-free	
SWEET SUBSTITUTES *	
Candy, hard, sugar-free	
Gelatin, sugar-free	
Gum, sugar-free	
Jam/jelly, sugar-free	2 tsp.
Pancake syrup, sugar-free	
Sugar substitutes (saccharin or aspartame)	
FRUITS	
Cranberries, unsweetened	½ cup
Rhubarb, unsweetened	½ cup
CONDIMENTS	
Ketchup, low-sodium	1 Tbsp.
Horseradish, freshly grated	
Mustard, low-sodium	
Pickles, dill, unsweetened, low-sodium	
Salad dressing, oil-free, low-sodium	
Vinegar	

* Sweet substitutes are listed for the benefit of those following diabetic diets.

EATING PLANS FOR CALORIE LEVELS HIGHER THAN 2,500 CALORIES

If you eat more than 2,500 calories a day, you can easily get more than 2,000 milligrams of sodium daily. If so, limit your intake of sodium by using all unsalted products, including unsalted bread and bread products. Be careful also to limit the sodium in the food you eat away from home.

YOUR DAILY EATING PLAN IN PORTIONS

Planning your meals to lower total fat, saturated fatty acids, dietary cholesterol and sodium will be easier if you plot them on a chart. The chart on page 321 shows a sample eating plan for a person on the

Step-Two Diet at 2,000 calories per day. Spreading the allowable portions listed below over all meals and snacks during the day, the chart reflects the daily numbers of portions allowed for each food group. Use the blank form on page 322 to chart your daily eating plan.

The sample menus that follow the chart are examples of how the Step-Two eating plan may be used. They include a variety of foods that can be eaten at home or in restaurants.

SAMPLE EATING PLANS: STEP-TWO DIET*

	Daily Portions			
Food Group	**2,500 Calories**	**2,000 Calories**	**1,600 Calories**	**1,200 Calories**
Meat, Poultry and Seafood (unsalted)	6 oz.	6 oz.	6 oz.	6 oz.
Eggs, whole (unsalted)	1/week	1/week	1/week	1/week
Dairy Products (unsalted)	3	2	2	3
Fats and Oils (unsalted)	8	7	5	2
Breads, Cereals, Pasta and Starchy Vegetables (unsalted)	10	8	5	4
Vegetables (unsalted)	5	4	4	4
Fruits	7	4	3	3
Optional Foods (unsalted)	2	2	2	0
Sodium from Food Groups, mg	1,520	1,201	922	798
Sodium from Water, mg	200	200	200	200
Additional Sodium,** mg	+250	+550	+850	+1,000
Total Sodium	1,970 mg	1,951 mg	1,972 mg	1,998 mg

* Your physician or dietitian can recommend an appropriate calorie plan. Sample eating plans for the Step-One Diet are on pages 285–306.

**Additional Sodium: A specific amount of sodium can be added to each of the eating plans. This "additional sodium" can be in the form of:

- Salt added at the table or in food preparation (home only)
  ¼ tsp. salt = 500 mg sodium
  ½ tsp. salt = 1,000 mg sodium
- Restaurant foods, see page 282–283

Your Daily Eating Plan in Portions*—Step-Two Diet

Calories 2,000 **Fat <30%** **Saturated fat <7%** **Cholesterol <200 mg** **Sodium 2,000 mg**

	Meat, Poultry & Seafood	Eggs	Dairy Products	Fats & Oils	Bread, Cereal & Starchy Vegetables	Vegetables	Fruit	Optional
Breakfast			1	1	2		1	
Snack								
Lunch	2 oz.			3	2	2	1	
Snack								
Dinner	4 oz.		1	3	3	2	1	2
Bedtime Snack					1		1	

* A blank form is provided on page 322 for your use. < = Less than.

Your Daily Eating Plan in Portions—Step-Two Diet

Calories _____ **Fat** _____ **Saturated fat** _____ **Cholesterol** _____ **Sodium** _____

	Meat, Poultry & Seafood	Eggs	Dairy Products	Fats & Oils	Bread, Cereal & Starchy Vegetables	Vegetables	Fruit	Optional
Breakfast								
Snack								
Lunch								
Snack								
Dinner								
Bedtime Snack								

SAMPLE MENU FOR THE STEP-TWO DIET—2,500 CALORIES

	Food Group Portions
BREAKFAST	
Apple Juice (1 cup)	2 Fruits
Shredded Wheat (1 cup) with	2 Breads
Sliced Banana (1)	2 Fruits
Milk, skim (1 cup)	1 Dairy
Whole-Wheat Toast (2 slices)	2 Breads
Margarine, unsalted (2 tsp.)	2 Fats
LUNCH	
Grilled Chicken Sandwich	
Grilled Chicken Breast (3 oz.)	3 Meats
Kaiser Roll (1 medium)	2 Breads
Mayonnaise (2 tsp.)	1 Fat
Lettuce (1 leaf), Tomato (2 slices)	Free
Corn on the Cob (6 in.)	1 Bread
Margarine, unsalted (1 tsp.), on corn	1 Fat
Tomato Wedges (1 tomato) and	1 Vegetable
Green Pepper Strips (½ pepper) in	Free
French Salad Dressing, unsalted (1 Tbsp.)	1 Fat
Fresh Bartlett Pear (1)	1 Fruit
Milk, skim (1 cup)	1 Dairy
DINNER	
Beef Shish Kabob	
Sirloin Steak (3 oz.)	3 Meats
Cherry Tomatoes (4)	1 Vegetable
Onion Wedges (1 small onion)	1 Vegetable
Mushrooms, fresh (4)	Free
White Rice, unsalted (⅔ cup) with	2 Breads
Margarine, unsalted (1 tsp.)	1 Fat
Steamed Green Beans (1 cup)	2 Vegetables
Margarine, unsalted (1 tsp.), on Green Beans	1 Fat
Fresh Strawberries (1¼ cups) and Pineapple Chunks, canned in juice (⅓ cup)	2 Fruits
Pumpernickel Bread (1 slice)	1 Bread
Margarine, unsalted (1 tsp.)	1 Fat
Milk, skim (1 cup)	1 Dairy
Oatmeal Cookies (4 cookies)	2 Optional

Additional Sodium: 250 mg allowed
Added: ⅛ teaspoon salt (250 mg sodium) in food preparation or at the table.

Nutrient Analysis:
1,941 mg Sodium (includes 200 mg sodium from water)
2,530 Calories, distributed as follows:

18% Protein	25% Fat	163 mg Cholesterol
60% Carbohydrate	5% Saturated Fatty Acids	

(The amount of cholesterol is less than 200 mg because no eggs were included in this menu.)

SAMPLE MENU FOR THE STEP-TWO DIET—2,000 CALORIES

	Food Group Portions
BREAKFAST	
Orange Juice (½ cup)	1 Fruit
Egg Substitute (equivalent to 1 egg) with Margarine, unsalted (1 tsp.)	1 Fat
Bagel (1 medium)	2 Breads
Margarine, unsalted (1 tsp.)	1 Fat
Cream of Wheat, unsalted (½ cup), with	1 Bread
Raisins (2 Tbsp.)	1 Fruit
Milk, skim (1 cup)	1 Dairy
LUNCH	
Roast Beef Pita Sandwich	
Roast Beef (2 oz.)	2 Meats
Pita Bread (1 medium)	2 Breads
Mayonnaise (2 tsp.)	1 Fat
Lettuce (1 leaf)	Free
Tomato (2 slices)	Free
Tossed Salad	
Lettuce (1 cup)	Free
Tomato Wedges (1 tomato)	1 Vegetable
Grated Carrots (½ cup)	1 Vegetable
French Salad Dressing, unsalted (2 Tbsp.)	2 Fats
Bread Sticks, unsalted (2)	1 Bread
Fresh Peach (1)	1 Fruit
Vanilla Frozen Yogurt (½ cup)	1 Dairy
DINNER	
Broiled Salmon (4 oz.) with Dill and	4 Meats
Margarine, unsalted (1 tsp.)	1 Fat
Steamed Broccoli and Cauliflower (1 cup)	2 Vegetables
Steamed Corn (½ cup)	1 Bread
Watermelon, cubed (1¼ cups)	1 Fruit
Whole-Wheat Dinner Roll (1)	1 Bread
Margarine, unsalted (1 tsp.)	1 Fat
Apple Pie (⅛ of 9-in. pie)	2 Optional

Additional Sodium: 550 mg allowed
Added: ¼ teaspoon salt (500 mg sodium) in food preparation or at the table

Nutrient Analysis:
1,929 mg Sodium (includes 200 mg sodium from water)
2,008 Calories, distributed as follows:

19% Protein	29% Fat	167 mg Cholesterol
54% Carbohydrate	6% Saturated Fatty Acids	

(The amount of cholesterol is less than 200 mg because no eggs were included in this menu.)

SAMPLE MENU FOR THE STEP-TWO DIET—1,600 CALORIES

	Food Group Portions
BREAKFAST	
Canteloupe, cubed (1 cup)	1 Fruit
Corn Flakes, unsalted (1 cup) with	1 Bread
Fresh Strawberries (1¼ cups)	1 Fruit
Milk, skim (1 cup)	1 Dairy
Whole-Wheat Toast (1 slice)	1 Bread
Margarine, unsalted (1 tsp.)	1 Fat
LUNCH (AT DELICATESSEN)	
Turkey Sandwich	
Turkey Breast, processed* (3 oz.)	3 Meats
Whole-Wheat Bread (2 slices)	2 Breads
Mayonnaise (2 tsp.)	1 Fat
Lettuce (1 leaf)	Free
Tomato (2 slices)	Free
Tossed Salad	
Lettuce (1 cup)	Free
Tomato Wedges (1 tomato)	1 Vegetable
French Salad Dressing* (2 Tbsp.)	2 Fats
Fresh Apple (1)	1 Fruit
DINNER	
Roast beef (3 oz.)	3 Meats
New Potatoes (½ cup) with Parsley and	1 Bread
Margarine, unsalted (1 tsp.)	1 Fat
Steamed Green Beans (½ cup)	1 Vegetable
Steamed Carrots (cup)	1 Vegetable
Green Salad	
Romaine Lettuce (1 cup)	Free
Tomato Wedges (1 tomato)	1 Vegetable
Vinegar	Free
Milk, skim (1 cup)	1 Dairy
Orange Sherbet (⅔ cup)	2 Optional

* *Additional Sodium:* 850 mg allowed
Added: 3 oz. processed Turkey Breast (360 mg sodium)
2 Tbsp. regular French Dressing (150 mg sodium)

Nutrient Analysis:
1,954 mg Sodium
1,592 Calories, distributed as follows:

21% Protein	25% Fat	152 mg Cholesterol
57% Carbohydrate	6% Saturated Fatty Acids	

(The amount of cholesterol is less than 200 mg because no eggs were included in this menu.)

SAMPLE MENU FOR THE STEP-TWO DIET—1,200 CALORIES

	Food Group Portions
BREAKFAST	
Fresh Blueberries (1 cup)	1 Fruit
Plain Nonfat Yogurt (1 cup)	1 Dairy
English Muffin (1)	2 Breads
Margarine, unsalted (1 tsp.)	1 Fat
LUNCH	
Tossed Salad	
Lettuce (2 cups)	Free
Tomato Wedges (1 tomato)	1 Vegetable
Grated Carrots (½ cup)	1 Vegetable
Vinegar	Free
Bread Sticks, unsalted (2)	1 Bread
Fresh Grapes (15)	1 Fruit
Milk, skim (1 cup)	1 Dairy
DINNER (AT RESTAURANT)	
Grilled Half Chicken* (6 oz.)	6 Meats
Broccoli Spears* (3)	1 Vegetable
Margarine (1 tp.), used in preparation of broccoli	1 Fat
Tossed Salad	
Lettuce (1 cup)	Free
Tomato Wedges (1 tomato)	1 Vegetable
French Salad Dressing* (1 Tbsp.)	1 Fat
White Roll (1)	1 Bread
Fresh Strawberries (1¼ cups)	1 Fruit

* *Additional Sodium:* 1,000 mg allowed
Added: 6 oz. Chicken (breast, thigh and drumstick) prepared with salt, skin removed after cooking (500 mg sodium)
½ cup frozen Broccoli prepared with salt (250 mg sodium)
1 Tbsp. regular French Dressing (225 mg sodium)

Nutrient Analysis:
1,945 mg Sodium
1,226 Calories, distributed as follows:

29% Protein	22% Fat	165 mg Cholesterol
51% Carbohydrate	6% Saturated Fatty Acids	

(The amount of cholesterol is less than 200 mg because no eggs were included in this menu.)

APPENDIX B

Herb, Spice and Seasoning Guide

Dips	Caraway, dill, garlic, oregano, parsley, freshly ground black pepper
Soups and Stews	
Bean soup	Dry mustard powder
Vegetable soup	Sugar, vinegar
Skim milk chowders	Bay leaf,* peppercorns
Pea soup	Bay leaf,* coriander, fresh parsley
Stews	Basil, bay leaf,* cayenne, chervil, chili powder, cinnamon, cumin, curry, fennel, garlic, ginger, marjoram, nutmeg, onion, parsley, saffron
Various	Basil, bay leaf,* burnet, cayenne, chervil, chili powder, cloves, curry, dill, garlic, ginger, marjoram, mint, mustard, nutmeg, onion, oregano, parsley, freshly ground black pepper, rosemary, sage, savory, sesame, tarragon, thyme, watercress
Salads	Basil, burnet, chervil, coriander, dill, fresh lemon juice, mint, fresh mushrooms, mustard, oregano, parsley, freshly ground black pepper, rosemary, sage, savory, sesame seeds, turmeric, vinegar, watercress
Meat, Fish and Poultry	
Fish and seafood	Allspice, basil, bay leaf,* cayenne, curry powder, cumin, fennel, garlic, green bell pepper, fresh lemon juice, mace, marjoram, mint, fresh mushrooms, Dijon mustard, dry mustard powder, green onion, paprika, saffron, sage, sesame, tarragon, thyme, turmeric, white wine

* Always remove bay leaf from dish before serving.

Poultry	Basil, bay leaf,* cinnamon, curry powder, garlic, green bell pepper, fresh lemon juice, mace, marjoram, fresh mushrooms, onion, paprika, fresh parsley, lemon pepper, poultry seasoning, rosemary, saffron, sage, savory, sesame, thyme, tarragon, white wine
Game	Bay leaf,* garlic, fresh lemon juice, fresh mushrooms, onion, rosemary, sage, savory, tarragon, thyme, vinegar
Beef	Allspice, bay leaf,* cayenne, cumin, curry powder, garlic, green bell pepper, marjoram, fresh mushrooms, dry mustard, nutmeg, onion, freshly ground black pepper, rosemary, sage, thyme, red wine
Pork	Apple, applesauce, cinnamon, cloves, fennel, garlic, mint, onion, sage, savory, red wine
Lamb	Curry powder, garlic, mint, mint jelly, onion, pineapple, rosemary, sage, savory, sesame, red wine
Veal	Apricot, bay leaf,* curry powder, ginger, fresh lemon juice, marjoram, mint, fresh mushrooms, oregano, saffron, sage, savory, tarragon, white wine
Various	Cayenne, chervil, chili powder, coriander, curry powder, dill, garlic, ginger, marjoram, onion, oregano, parsley, freshly ground black pepper
VEGETABLES	
Asparagus	Garlic, fresh lemon juice, onion, vinegar
Beans	Caraway, cloves, cumin, mint, savory, tarragon, thyme
Beets	Anise, caraway, fennel, ginger, savory
Carrots	Anise, cinnamon, cloves, mint, sage, tarragon
Corn	Allspice, green bell pepper, pimiento, fresh tomato
Cucumbers	Chives, dill, garlic, vinegar
Green Beans	Dill, fresh lemon juice, marjoram, nutmeg, pimiento
Greens	Garlic, fresh lemon juice, onion, vinegar
Peas	Allspice, green bell pepper, mint, fresh mushrooms, onions, fresh parsley, sage, savory
Potatoes	Chives, dill, green bell pepper, onion, pimiento, saffron
Squash	Allspice, brown sugar, cinnamon, cloves, fennel, ginger, mace, nutmeg, onion, savory
Tomatoes	Allspice, basil, garlic, marjoram, onion, oregano, sage, savory, tarragon, thyme
Various	Basil, burnet, cayenne, chervil, dill, marjoram, mint, fresh mushrooms, nutmeg, oregano, parsley, freshly ground black pepper, poppy seeds, rosemary, sage, sesame seeds, sunflower seeds, tarragon, thyme, turmeric, watercress

* Always remove bay leaf from dish before serving.

BAKED GOODS	
Breads	Anise, caraway, cardamom, fennel, poppy seeds, sesame seeds
Desserts	Anise, caraway, cardamom, cinnamon, cloves, coriander, fennel, ginger, mace, mint, nutmeg, poppy seeds, sesame seeds
FRUITS	Allspice, anise, basil, cardamom, cinnamon, cloves, cumin, curry, ginger, mint, nutmeg, poppy seeds, rosemary, watercress
EGGS	Basil, chervil, chili powder, cumin, curry, fennel, marjoram, mustard, oregano, parsley, freshly ground black pepper, poppy seeds, rosemary, saffron, savory, sesame seeds, tarragon, thyme, turmeric, watercress

APPENDIX C

American Heart Association Affiliates

American Heart Association
National Center
Dallas, TX

American Heart Association
Alabama Affiliate, Inc.
Birmingham, AL

American Heart Association
Alaska Affiliate, Inc.
Anchorage, AK

American Heart Association
Arizona Affiliate, Inc.
Phoenix, AZ

American Heart Association
Arkansas Affiliate, Inc.
Little Rock, AR

American Heart Association
California Affiliate, Inc.
Burlingame, CA

American Heart Association of
Metropolitan Chicago, Inc.
Chicago, IL

American Heart Association of
Colorado, Inc.
Denver, CO

American Heart Association
Connecticut Affiliate, Inc.
Wallingford, CT

American Heart Association
Dakota Affiliate, Inc.
Jamestown, ND

American Heart Association
of Delaware, Inc.
Wilmington, DE

American Heart Association
Florida Affiliate, Inc.
St. Petersburg, FL

American Heart Association
Georgia Affiliate, Inc.
Marietta, GA

American Heart Association
Hawaii Affiliate, Inc.
Honolulu, HI

American Heart Association of
Idaho, Inc.
Boise, ID

American Heart Association
Illinois Affiliate, Inc.
Springfield, IL

American Heart Association
Indiana Affiliate, Inc.
Indianapolis, IN

American Heart Association
Iowa Affiliate, Inc.
Des Moines, IA

American Heart Association
Kansas Affiliate, Inc.
Topeka, KS

American Heart Association
Kentucky Affiliate, Inc.
Louisville, KY

American Heart Association
Greater Los Angeles Affiliate, Inc.
Los Angeles, CA

American Heart Association
Louisiana, Inc.
Destrehan, LA

American Heart Association
Maine Affiliate, Inc.
Augusta, ME

American Heart Association
Maryland Affiliate, Inc.
Baltimore, MD

American Heart Association
Massachusetts Affiliate, Inc.
Needham Heights, MA

American Heart Association of
Michigan, Inc.
Lathrup Village, MI

American Heart Association
Minnesota Affiliate, Inc.
Minneapolis, MN

American Heart Association
Mississippi Affiliate, Inc.
Jackson, MS

American Heart Association
Missouri Affiliate, Inc.
Columbia, MO

American Heart Association
Montana Affiliate, Inc.
Great Falls, MT

American Heart Association
Nation's Capital Affiliate, Inc.
Washington, DC

American Heart Association
Nebraska Affiliate, Inc.
Omaha, NE

American Heart Association
Nevada Affiliate, Inc.
Las Vegas, NV

American Heart Association
New Hampshire Affiliate, Inc.
Manchester, NH

American Heart Association
New Jersey Affiliate, Inc.
North Brunswick, NJ

American Heart Association
New Mexico Affiliate, Inc.
Albuquerque, NM

American Heart Association
New York City Affiliate, Inc.
New York City, NY

American Heart Association
New York State Affiliate, Inc.
North Syracuse, NY

American Heart Association
North Carolina Affiliate, Inc.
Chapel Hill, NC

American Heart Association
Northeast Ohio Affiliate, Inc.
Cleveland, OH

American Heart Association
Ohio Affiliate, Inc.
Columbus, OH

American Heart Association
Oklahoma Affiliate, Inc.
Oklahoma City, OK

American Heart Association
Oregon Affiliate, Inc.
Portland, OR

American Heart Association
Pennsylvania Affiliate, Inc.
Harrisburg, PA

Puerto Rico Heart Association, Inc.
Hato Rey, Puerto Rico

American Heart Association
Rhode Island Affiliate, Inc.
Pawtucket, RI

American Heart Association
South Carolina Affiliate, Inc.
Columbia, SC

American Heart Association
Southeastern Pennsylvania Affiliate, Inc.
Philadelphia, PA

American Heart Association
Tennessee Affiliate, Inc.
Nashville, TN

American Heart Association
Texas Affiliate, Inc.
Austin, TX

American Heart Association
Utah Affiliate, Inc.
Salt Lake City, UT

American Heart Association
Vermont Affiliate, Inc.
Williston, VT

American Heart Association
Virginia Affiliate, Inc.
Glen Allen, VA

American Heart Association
Washington Affiliate, Inc.
Seattle, WA

American Heart Association
West Virginia Affiliate, Inc.
Charleston, WV

American Heart Association
Wisconsin Affiliate, Inc.
Milwaukee, WI

American Heart Association of
Wyoming, Inc.
Cheyenne, WY

APPENDIX D

FOR MORE INFORMATION

American Heart Association
7320 Greenville Avenue
Dallas, TX 75231

The American Heart Association Low-Fat, Low-Cholesterol Cookbook
Times Books

"About High Blood Pressure"
American Heart Association

"Dining Out: A Guide to Restaurant Dining"
American Heart Association

"Facts About Potassium"
American Heart Association

"Salt, Sodium and Blood Pressure"
American Heart Association

INDEX

A

alcohol:
  about, 272, 317
  portion sizes for step-one diet (table), 297
  portion sizes for step-two diet (table), 318
ambrosia, 65
American Heart Association:
  address, 333
  affiliates, 330–32
analyses, recipe, 26–27
angel food cake, 217
appetizers, *see* snacks
apple(s):
  crisp, 236
  filled crepes, 227
  pie, 233
  in Waldorf salad, 64
applesauce cake, 216
arroz con pollo (chicken with rice), 110–11

B

baked beans, 160
baked custard, 241
baked pears, 237
baked tomatoes, 157
baking, 17
banana:
  bread, 206
  crepes, 228
    with powdered sugar (variation), 228
    with yogurt and nutmeg (variation), 229
barbecue sauce, 186
basic salad dressing I, 74
basic salad dressing II, 75
basic white bread, 196–97
bean and sprout salad (variation), 56
bean sprouts:
  and bean salad (variation), 56
beans, green:
  and corn, 162
  sweet and sour, 161
  in three-bean salad, 56
beans, kidney:
  in three-bean salad, 56
beans, lima:
  in succotash, 162
beans, navy:
  baked, 160
beans, yellow:
  in three-bean salad, 56
beef:
  appropriate, for step-one diet (table), 286
  appropriate, for step-two diet (table), 308
  bourguignon, 124

beef (*cont'd*)
broth, 43
chili, 128
goulash, 130
meat loaf, 129
in meat sauce, spaghetti with, 132
portion sizes for step-one diet (table), 287
portion sizes for step-two diet (table), 309
roast, peppered, 125
seasonings for, 328
steak, lime marinated, 127
stroganoff, 126–27
in tacos, soft, 131
vegetable soup, 44
beverages:
about, 15
portion sizes for step-one diet (table), 298
portion sizes for step-two diet (table), 319
see also alcohol
biscuits, 202
drop, 202
herb-seasoned, 202
see also muffins; rolls
black-eyed pea salad (Texas caviar), 57
blood cholesterol, *see* cholesterol, blood
blood pressure:
and dietary factors affecting, 268–73
measurement, 4
measuring, 267
see also blood pressure, high
blood pressure, high, vii-viii, 4, 267
and bringing under control, 4
blueberry:
crisp (variation), 237
muffins, 204
pancakes (variation), 208
pie (variation), 232
bouillon, *see* broth
braising, 17–18
bread(s), 195–211
about, 12–13, 195
baking tips for, 295, 315–16
banana, 206
basic white, 196–97
cinnamon, 200
corn, 203
in croutons, seasoned, 211
dough; raising, 195
ginger, 207
herb, 199
portion sizes for step-one diet (table), 294, 295
portion sizes for step-two diet (table), 314, 315
raisin, 199
rye, 198
seasonings for, 329
shopping tips for, 293, 315
and step-one diet, 293–95
and step-two diet, 313–16
Swedish, 200
whole-wheat, 198
see also biscuits; muffins; rolls
bread-and-butter pickles, 256
broiling, 18
broth:
beef, 43
chicken, 42
substitutions for, 23
see also soups
brown rice, *see* rice
brownies, 245
butter:
substitutions for, 24
butterscotch pudding (variation), 243

C

cabbage:
coleslaw
creamy, 62
pineapple, 63
stir-fried, with noodles, 159
cakes:
angel food, 217
applesauce, 216
carrot, 221
chocolate, 218–19
chocolate pudding, Denver, 220
gingerbread, 207
and quick frosting for, 219
calcium, 273
in dairy products (table), 291
California onion dip, 262
calories:
and checking product labels for, 8
canned fruit cobbler (variation), 240–41
cardiovascular disease:
risk factors, 266–68
carrot(s):
cake, 221
gingered, 154
in rice and vegetable pilaf, 174
casseroles:
cooking tips for, 21
tuna-macaroni, 94–95
catfish fillets, Southern, 91
cauliflower, sautéed, 158
cereals:
about, 12, 13
portion sizes for step-one diet (table), 294
portion sizes for step-two diet (table), 314
shopping tips for, 293, 315
and step-one diet, 293–95
and step-two diet, 313–16
cheese blintzes, 147
cheese, cottage:
blintzes, 147
in mock cream cheese, 261
in mock sour cream, 178
cheese, cream:
mock, 261
substitution for, 24
cherry pie, 232
chicken:
à l'orange, 104
in arroz con pollo, 110–11
broth, 42
cacciatore, 111
Dijon, 105
enchiladas, 112–13
with ginger and snow peas, 114
golden baked, 100
lemon-baked, 101
lemon-barbecued, 115
marengo, 109
mushroom and herb dressing for, 164
oven-fried, 103
paprikash, 107
portion sizes for step-one diet (table), 287
portion sizes for step-two diet (table), 309
primavera, 108
with rice, 110–11
roast, 102
salad, 67
Hawaiian, 68
skinning, 20
in stuffed mushrooms, 253
Tuscany, 113
with yogurt-cilantro sauce, 106
see also turkey
chili, 128
vegetarian, 146
chili dip, 263
chili powder, 37
chili sauce, 183

chilies:
and releasing flavor from, 21
chocolate:
baking, substitutions for, 24
cake, 218–19
pudding (variation), 242
pudding cake; Denver, 220
sauce, 191
cholesterol, blood:
categories (table), 268
and dietary factors affecting, 273–76
and dietary factors that help lower, 268
high (hypercholesterolemia), 267–68
measuring, 267–68
see also cholesterol, dietary
cholesterol, dietary, 276
and checking product labels for, 8
and foods high in (table), 278
see also cholesterol, blood
chowders, *see* soups
chunky tomato sauce, 185
cinnamon:
bread, 200
rolls, 201
citrus:
chiffon, 235
juice, 21–22
zest, 21
see also individual names
cod fillets supreme, 87
coleslaw:
creamy, 62
pineapple, 63
condiments:
portion sizes for step-one diet (table), 299
portion sizes for step-two diet (table), 319
see also sauces; *individual names*
cookies:
brownies, 245
date rounds, 225
oatmeal, 222
peanut butter, 223
pralines, 226
walnut delights, 224
cooking techniques, 17–19
cooking tips, 19–22
Cooking Without Your Salt Shaker, ix
corn:
and green beans, 162
in succotash, 162
corn bread, 203
corn muffins, 203
coronary heart disease, *see* cardiovascular disease
cottage cheese, *see* cheese, cottage
crabmeat:
in seafood salad, 69
crackers:
portion sizes for step-one diet (table), 294
portion sizes for step-two diet (table), 314
cream:
mock whipped, 179
substitutions for, 24
whipped, substitutions for, 23
cream cheese, *see* cheese, cream
creamy coleslaw, 62
crepes, 210–11
apple-filled, 227
banana, 228
with powdered sugar (variation), 228
with yogurt and nutmeg (variation), 229
strawberry (variation), 229
see also pancakes
crispy baked fish, 90
croutons, seasoned, 211
cucumber raita, 64

custard:
baked, 241
see also pudding

D

dairy products:
about, 9–10, 290–91, 311–12
and calcium (table), 291
portion sizes for step-one diet (table), 290
portion sizes for step-two diet (table), 311
shopping tips for, 290–91, 312
substitutions for, 24
see also individual names
date rounds, 225
Denver chocolate pudding cake, 220
desserts, 215–47
about, 215
brownies, 245
citrus chiffon, 235
cobbler
canned fruit (variation), 240
fresh fruit, 240
crepes
apple-filled, 227
banana, 228
banana, with powdered sugar (variation), 228
banana, with yogurt and nutmeg (variation), 229
strawberry (variation), 229
crisp
apple, 236
blueberry (variation), 237
peach (variation), 236
fudge, 246
nut (variation), 246
peanut butter (variation), 247
pears, baked, 237
portion sizes for step-one diet (table), 297
portion sizes for step-two diet (table), 318
raspberry sorbet, 239
seasonings for, 329
shopping tips for, 298, 317–18
spiced fruit, 244
with ice milk (variation), 244
see also cakes; cookies; custard; pies; pudding; sauces, dessert
diet, low-sodium, 266–83
and daily food choices for, 9–16
and special instructions for, 5–6
step-one, 285–306
step-two, 307–26
see also diet, step-one; diet, step-two
diet, step-one, 285–306
about, 285
and appropriate foods for (table), 286
and breads, 293–95
and cereals, 293–95
daily eating plan for, 300–302
and dairy products, 290–91
and eggs, 288–89
and fats and oils, 291–93
and food preparation for, 287–88
and free foods, 298–99
and fruits, 295–96
and meats, 285–88
and optional foods, 297–98
and pasta, 293–95
and portion sizes of cooked meat for (table), 287
and poultry, 285–88
sample eating plans for (table), 299
sample menus for, 303–306
and seafood, 285–88
and starchy vegetables, 293–95

and vegetables, 295–96
see also diet, step-two
diet, step-two, 307–26
about, 307
and appropriate foods for (table), 308
and breads, 313–16
and cereals, 313–16
daily eating plan for, 319–22
and dairy products, 311–12
and eggs, 310–11
and fats and oils, 312–13
and food preparation for, 310
and free foods, 318–19
and fruits, 316–17
and meats, 308–10
and optional foods, 317–18
and pasta, 313–16
and portion sizes of cooked meat for (table), 309
and poultry, 308–10
sample eating plans for (table), 320
sample menus for, 323–26
and seafood, 308–10
and starchy vegetables, 313–16
and vegetables, 316–17
see also diet, step-one
dietary cholesterol, *see* cholesterol, dietary
dill pickles, 255
dilled summer squash, 155
dining out, 279–83
and sodium values in restaurant/commercial foods (table), 282–83
dips:
chili, 263
onion, California, 262
seasonings for, 327
dressing, mushroom and herb, 164
drop biscuits, 202

E

eggplant Mexicana, 163
eggs:
about, 10, 288, 310
cooking tips for, 20, 288–89, 310–11
omelet, no-cholesterol, 149
scrambled, no-cholesterol, 149
seasonings for, 329
substitute; no-cholesterol, 149
substitutions for, 24
enchiladas, chicken, 112–13

F

Fannie Farmer Cookbook, 153
fats and oils:
about, 13–14, 273–75, 291–92, 312
and foods high in saturated fatty acids (table), 278
hydrogenated, 14, 274–75
low, 5
monounsaturated, 14
polyunsaturated, 14
portion sizes for step-one diet (table), 292
portion sizes for step-two diet (table), 313
recommended (table), 14
saturated, 13–14, 274
shopping tips for, 291–93, 312–13
unsaturated, 274–75
and unsaturated content of selected foods (table), 275
fettucine, *see* pasta
fiber, 276
fish, 85–95
about, 11, 85
canned, removing oils from, 21
catfish fillets, Southern, 91
chowder with thyme; New England, 51
cooking tips for, 20

crispy baked, 90
fillets
rolled, 88
supreme, cod, 87
oven-fried, 89
portion sizes for step-one diet (table), 287
portion sizes for step-two diet (table), 309
salmon steaks, poached, 93
seasonings for, 327
sole, herbed fillet of, 86
steak with thyme, 92
tuna
macaroni casserole, 94–95
oriental, 95
salad, 68
see also seafood
flavor enhancers, *see* herbs; seasonings; spices
flounder, oven-fried, 89
food labels, *see* labels
foods, processed:
high in sodium (table), 270
free foods:
portion sizes for step-one diet (table), 298–99
portion sizes for step-two diet (table), 319
French dressing, tomato, 75
French toast, 148
fresh fruit cobbler, 240
fresh vegetable platter, 252
frittatas, zucchini, 144
frosting, quick, 219
fruit:
about, 12, 295–96, 316
chilled with liqueur, 215
cobbler
canned (variation), 240–41
fresh, 240
dried, 22
nut snack mix, 259
portion sizes for step-one diet (table), 296
portion sizes for step-two diet (table), 316
pudding (variation), 238
rice pudding, 243
seasonings for, 22, 329
shopping tips for, 296, 317
spiced, 244
with ice milk (variation), 244
see also individual names
fudge, 246
nut (variation), 246
peanut butter (variation), 247

G

game:
appropriate, for step-one diet (table), 286
appropriate, for step-two diet (table), 308
seasonings for, 328
garlic:
and releasing flavor from, 21
gazpacho, 50
gelatin, *see* custard; pudding
ginger, fresh:
grating, 21
gingerbread, 207
gingered carrots, 154
golden baked chicken, 100
grains, 12
grapefruit-orange salad, 66
gravy, 20
green beans, *see* beans, green
grilling, 18

H

hash-brown potatoes, 167
Hawaiian chicken salad, 68
herb(s):
blend; salad, 36
bread, 199

herb(s) (*cont'd*)
fresh, releasing flavors from, 21
guide, 327–29
seasoned biscuits, 202
seasoning, 34
lemon, 35
see also seasonings; spices; *individual names*
herbed fillet of sole, 86
high blood cholesterol, *see* cholesterol, blood
high blood pressure, *see* blood pressure, high
horseradish:
fresh, grating, 21
sauce, 182
hot prepared mustard, 182
Hungarian pork chops, 136
hypercholesterolemia, *see* cholesterol, blood
hypertension, *see* blood pressure, high

I

ice cream:
substitutions for, 24
ice milk:
spiced fruit with (variation), 244
ingredient substitutions, 23–25
table, 23–24
Italian dressing, 76

K

ketchup, 181
kidney beans, *see* beans, kidney

L

labels, 7–9, 277–79
and how to read, 8–9
and nutritional information on (table), 279
and sodium, saturated fatty acids and cholesterol information on (table), 278
and terms used on, indicating reduced sodium (table), 278
lamb:
appropriate, for step-one diet (table), 286
appropriate, for step-two diet (table), 308
curry, 134
portion sizes for step-one diet (table), 287
portion sizes for step-two diet (table), 309
seasonings for, 328
see also beef; game; pork; veal
lasagna, *see* pasta
legumes, 12
see also individual names
lemon(s):
baked chicken, 101
barbecued chicken, 115
in citrus chiffon, 235
herb seasoning, 35
lentil soup with, 49
poppy seed dressing, 80
veal with spinach, 133
lentil soup with lemon, 49
lima beans, *see* beans, lima
lime marinated steak, 127
low-sodium diet, *see* diet, low-sodium

M

macaroni, *see* pasta
mako shark steak with thyme, 92
matzo crumb piecrust, 230
mayonnaise, tofu, 81
meats, 123–36
about, 10–11, 123
appropriate, for step-one diet (table), 286

appropriate, for step-two diet (table), 308
cooking tips for, 19–20, 287–88, 310
ground, 19–20
loaf, 129
seasonings for, 328
shopping tips for, 286–87, 308–309
and step-one diet, 285–88
and step-two diet, 308–10
see also beef; game; lamb; pork; veal
Mediterranean pork chops, 135
Mexican salsa, 187
microwave cooking, 18–19
milk products, *see* dairy products
minestrone, 45
mock cream cheese, 261
mock sour cream, 178
mock whipped cream, 179
muffins:
blueberry, 204
corn, 203
oat bran and yogurt, 205
see also biscuits; rolls
mushroom(s):
cleaning, 20
and herb dressing, 164
in rice and vegetable pilaf, 174
sauce, 180
spaghetti with, 140
sautéed, on toast, 254
stuffed, 253
mustard, 22
Dijon, white sauce with, 189
hot prepared, 182

N

navy beans, *see* beans, navy
New England fish chowder with thyme, 51
no-cholesterol egg substitute, 149
no-cholesterol omelet, 149
no-cholesterol scrambled eggs, 149
nuts and seeds:
about, 12
fruit-nut snack mix, 259
nut fudge (variation), 246
spiced nuts, 258
toasting, 21
see also individual names

O

oat bran and yogurt muffins, 205
oatmeal cookies, 222
oils, *see* fats and oils
onion(s):
dip; California, 262
soup, 47
in vegetable medley, 156
orange(s):
in citrus chiffon, 235
grapefruit salad, 66
mandarin, in ambrosia, 65
pudding, 238
whip (variation), 238
yogurt dressing, 80
organ meats, 11, 287, 309
oven-fried chicken, 103
oven-fried fish, 89
oven-fried potatoes with oregano, 169

P

pancakes, 208
blueberry (variation), 208
potato, 168
with applesauce and cinnamon (variation), 168
with walnuts (variation), 209
wheat-germ (variation), 209
see also crepes
Parmesan cheese:
white sauce with (variation), 188
party mix, 260

pasta:
about, 12, 13
fettucine Alfredo, 145
lasagna, spinach, 142–43
macaroni
salad, 61
tuna casserole, 94–95
portion sizes for step-one diet (table), 294
portion sizes for step-two diet (table), 314
salad; summer, 59
shopping tips for, 293, 315
spaghetti
with meat sauce, 132
with mushroom sauce, 140
and step-one diet, 293–95
and step-two diet, 313–16
peach:
crisp (variation), 236
pie (variation), 233
peanut butter:
cookies, 223
fudge (variation), 247
peanuts, sugared, 257
pears, baked, 237
pecans:
in pralines, 226
spiced, 258
peppered roast beef, 125
peppers, hot:
about, 22
handling, 21
pickle(s):
bread-and-butter, 256
dill, 255
relish (variation), 256
piecrusts, *see* pies
pies:
apple, 233
blueberry (variation), 232
cherry, 232
matzo crumb piecrust for, 230
peach (variation), 233
piecrust for, 231
pumpkin, 234
vanilla pudding (variation), 242
pineapple:
in ambrosia, 65
coleslaw, 63
pizza hero, 143
poached salmon steaks, 93
poaching, 18
pork:
appropriate, for step-one diet (table), 286
appropriate, for step-two diet (table), 308
chops
in baked beans, 160
Hungarian, 136
Mediterranean, 135
portion size for step-one diet (table), 287
portion size for step-two diet (table), 309
seasonings for, 328
see also beef; game; lamb; veal
potassium, 272–73
source (table), 272–73
potato(es):
about, 153
hash-brown, 167
O'Brien, 166
oven-fried, with oregano, 169
pancakes, 168
with applesauce and cinnamon (variation), 168
salad, 60
scalloped, 165
potato(es), sweet:
casserole, 171
scalloped, 170
poultry, 99–119
about, 11, 99

appropriate, for step-one diet (table), 286
appropriate, for step-two diet (table), 308
cooking tips for, 19–20, 287–88, 310
mushroom and herb dressing for, 164
seasonings for, 328
shopping tips for, 286–87, 308–309
and step-one diet, 285–88
and step-two diet, 308–10
see also chicken; turkey
pralines, 226
product labels, *see* labels
pudding:
butterscotch (variation), 243
chocolate (variation), 242
fruit (variation), 238
fruit-rice, 243
orange, 238
whip (variation), 238
vanilla, 242
see also custard
pumpkin pie, 234

Q

quick frosting, 219

R

raisin bread, 199
raita, cucumber, 64
ranch dressing, reduced-calorie, 79
raspberry sorbet, 239
reduced-calorie ranch dressing, 79
relish, pickle (variation), 256
rice:
fruit pudding, 243
pilaf; brown, 173
portion size for step-one diet (table), 294
portion size for step-two diet (table), 314
seasoned, 172
and vegetable pilaf, 174
roast chicken, 102
roast turkey, 116
roasting, 17
rolled fish fillets, 88
rolls:
cinnamon, 201
dinner, 197
see also biscuits; muffins
Russian dressing, 76
rye bread, 198

S

salad dressings, 73–81
about, 15, 73
basic I, 74
basic II, 75
creamy, 21
French, tomato, 75
Italian, 76
lemon-poppy seed, 80
orange-yogurt, 80
ranch, reduced-calorie, 79
Russian, 76
Thousand Island, 77
tofu mayonnaise, 81
vinaigrette, 78
yogurt, 77
see also salads; sauces
salad herb blend, 36
salads, 55–69
about, 55
ambrosia, 65
bean and sprout (variation), 56
chicken, 67
Hawaiian, 68
coleslaw
creamy, 62
pineapple, 63
cucumber raita, 64
macaroni, 61
marinated vegetables, spicy, 58

salads (*cont'd*)
orange-grapefruit, 66
pasta, summer, 59
potato, 60
seafood, 69
seasonings for, 327
Texas caviar (black-eyed pea salad), 57
three-bean, 56
tuna, 68
turkey (variation), 67
Waldorf, 64
see also salad dressings
salmon steaks, poached, 93
salsa, Mexican, 187
salt, 4–5
and checking product labels for, 7
substitutions for, 23
see also salts, flavor; sodium
salts, flavor:
substitutions for, 23
sauces, 177–91
about, 15, 177
barbecue, 186
chili, 183
horseradish, 182
ketchup, 181
mock sour cream, 178
mushroom, 180
mustard, hot prepared, 182
salsa, Mexican, 187
tomato, 184
chunky, 185
white, 188
with Dijon mustard (variation), 189
with Parmesan cheese (variation), 188
yogurt-cilantro, chicken with, 106
yogurt-dill, 189
see also sauces, dessert
sauces, dessert:
chocolate, 191
strawberry, 190
whipped cream, mock, 179
sausage patties, *see* turkey sausage patties
sautéed cauliflower, 158
sautéed mushrooms on toast, 254
sautéing, 18
scalloped potatoes, 165
scalloped sweet potatoes, 170
seafood:
appropriate, for step-one diet (table), 286
appropriate, for step-two diet (table), 308
cooking tips for, 287–88, 310
salad, 69
seasonings for, 327
shopping tips for, 286–87, 308–309
and step-one diet, 285–88
and step-two diet, 308–10
see also fish
seasoned croutons, 211
seasoned rice, 172
seasonings, 21–22, 33–37
about, 15, 33
chili powder, 37
guide, 327–29
herb, 34
lemon herb, 35
salad herb blend, 36
suggestions, 33
see also herbs; spices; *individual names*
seeds, *see* nuts and seeds
shortening:
substitutions for, 24
shrimp:
in seafood salad, 69
snacks, 251–63
about, 16, 251
cream cheese, mock, 261

dips
chili, 263
onion, California, 262
fruit-nut mix, 259
mushrooms
on toast; sautéed, 254
stuffed, 253
party mix, 260
pickles
bread-and-butter, 256
dill, 255
relish (variation), 256
shopping tips for, 298, 318
spiced nuts, 258
and step-one diet, 297–98
and step-two diet, 318
sugared peanuts, 257
vegetable platter, fresh, 252
snow peas and ginger, chicken with, 114
sodium, 4–5, 269–71
and checking product labels for, 7
compounds (table), 278
food preparation and, 269–70
naturally occurring in food, 271
in processed foods, 270–71
and product label terms indicating reduced (table), 278
values in restaurant/commercial foods (table), 282–83
see also salt
sodium chloride, *see* salt
soft tacos, 131
sole, herbed fillet of, 86
sorbet, *see* desserts
soups, 41–51
about, 41
beef vegetable, 44
broth
beef, 43
chicken, 42
cooking tips for, 21
fish chowder with thyme, New England, 51
gazpacho, 50
lentil, with lemon, 49
minestrone, 45
onion, 47
seasonings for, 327
split pea, 48
turkey vegetable, 46
see also soups, commercial; stews
soups, commercial:
about, 293
portion sizes for step-one diet (table), 294
portion sizes for step-two diet (table), 314
sour cream:
mock, 178
substitutions for, 23
southern catfish fillets, 91
spaghetti, *see* pasta
spaghetti squash, *see* squash
spiced fruit, 244
spiced fruit with ice milk (variation), 244
spiced nuts, 258
spices:
fresh, releasing flavors from, 21
guide, 327–29
whole, 22
toasting, 21
see also herbs; seasonings; *individual names*
spicy marinated vegetables, 58
spinach:
lasagna, 142–43
lemon veal with, 133
split pea soup, 48
squash:
spaghetti, 141
summer
dilled, 155
in vegetable medley, 156

squash (*cont'd*)
see also zucchini
steaming, 18
step-one diet, *see* diet, step-one
step-two diet, *see* diet, step-two
stewing, 17–18
stews:
chili, 128
cooking tips for, 21
seasonings for, 327
turkey, 117
see also soups
stir-fried cabbage with noodles, 159
stir-frying, 18
strawberry:
crepes (variation), 229
sauce, 190
stroke, *see* cardiovascular disease
stuffed mushrooms, 253
succotash (variation), 162
sugared peanuts, 257
summer pasta salad, 59
summer squash, *see* squash
Swedish bread, 200
sweet and sour green beans, 161
sweet potatoes, *see* potatoes, sweet
sweet substitutes:
portion sizes for step-one diet (table), 298
portion sizes for step-two diet (table), 319
sweets, *see* desserts
swordfish steak with thyme, 92

T

tacos, soft, 131
Texas caviar (black-eyed pea salad), 57
Thousand Island dressing, 77
three-bean salad, 56
tofu mayonnaise, 81
tomato(es):
baked, 157
French dressing, 75
juice substitutions, 23
puree substitution, 23
sauce, 184
chunky, 185
in vegetable medley, 156
tuna:
macaroni casserole, 94–95
oriental, 95
salad, 68
steak with thyme, 92
turkey:
cooking tip for, 99
roast, 116
with rosemary, 118
salad (variation), 67
sausage patties, 119
stew, 117
vegetable soup, 46
see also chicken

V

vanilla pudding, 242
veal:
appropriate, for step-one diet (table), 286
appropriate, for step-two diet (table), 308
seasonings for, 328
with spinach; lemon, 133
see also beef; game; lamb; pork
vegetable oil, appropriate, *see* fats and oils, recommended
vegetables, 153–74
about, 12, 153, 295–96, 316
beef soup, 44
cooking tips for, 20, 296, 317
dried, 22
in gazpacho, 50
marinated, spicy, 58
medley, 156
platter; fresh, 252

portion sizes for step-one diet (table), 296
portion sizes for step-two diet (table), 316
and rice pilaf, 174
roasting, 21
seasonings for, 22, 328
shopping tips for, 296, 317
succotash (variation), 162
turkey soup, 46
see also vegetables, starchy; vegetarian dishes; *individual names*
vegetables, starchy:
portion sizes for step-one diet (table), 294
portion sizes for step-two diet (table), 314
shopping tips for, 293, 315
and step-one diet, 293–95
and step-two diet, 313–16
vegetarian dishes, 139–49
about, 139
cheese blintzes, 147
chili, 146
fettucine Alfredo, 145
French toast, 148
omelet, no-cholesterol, 149
pizza hero, 143
scrambled eggs, no-cholesterol, 149
spaghetti squash, 141
spaghetti with mushroom sauce, 140
spinach lasagna, 142–43
zucchini frittata, 144
see also vegetables
vinaigrette dressing, 78
vinegar, 21–22

W

Waldorf salad, 64
walnut(s):
delights, 224
in nut fudge (variation), 246
pancakes with (variation), 209
weight control, 273, 276–77
wheat-germ pancakes (variation), 209
whipped cream, *see* cream
white sauce, 188
with Dijon mustard (variation), 189
with Parmesan cheese (variation), 188
whole-wheat bread, 198

Y

yellow beans, *see* beans, yellow
yogurt:
cilantro sauce; chicken with, 106
dill sauce, 189
dressing, 77
and nutmeg; banana crepes with (variation), 229
and oat bran muffins, 205
orange dressing, 80
and suggested uses for, 21
sweetening, 21

Z

zucchini:
frittata, 144
in vegetable medley, 156
see also squash

Notes

Notes

Notes

Notes

Notes

ALSO FROM THE AMERICAN HEART ASSOCIATION

Concerned about your cholesterol level? The American Heart Association is too.

That's why the nation's most trusted authority on heart disease has prepared an important new guide for avoiding high-saturated fat and high-cholesterol foods that may increase your risk of high cholesterol.

The Low-Fat, Low-Cholesterol Cookbook shows you:

- How to shop for the best foods
- How to adapt your favorite recipes for better eating
- How to avoid high-cholesterol dishes in restaurants
- How to distinguish between "good" cholesterol and "bad."

The Low Fat, Low-Cholesterol Cookbook also gives you 200 step-by-step recipes for innovative, delicious dishes such as:

- Oriental Grilled Chicken
- Crispy Fish with Fennel
- Mexican Beef and Cornbread Pie
- Pizza
- Mocha Cheesecake . . . and more.

American Heart Association

Each recipe has been tested by the American Heart Association and specifically formulated to help keep your blood cholesterol within medically accepted guidelines.

So you can reduce the risk of heart disease and live a healthier life.

The Low-Fat, Low-Cholesterol Cookbook belongs in every kitchen. And it makes the perfect gift for anyone you truly care about.

Order your copies of this important 342-page resource today. Because the Low-Fat, Low-Cholesterol Cookbook makes eating a pleasure for everyone who has a heart.

AVAILABLE AT BOOKSTORES EVERYWHERE

Times Books/Random House, Mail Service Dept. AHA2
201 East 50th Street, New York, NY 10022

Please send me ____ copy(ies) of THE AHA LOW-FAT, LOW-CHOLESTEROL COOKBOOK (91783) at $19.95 each (plus $2.00 handling and postage for the first book, and $.50 for each additional book ordered). Please add sales tax where applicable.

____ Enclosed is my check or money order payable to Times Books.

Charge my account with ____ American Express ____ Visa ____ Mastercard.

Acct. # _____ Exp. date _____ Sig. _____

Name (print) _____

Address _____

City _____ State _____ Zip Code _____

005 35 LS1

TIMES BOOKS

RANDOM HOUSE